D1022045

Since You Went Away

SINCE YOU WENT AWAY

Donald I. Rogers

ARLINGTON HOUSE
NEW ROCHELLE, N. Y.

Library of Congress Catalog Card Number 72-91642

Manufactured in the United States of America

Library of Congress Cataloging in Publication Data

Rogers, Donald I
   Since you went away.

   Bibliography: p.
   1. United States--History--1933-1945.
2. World War, 1939-1945--United States. I. Title.
E806.R726   973.917   72-91642
ISBN 0-87000-195-7

This Book Is Dedicated To
Nancy Elizabeth Rogers
With Love From Her Father

Contents

Foreword

Their ranks are beginning to thin, now. They are in the bifocal set, no longer worried about receding hair, for it has long been a *fait accompli*. Some are paunchy, some are stooped, but most of them can still swing along Main Street on Memorial Day or July Fourth at a cadence of 128 steps per minute, and to those of us who can remember, they seem, for a brief time, to be once again the strong vigorous young people who wore the uniform of their nation from 1940 through 1945.

They went off to their wars to ancient battlefields in Africa and Europe and to new ones in Asia and the Pacific and performed the dull, boring duties of military people, and some of them performed astonishing feats of valor and bravery, astonishing because by nature they were by and large a gentle, easygoing folk who came from peaceful, law-abiding places in our vast land. They were the sons of peacemakers, engaging in an unpleasant and alien rite.

Some were away from home for as long as six or seven years, others for as brief a period as one year, but no matter how long or short their absence, they returned to a land that had changed drastically.

Very little was as they remembered it.

America, in their absence, had undergone yet another giant industrial revolution, and a technical revolution. Whole landscapes had been changed by wartime construction. The cities were bursting their seams and rural villages and hamlets had begun their sprawl across the adjacent countrysides.

A new man was in the White House and politics was seething. The songs were different. The literature had changed. Mores, manners and morals were not the same. A feeling of permissiveness was in the air. In many instances the younger generation seemed ill at ease with the returning men who had seen such distant horizons.

9

But the men adjusted quickly and settled down to the challenging job of living, loving, building homes and families and becoming good peacetime citizens, just as they had been good wartime citizens.

I was one of the ones who was away some of the time, and my research for this book brought back many vivid memories of things and incidents I had forgotten, and caused me to wallow, luxuriously, in the warm baths of nostalgia.

As I write this, I can look from my studio window and see a giant pileated woodpecker cleaning out his home atop a maple trunk that was hit by lightning two summers ago. A grey squirrel on my stone wall is lashing his tail in anger at a bluejay that has stolen a food morsel. The war seems unreal, a dream, something that couldn't possibly happen.

But it did happen, and this book, a chronicle of what life was like on the home front while the big news was being made in distant lands, is offered, with the author's deep gratitude, to the guys who came back to take up their chores in the land they had defended.

Quite aside from the fact that she is a keenly intelligent, very special and an extremely beautiful young lady, I have dedicated this book to my daughter Nancy for a specific reason. She is sixteen years old as of this writing and through her I have learned that young people today are seeking a point of reference. They don't know what we mean when we say the war changed things. What war? they ask. What *things* were changed? What were the differences, and were they good or bad? Perhaps this book can help provide a frame of reference.

To my wife Marjorie who helped me with so much of the research of this book as well as all my others, who coddled me when the going was rough, whose wise counsel guided me, and whose steadfastness provides my life with its chief navigational aid my deepest thanks and love. My thanks also to Mrs. Dolores Peto who cheerfully typed and retyped the pages of this manuscript; to Miss Donna L. Meade, whose research and criticism were of immeasurable value; and to my dear daughter, Lynn Wallrapp, whose encouragement and friendly, on-target criticism helped guide me all the way.

Donald I. Rogers
Ridgefield Connecticut

Since You Went Away

1

The Distant Boots
1940

Is there *always* a calm before the storm? Americans asked themselves that question in later years as they looked back on the beginning of the fifth decade of the twentieth century. The sunshine of promise shone brightly over America in 1940 as millions began to emerge from the hopeless winter of a ten-year depression, the gravest and longest economic illness in recorded history.

There were terrible problems in Europe, of course. The headlines of American newspapers screamed them in outsize bold type. German troops invaded Denmark and Norway simultaneously, aided by the softening political activity of Vidkun Quisling who was to become later the Nazis' minister president in Norway. Borrowing a phrase that came from the Spanish Civil War, Hitler said the invasion was accomplished with a "Fifth Column," four from without and one from within—the traitors around Quisling.

These were serious headlines, disturbing headlines. But beside them on page one there were other headlines. They revealed that auto manufacturing was turning in one of its best years, that steel production was on the increase, that the armed services were growing—up to about 1 million men—and that employment was increasing and unemployment was dropping.

Economists predicted that the Gross National Product, the total value of the output of all goods and services, would reach $125.3 billion by the beginning of 1941, and since this was more than twice the figure recorded in the depths of the depression, many people were prone to feel twice as good about things. America had had its own problems, only now beginning to end.

There were 56 million in the American labor force, not all of them employed, of course, but most of them optimistic about their chances—unless one looked beneath the surface in the cities, where poverty-level wages were paid in many jobs not covered by the New Deal's new laws, or in the potholes of poverty occupied by sharecroppers, pieceworkers, fishermen, farmers and even many retail employees. Earnings of $2,000 gave a worker the average median income, and many of the aforementioned earned well below that.

But such a large proportion of Americans were earning $3,500 to $5,000 or more, that it was as easy to overlook the darker side of the domestic economy as it was to ignore the idiotic antics of the madman in Berlin and that strutting bag of wind in Rome who called himself the Duce.

Casting aside the shroud of economic despair, the grocery stores and the very few newfangled supermarkets were taking on new life and color, broadening and upgrading their offerings to the public. A person could buy a loaf of bread for 8 cents; a pound of choice hot dogs in natural skins for 13 cents; a bakery pie for 12 cents; a pound of good-quality hamburger for 25 cents; a pound of coffee for about 39 cents; excellent steaks at 23 cents a pound; a leg of lamb at 19 cents a pound; a one-pound roll of fresh creamery butter for less than 40 cents. Vegetables were sold by the bunch, the pint, the quart, the peck, and not by weight. Carrots were 5 cents a bunch; radishes two bunches for 5 cents; fresh peas, 30 cents a peck.

Magnificent new cars were rolling out of Detroit in 1940, with prices to attract customers who had been riding makeshift cars since 1930. A total of $1,200 would buy an outstanding new motorcar with all optional equipment, and $1,400 would get a luxury vehicle. A year-old Dodge sold for about $950, equipped with radio, heater and hydraulic brakes, plus many other "extras."

Gasoline to power the new cars ranged in price from 14 cents to 19 cents a gallon, depending on the octane rating and local marketing conditions. High-grade motor oil, in quantity, was less than 25 cents a quart.

The movies, in a majority of cities, cost 15 cents in the afternoon and 25 cents at night, except for weekends, when the matinee price was 25 cents and the evenings ranged up to 50 or 60 cents. Moving picture tickets cost more, of course, in the downtown theatres of the big cities like New York, Chicago and Los Angeles.

And there was radio. The 1916 prediction of RCA's president, David Sarnoff, had come true and by 1940 nearly every home in America had a radio set of some kind, except in isolated ultra-rural areas. Most of them were much smaller than their predecessors and were, by now, all electric. The frequencies were not overcrowded and it was possible, after local and nearby stations signed off, to get the big 50,000-watt stations from many miles away.

The Crossley rating in 1940 showed that Americans were listening most to a blend of serials and comedy shows. Leading all the rest was Jack Benny and his co-stars, Mary Livingston, Rochester, Dennis Day and Don Wilson. Their names were as familiar as any in the land. Only shortly behind Benny, as far as ratings went, were Edgar Bergen with his monocled, top-hatted, saucy, wooden offspring, Charlie McCarthy, and the puppet's foil, Mortimer Snerd. Americans also listened avidly to Fibber McGee and Molly, Bob Hope, Kate Smith, "Major Bowes' Amateur Hour" "Lux Radio Theatre," "The Aldrich Family," "One Man's Family," Kay ("Hi Y'all") Kayser's schmaltzy band, "The Goldbergs," "Amos 'n' Andy" (in their twelfth year on radio), "Ma Perkins," "Backstage Wife" and "Our Gal Sunday." Kids, who said "Keemo Sabe" almost universally, listened to the Lone Ranger and his trusted Tonto.

Radio still had a bit of growing to do. It would mature quite a bit in the following year and reach full growth after Pearl Harbor. In 1940 it was clomping into adulthood, bursting the seams of its adolescent attire and sizing up a conquerable world. The names of serious commentators were becoming familiar to millions, names like Boake Carter, Lowell Thomas, Fulton Lewis, Jr., Edward Morgan, Edward R. Murrow and the scholarly-sounding H. V. Kaltenborn, whose crispy-dry diction, replete with rolling r's, set a fashion in news delivery.

In looking back at the year on the silver screen, most Americans would say that *Gone with the Wind* was the big movie of 1940. Its star-studded cast did, indeed, carve a place in motion picture history—Vivien Leigh as Scarlett, Clark Gable as Rhett Butler, Thomas Mitchell, Olivia de Haviland and Leslie Howard. The names of the characters endured—O'Hara, Melanie, Ashley, as did the name of the plantation, Tara. The haunting theme song lingered like jasmine.

Margaret Mitchell's great story of the fall of Atlanta was not alone, however, for it was a year jammed with brilliant screen performances and memorable scripts. Hollywood, too, was emerging from the doldrums, and its moguls figured they had a lot of catching-up to do. *The Grapes of Wrath* brought Okies to the screen, victimized by corporate farming and the employers of migrant workers, and brought worldwide stardom to Henry Fonda and Jane Darwell. *The Philadelphia Story* set a new mark in sophisticated, brittle comedy, with Katharine Hepburn, Cary Grant and James Stewart.

There were historic tear-jerkers—*Our Town* with William Holden; Christopher Morley's *Kitty Foyle*, with Ginger Rogers, one of the earlier serious treatments of illicit sex; and *The Mortal Storm* with Margaret Sullavan and James Stewart.

A memorable and moving performance was turned in by veteran Raymond Massey in *Abraham Lincoln in Illinois*. Bette Davis and Charles Boyer pulled in record crowds to see them in *All This and Heaven Too*. There were Gable, Spencer Tracy and Claudette Colbert in *Boom Town*, and unforgettable performances by Tracy, Robert Young, Bruce Cabot and Henry Wilcoxon in *Northwest Passage*, from the book by the very popular novelist-historian, Kenneth Roberts.

Walt Disney packed theatres with a cartoon story of what was to become one of his most lovable and unforgettable characters, *Pinocchio*. Later in the year he backed up his success with the spectacular *Fantasia*, with musical accompaniment by Leopold Stokowski and an enormous symphony orchestra. But Pinocchio and his father, Gepetto, and his pal, Jimminy Cricket, stayed around a long while.

It was a good time for musicals. On Broadway, tuneful productions included *Boys and Girls Together*, *Louisiana Purchase*, *Pal Joey*, *Panama Hattie* and *It Happens on Ice*.

The Great White Way, still great and still bright with millions of lights in 1940, attracted throngs to see such theatre as *Separate Rooms*, *The Male Animal*, Robert E. Sherwood's *There Shall Be No Night*, *George Washington Slept Here*, *Johnny Belinda*, *The Corn Is Green*, *Charley's Aunt* and *My Sister Eileen*. In the fall, for serious theatre-goers, Helen Hayes revived *Twelfth Night*. *Life With Father*, which opened in 1939, was, of course, playing on Broadway, where it set records until 1947.

It seemed that no part of America was very far from a jukebox as the fifth decade began. In towns and cities there were many on each block. In the most remote hamlets, they were found in

16

the diners, the tearooms, the taverns, the variety stores and even in the gas stations and barbershops.

Big and gaudy, with flickering multicolored lights, with a visible storage file of dozens of records and a complex of selection buttons, the jukes operated for a nickel. Many of them had remote-control boxes that were strategically located at tables or at the corners of bars or on the marble-top counters of diners. For a quarter one music lover could get six plays, for a half-dollar, sixteen selections.

Throughout the land, they blared from early morning until late at night, playing popular music, selections from Broadway shows and movies, country music, even devotional music. Instrumentalists vied for popularity with trumpet, clarinet, saxophone, piano and guitar. Vocalists ran the gamut from operatic performers to crooners, to such sweet harmonizers as Ginny Sims and Harry Babbitt, and on to the nasal twangers of the country set, some of whom in later years were to enjoy much greater nationwide popularity. Large choral groups were becoming popular, epitomized by Fred Waring and his Pennsylvanians. And for a nickel, on some machines, you could buy three minutes of silence.

Americans did a lot of humming, singing and dancing in 1940.

From the film *Pinocchio*, they vocalized the sweet lyrics of "When You Wish upon a Star," but were likely to follow it with one of the first hoedown country tunes to gain nationwide popularity, "You Are My Sunshine."

The kooky 1939 smash hit, "Three Little Fishies" remained in many jukes throughout 1940, as did several other hits from the previous year, including, of course, Irving Berlin's timely "God Bless America," "The Beer Barrel Polka," "Frenesi" and Andre Kostelanetz' rendition of "Moon Love," adapted from Tchaikovsky's Fifth Symphony.

On most jukeboxes one could find "If I Didn't Care," sung by Nat King Cole. Judy Garland's inimitable recording of "Over the Rainbow," from her film *The Wizard of Oz*, was also popular, as were "I Concentrate on You," from *Broadway Melody of 1940*, and "All the Things You Are," from *Very Warm For May*. Other carry-overs on the jukes were Cole Porter's "Do I Love You?" (1939), Ella Fitzgerald's "A-Tisket a-Tasket" (1938), "I'll Be Seeing You" (1938), "The Donkey Serenade" (1937) and "Deep

Purple" (1934). On every jukebox throughout the entire war was Hoagy Carmichael's immortal "Stardust" (1929).

Shortly after France fell and sued for armistice on June 17, Oscar Hammerstein II and Jerome Kern hit the music stalls and stores with the Academy Award-winning "The Last Time I Saw Paris," and box-office record-breaker Judy Garland, who at that time had never been to Paris, vocalized it from every jukebox in the land. Later, the incomparable Hildegarde pulled huge crowds to hear her sing it at the Savoy Room. Americans who had been to Paris only vicariously in the movies or in *Life* magazine, stood and wept as Miss Garland's tribute to the city on the Seine echoed from beery barrooms, crowded dancehalls and steamy diners.

For lovers and romantics there were "Fools Rush In," "How High the Moon," "Only Forever" and the instrumental rendition of "A Love Story—Intermezzo," from the movie *Intermezzo*.

The civil war in Spain, which had been slipping from the consciousness of most Americans, was brought home suddenly and dramatically by Ernest Hemingway's powerful *For Whom the Bell Tolls*, which became an overnight best seller.

Hardly had avid readers become accustomed to the lilting Spanish names in Hemingway's novel than they were obliged to try their prowess on the furry, lispy names of the Welsh when Richard Llewellyn brought out his evocative *How Green Was My Valley*. Many an American lady, upon encountering the name of the principal female character, Angharyd, simply called her Anna. John O'Hara wrote *Pal Joey* that year (not to be confused with the play) and William Saroyan came out with *My Name Is Aram*. Thomas Wolfe's *You Can't Go Home Again* caused a stir in literary circles. James Truslow Adams published the sixth volume of his *Dictionary of American History*.

The war rolled across the flatlands and rivers of Europe, through Belgium, Luxembourg and the Netherlands. The Dutch and Belgian armies capitulated and surrendered to the German armies after suffering fantastic casualties.

The Maginot line, behind which the French armies huddled, stretched for 100 miles and was said by the experts at l'Ecole du Militaire at St. Cyr to be absolutely impregnable, the finest fortification in the world. It had its own air-conditioning, its own kitchens and hospitals and supply rooms and power plants. It bristled with the full range of the French Field Artillery's modern weaponry, pointing across the border into Germany.

Hitler laughed, and his armies swept around the "impregnable" Maginot into the low countries, while the Luftwaffe roared overhead. Never mind the French fortifications, Hitler said. "We will make a fortress of all of Europe—Festung Europa."

The British and French, driven to the coast, huddled under withering attacks on the beaches at Dunkirk. It was there that the British Royal Navy performed the evacuation that was to be hailed later as one of the most heroic actions of the war. Under incessant attack from the Nazis who were well-supplied from nearby Calais and Boulogne, officers and men of the Royal Navy brought small craft right up to the beaches to rescue the entrapped forces.

When they ran out of small craft because of the heavy shelling and machine-gunning, the Navy asked for help and there was launched from Dover a civilian navy consisting of fishing boats, pleasure craft, skiffs, dories, small sailboats—anything that would float and could muster some kind of power—to help in the rescue operation. An armada of some 850 shallow-draft craft went to the beach, unarmed, unprotected, to pick up the beleaguered troops, while the Naval vessels stood off, in water barely deep enough to float them, and poured a torrent of steel at the enemy.

When it had ended, more than 335,000 British and French troops had been saved. Besides tens of thousands of casualties, however, the British lost much of their armament at Dunkirk and, once home, turned with almost empty hands to face a rampaging enemy across the channel that was threatening imminent invasion.

The Germans pushed on toward Paris, and in Rome, now emboldened by the British defeat at Dunkirk and the German advance toward the French capital, Mussolini declared war on Great Britain and France. *"Vive il Duce!"* the Romans shouted, but in Sicily, where Mussolini had caused many problems by clamping down on the Mafia, there was sullen silence, a fact that was noted by Allied intelligence units as well as by the American

G-2. If ever it would be decided to invade Italy, this intelligence would be useful. As France fell to the Nazis and sued for an armistice, and General Charles de Gaulle shouted defiance at the Pétain government from England, Mussolini opened a new front by sending his army against Greece. At the border he found, to his surprise, that the Greeks were prepared to stop him. Hitler had to come to his rescue and in so doing sent armored German columns through Greece and Yugoslavia, formed alliances with Hungary, Bulgaria and Rumania, and declared them all under German domination and control. A deflated if not defeated Italian army trudged along behind, picking up the pieces and helping the Germans with the chores of occupation.

It bothered Americans to read of these events, but Europe was many miles from America, even though the Pan American Airways "Yankee Clipper" had flown from New York to Lisbon, Portugal, in the record time of eighteen hours and thirty-five minutes, with a stiff tailwind most of the way. Pan American was becoming known worldwide, and it was becoming clear that Lisbon would be the open gateway to "Fortress Europe," a gate that opened either way.

There were other things to think about on the home front. Steel scrap, for instance. American junk-dealers were still selling it to Japan—almost 200 million tons in the last five years—and it was said in Pittsburgh that there was an insufficient amount of scrap on hand to operate the open-hearth furnaces for more than a few weeks.

And then there was the economy—an intriguing thing to watch.

It kept perking up, and was actually beginning to show signs of prosperity. The government was pouring the first of billions into defense spending (it was to total $8.3 billion in the next year) and the money was starting to trickle down to the man on the street. National income was reaching up to $90 billion, the newspapers reported.

A war? Sure a war in *Europe*. But no war for Americans. Europe was far away and was embroiled and ensnared in ancient problems. We had been suckered into their affairs once before, but not again. Let them fight their own battles. The United States of America was uncommitted and it seemed certain that a majority intended that it would stay that way.

It was too bad about the Jews in Germany, but Germany was a sovereign state and there was little one could do to interfere except *condemn* what the Germans were doing. Besides, there were several speakers touring America who said that the Jews had taken advantage of Germany's devastating poverty after World War I and had gobbled up all of the wealth. Thus, they implied, this military seizure of private property from the Jews might, in some circumstances, be justified. That this was being said by Americans who supposedly placed supreme value on individual life and on the sanctity of the right to own private property, wasn't challenged in many places.

We had just recovered from a serious ten-year illness. We were still convalescing. We really couldn't do much about the rest of the world. We owed it to ourselves to get our own health fully restored. So went the basic thinking.

And the money filtered down.

Nightclubs, which had burst open in the bigger cities the week after Prohibition was repealed, suggesting to some skeptics that they might have been operating right along, now began to spring up in all of the smaller cities and towns and in the villages and on the highways leading to town. Most were just drinking spots, often boasting a dance floor and a loud jukebox, with perhaps a live band on Friday and Saturday nights. But in or near any town of any size there was a genuine "nightclub" patterned after famous ones in New York. To supply them with talent (singers, dancers, stand-up comedians and magicians), booking "circuits" came into existence throughout the country, sharply reminiscent of the old vaudeville circuits, which had died a decade earlier with the advent of the talking picture.

People were beginning to spend the money they earned. It was the first time they had been so free with cash since 1930, when they tightened up through necessity in the aftermath of the great stock market crash of October 24, 1929 and Wall Street's deathblow to prosperity on October 29, 1929.

For the first time in ten years they bought such things as jewelry, watches, radios, kitchen appliances and prime steaks. They drank scotch and bourbon and rye and gin instead of beer. Kids got their teeth straightened; adults had old and bothersome

21

teeth extracted and ordered bridgework. Those who had delayed having children, started families. Those who had put off
marriage, bought rings and licenses and set up housekeeping.

Prices began to rise, but only a little. Only the elderly and the
retired grumbled about the diminishing purchasing power of
their fixed incomes.

The war? That was far away. Here there were vacations to
be had, the first ones in ten years, and there were new things
to buy. The larder was being restocked. Wardrobes were being
outfitted. You realized, of course, that mother hadn't had a new
coat in five years. The priorities were *here*.

In May, on the third Sunday, by Presidential Proclamation,
Americans observed I Am An American Day for the first time.
There were parades in most cities. The National Guard units
marched, and in some areas it could have been noted (but probably wasn't) that some companies had been outfitted with the
new combat steel helmets to wear instead of the round-brimmed
campaign hats. Some wore helmet liners, made out of what
seemed to be hard plastic.

They were smart-looking soldiers, and they carried their
twenty-three-year-old World War I-issue Springfield '03 bolt-
action rifles as though they knew how to use them. Field Artillery and Coast Artillery units paraded behind motor-drawn cais-
sons attached to businesslike split-trail 105-millimeter howitzers.
Friendly faces were among the marchers, known faces, the faces
of townspeople who drilled at the armory every Thursday night
and spent a couple of weeks at camp in the summer. This was
the first time many of their neighbors had seen them in full
uniform. They marched in thrilling cadence, 128 steps to the
minute, the drugstore clerk, the insurance man, the shoe salesman, the lawyer, the city employee, the cop at the school crossing, the newspaper editor. Fellow Americans waved flags and
applauded as they passed in review on the first I Am An American Day.

Portentous?

The guardsmen thought so. From scuttlebutt and from intensifying training schedules they suspected that mobilization was
not far off. Some among the spectators thought so too, especially
those who read the papers carefully. But not many.

In the White House a troubled Franklin Delano Roosevelt

read the alarming dispatches from Europe, and now, suddenly, from Asia and the Far East, and pondered on the isolationism and pacifism that seemed lodged in the land. Americans were peace-lovers. Also, they were disenchanted with war. World War I, despite the promises, had failed to make the world safe for democracy; it had failed to bring everlasting peace. If you won a war, the average fellow asked, what did you win? And then he answered his question: Nothing. You won nothing.

There was no way, Roosevelt realized, that Americans, in 1940, could have been persuaded to enter the war. Instead, he resolved, we would make America the "Arsenal for Democracy." The British, pleased, of course, but not as happy as they would have been if Americans had come to their aid with men as well as machines and weapons, cracked that Americans were willing to fight Hitler until there wasn't an Englishman left.

Roosevelt swapped fifty old destroyers to Britain for some naval and air bases in Western Hemisphere waters and quietly negotiated a deal with Iceland to allow the building of an American base there when, as and if needed. On paper, the SeaBees (naval construction battalions) came into existence.

Then, without warning or build-up, the President announced that he wanted to build a peacetime army so that if America had to go to war, she would, for the first time in history, do so *fully prepared*. He called up the National Guard and all other auxiliary services—Naval Reserve and Marine Corps Reserve, (the Coast Guard had already been absorbed into the Navy)—in a general mobilization, and asked Congress to authorize a national selective service act so that the nation could embark on its first peacetime draft in history,

It was a daring move for the President, but Hitler's hordes were marching on, and Americans, finding the President's concern to be infectious, were losing much of their isolationism, except, perhaps, in the Midwest, where British-hating Roosevelt-loathing Robert McCormick, publisher of the powerful *Chicago Tribune*, one of the most respected newspapers in the nation, garnered many followers who agreed with him that America should keep its nose out of foreign affairs.

Congress, weighted in the Democrat column, responded to Roosevelt's command and on August 27 enacted the Selective Service and Training Act. The same measure also required that all alien residents register with the government. The President signed the draft into law on September 16, a hot, bright, sunshiny day in Washington.

He set one month from the day of signing—October 16, 1940—as the day of registration for all male citizens from ages eighteen through thirty-five.

The first American peacetime draft was underway.

In all, 16,313,240 men received their registration cards. In Washington, Secretary of War Henry L. Stimson, having been blindfolded by the selective service director, plunged his hand into a giant glass bowl and drew the card of the first selectee, and the draft machinery was set in inexorable motion. Selectees, in short order, became inductees—into the armed forces.

The day that Roosevelt signed the Selective Service Act into law, was four days after the forty-seventh birthday of a general staff colonel, a former schoolteacher and high school principal from Indiana, Lewis B. Hershey. Just before the day of the drawing, on October 15, Hershey was appointed a brigadier general and named director of selective service, a post he was to occupy until his retirement in 1971, probably the most thankless job in government.

To mark that important day October 16, the Post Office Department issued three patriotic postage stamps calculated to impress upon the public the need'for adequate national defense. The 1-cent stamp bore the picture of the Statue of Liberty; the 2-cent stamp an antiaircraft gun; and the 3-cent stamp showed an uplifted torch (whether Columbia's or Miss Liberty's no one seemed to know). Each stamp bore the words "For Defense."

There were some people, Republicans and defecting Democrats, who said that Roosevelt was pushing the country nearer to wartime footing to scare the voters into supporting him for the third term for which he had been nominated in July at a tumultuous, rifting Democratic National Convention in Chicago. The chief executive ignored such gibes and implied that he was going to limit his campaigning because of the increasing pressures of office. Those who wished to could infer from that that he was already a wartime president, too busy for the trivia of politics.

Unlimited in his campaign efforts or his campaign spending was Wendell Willkie, an Indiana utilityman turned Wall Street lawyer, the Republican nominee, who made whistle-stop tours throughout the country, attracting large, exuberant crowds. For a candidate of the "outs," he was very well financed. He was backed by an ultra-rich faction of the eastern Establishment, which had, for sundry reasons, broken with Roosevelt. Perhaps reflecting the sympathies of his strongest and richest supporters, Willkie differed from Roosevelt mainly in domestic matters and policies, which he claimed had been neglected, and spoke eloquently of "One World," maintaining that the earth had become too small to endure isolationism on the part of any leading nation.

Before November, however FDR and his wife Eleanor managed to do a considerable amount of campaigning to cheering crowds in the most politically sensitive or politically significant parts of the nation.

And on Tuesday, November 4, Roosevelt won by another landslide (440 electoral votes), the first President to be elected for more than two terms of office in the history of the country.

It was, he said, a mandate to forge ahead with his plans for defense. Other, more ambitious plans were to be revealed after the first of the year.

A couple of weeks after the election, New Yorkers and Long Islanders celebrated the opening of the Queens Midtown Tunnel (cost $58 million) with festivities on both sides of the East River. It was just a bit too late for the 1939 World's Fair at Flushing Meadows, for which the Bronx Whitestone Bridge had been completed to handle traffic from the north and east. The Fair had run through the summer and autumn of 1940, and had closed before the tunnel was opened.

Variety noted that trumpeter Harry James had left the Benny Goodman orchestra to form his own band, and had brought along with him from the Goodman group an unknown young vocalist named Francis Albert Sinatra. Some of the old hands in the dance band business said they thought the kid didn't sing too well. And he was awfully skinny.

"Defense" was becoming a more important word as the year waned. "Defense plants" seemed, suddenly, to be everywhere, with new buildings springing up where there had been farmland a year before. In New England, in upstate New York, in New Jersey, in Pennsylvania and in the Midwest, old factories that had been abandoned or only partially used, were spruced up, cleaned out and reactivated.

Throughout the country, defense plants geared up to work around the clock, seven days a week. Long freight trains hooted and clattered and snaked their cars along the railroads all night long, every night in the week. Extra passenger trains were seen streaking along the rights-of-way during the daytime with white flags on the engines denoting they were "specials." If they slowed down, uniformed men could be seen inside.

Small inconveniences began to occur. Fold-down paper match-books began to disappear from the stores, and smokers had to switch back to the old-fashioned wooden "kitchen matches," which came in a big rectangular box and cost a nickel. Zippers, only recently introduced, disappeared from the flies of new trousers. Silk stockings fell into short supply because the material was needed for parachutes, so women painted makeup on their legs to give them that taupe tone, and some even painted stripes on the backs of their calves with eyebrow pencils. The telephone companies, which had converted the biggest cities to dial phones, as well as some of the smaller rural communities, postponed the dial conversions in hundreds of medium- and small-sized cities because copper and other materials were in shortening supply.

As winter approached, it was announced by various experts that there might be a shortage of both coal and oil because of the diversion of transportation equipment, including barges and tankers.

In many parts of the country, people who looked smugly at the gas cooking stoves in their kitchens were disappointed to learn that companies that manufactured their own "illuminating gas" would also likely be short of coking coal.

Stores reported a run on sugar and retail spokesmen cautioned against hoarding, but housewives, who either remembered the sugar shortages of World War I or had heard the older folks discuss them, paid little heed.

But the money kept coming faster and faster. There was not much consumer credit around in those days, so the wage-earners worked and spent—and spent.

Automobile production set a record. New cars filled the highways, despite warnings from Interior Secretary Harold L. Ickes that motorists were going to use up all the gasoline we had. Huge quantities, he cautioned, were being diverted to military needs.

At Christmastime, most of the boys who had been drafted or

26

mobilized were sent home on furlough, and it turned into one of the merriest Christmases in the memory of most.

Retail sales smashed through and set a record.

The Depression was forgotten. Erased from memory was the fact that only two years before, in the spring of 1938, the economic slump had hit bottom and 12 million Americans had been out of work. Now everybody was working—everybody, that is, who really *wanted* to work. Or so it seemed.

The figures didn't bear that out. Poverty persisted in a great many parts of the country, notably in the South and the Middle South, where, as yet, there weren't many factories to get defense orders. But if you weren't in those sections, you didn't notice it.

In the service, a buck private got $21 a month, plus all his clothes, supplies, meals, lodging and medical and dental care. That was $21 free and clear, to spend as he wished.

America was gearing up for war, and by and large the people were enjoying it—or the results of it. It was exhilarating and it brought prosperity.

It was called "defense," not "war," and it was easy to think that the whole thing would roll along as it was going for many years to come. It was easy to think this because most Americans were simply not ready for war. Not in any way were they ready.

Especially unready for war were the military. The new draftees were sent to training camps in World War I gear, hand-me-downs from 1918. In the Carolinas and Georgia and Tennessee, woodworking factories were pressed into service to turn out wooden rifles for the trainees so they could get the "feel" of them. At Fort McClellan, soldiers used broomsticks to learn the manual of arms. At the Springfield Armory and Arsenal in Massachusetts, the blueprints for the Garand semiautomatic, recoilless, gas-ejection rifle were being studied. It was called the M-1.

As prosperity washed and laved the land there was evidence that labor unrest, long postponed, was emerging, and there were threats of strikes. Most of them, however, were threatened for the following year. Crotchety, bristly-browed John L. Lewis, one of the most vocal Roosevelt-haters, resigned as president of the Congress of Industrial Organizations, the CIO, which he had founded in 1935. He remained as president of the United Mine Workers Union, and was preparing to do battle with the White House in the coming year.

27

Booming, bustling, even bristling, America ended the first year of the fifth decade of the twentieth century in feverish activity, with most people *saying* that the nation would never again go to war, but growing numbers of them fearing that sooner or later it was bound to come.

New Year's Eve of 1940 was certainly the gayest, noisiest, costliest, celebratingest night since 1928, before the market crashed.

The lights were on all over America, and they glowed 'til dawn had brought the first daylight of 1941 from coast to coast.

2

The Hero's Hero of
1941

There were a great many fight fans who were disappointed with the way the heavyweight champion of the world, Joe Louis, was mowing down his competitors, a job he had undertaken in the late fall of 1940 and was continuing into the deep spring of 1941. Louis was taking on all comers, eliminating all possible contenders. Once a month a challenger was presented to the hulking, warm-hearted champ, and with what seemed to be clockwork precision, he would be eliminated, not always painlessly.

The ringside press corps took to calling the victims by uncomplimentary names and saying that they were from the "Bum-of-the-Month Club." The Bum-of-the-Month in January was a fellow named Red Burman, who was smashed into unconsciousness in the fifth round. In February it was Gus Dorazio, who was stuck to the canvas in the second round.

Lined up for March was a twenty-six-year-old, meaty, 255-pound Abe Simon of Queens, Long Island, and the newspapers identified him immediately as coming from the same old club of bums. "Simple Simon" they called him and generally predicted he wouldn't last through the fifth round.

Simon, appearing a little awkward, started the contest with a hard right to the champ's head. Stung, Louis came out of his crouch and began his famed battering attack. A right, a left, a right, a left. Simon took them all.

Round after round, Simon stood up to the unbelievable assault. He seemed to Louis a barely resisting punching bag. The crowd cheered wildly. In the thirteenth round dazed and unable to lift his dead-weight arms, Simon staggered over to the ropes, calling an end to the match. For his unbelievably courageous stand against the invincible Joe Louis, Simon was ousted from the Bum-of-the-Month Club and his proper first name of Abe was restored to him in the sports columns.

Another member of the club came along in April, however—one Tony Musto, who was disposed of in nine rounds. People began to say that nobody—just *nobody*—could stand up to world heavyweight champion Joe Louis, the toughest gladiator of them all, and, beyond question, the most universally loved of all the heavyweight champions of the world, past or present, including the ultra-popular Jack Dempsey.

Three times more in 1941 Joe Louis was to defend his championship, each time with a spectacular display of his special prowess and, it turned out, with his crown at one time in serious jeopardy.

He had fought almost constantly for four years since becoming champ. He took on all applicants, never grumbling, not even at the offerings from the Bum-of-the-Month Club. He was never accused of a deliberately low blow, of sneering at his opponents or of a fixed fight.

"I want to fight honest," he said, "so the next colored boy can get the same break I got."

Fetched from Alabama to Detroit when he was twelve years old, Joseph Louis Barrow grew up on the streets, primarily because of his ineptitude in the classroom, and because his family was poor. A good street-brawler, he was persuaded by his friends to try a hand at boxing at a settlement house. He disliked it at first, but soon had floored so many opponents with the big, puffy sixteen-ounce gloves that he attracted the notice of professionals and his magic career was opened before him.

Among all celebrities, even if you included the top movie stars, the politicians and the radio personalities, Joe Louis was *the* hero to most Americans in 1941 and for a long time after that.

He was the benchmark from which one measured the great virtues—strength, skill, courage, honesty, integrity, steadfastness and, above it all, humility. In the newsreels he appeared a bit dull, perhaps lugubrious, but only to people who didn't know him. He was a fast man with a funny line (never smutty or scatological), enjoyed a good sense of humor, and his mother confided that as a kid he was a genuine hell-raiser who spent a good deal of his time soothing the seat of his oft-spanked britches. As a national hero, though, he didn't drink, smoke, chew, swear or display evidence that he recognized any differences between boys and girls, though in the presence of the latter he always stood, awkward and embarrassed.

America loved him, revered him, held him in awe.

When he waved his great hamlike hands, Americans cheered and wept with almost the same frenzy that the newsreels showed the Germans exhibiting when Hitler spoke in the *sportplatz*.

In May, Joe Louis defended his laurels in Washington, the first world championship fight ever to be held in the nation's capital. Not yet called "Wartime Washington," the district, nevertheless, was already jammed with newcomers from all walks of life and all parts of the country, and Griffith Stadium was filled to capacity with excited fans. They got their money's worth.

Hardly had the first round gotten underway than the great, the invincible Joe Louis, stunned and dazed, was hanging over the ropes, head down, teetering between the canvas and the floor. The contender, who had sent the king of champs against the ropes and nearly across the ring's apron, was twenty-five-year-old Buddy Baer, the kid brother of former champion Max Baer, who as an underdog had won the heavyweight title from the mammoth Primo Carnera in 1934, the same Maxie Baer who in 1942 was to enlist in the U.S. Army as a foot soldier.

Embarrassed by the shattering sledgehammer blow that had sent him into the ropes, Louis unleashed his thunder and lightning in sporadic bursts as he circled Baer in his now-famous stalker's crouch. To the delight of the spectators, who, as always, wanted full value in gladiators' blood, he seemed to miss a lot and in the fifth round Baer opened a gash over the champ's left eye. It was the first time in his career that anyone had drawn blood on Joseph Louis Barrow. If not really angry, he was disturbed by the development.

Buddy Baer was a giant who towered over Louis, and somehow he was getting to him. Apparently the situation called for a change in strategy. With blood streaming down his round cheek, Louis changed his pace a bit in the sixth, threw the giant off and then attacked with his unparalleled assault of rights and lefts, like a woodchopper reducing a towering oak, and the Big Baer fell to the canvas.

At the count of seven Baer regained his feet, to be cut down again by a blasting right to the jaw. Hearing the count in his dreams, Baer managed to lift both gloves from the floor just before the timekeeper shouted "ten" and the referee motioned Louis from his neutral corner to continue the fight. Baer arose,

31

faced Louis, accepted another smashing right to the same abused jaw and slumped to the floor, out cold. It was a Joe Louis fight at its best, a crowd-pleaser that would have been hard to duplicate in fact or fiction.

Thus was eliminated the sixteenth consecutive challenger to the world's heavyweight crown since it had come to repose on Joe Louis' close-cropped head. But like the fastest gunman in a western bad town Louis was never to be without a challenger.

A month later he was in New York City's Polo Grounds before a crowd of more than 54,000 eager fans, all mindful of the fresh scar over his left eye, when he faced twenty-three-year-old Billy Conn, a Pittsburgh kid whose fans said he was specially forged of formidable secret alloys. Right from the start, young Conn (five years younger than the champ) began a sight-blurring tattoo of strokes and pokes, some of which got through the defense of the big, shuffling hero.

In the fourth, Conn's jabs became lightninglike, and Louis was seen to shake his head. In the eighth they had begun to sting, and besides, Conn was piling up points.

Louis maintained his flatfooted circling of the kid, the deadly right fist ever-cocked but seemingly always just a little off target. By the end of the twelfth, Conn's relentless parries and thrusts, more of them scoring now, had the huge crowd on its feet crying in a sustained cheer blended with moans.

As he bounced from the corner on the bell at the opening of the thirteenth round, Conn sneered, "I got you, Joe," breaking, as far as Louis was concerned, a cardinal rule. The champ never spoke in the ring, hardly ever grunted. He never did or said anything to disparage his adversary. It just wasn't gentlemanly.

Louis continued his shuffle, and the cocky Conn did exactly what he was cautioned against—he plowed into Joe and began to trade punch for punch. It was a kid with a water pistol going after a tank. With the very first swap Louis' right hand exploded in Conn's face.

Conn fell back, but before he could reorganize, the rain of destruction was upon him, rights and lefts slamming into his face, his chest, his body with a deadly uppercut awaiting him as soon as he dropped his guard. He fell to the canvas, bounced once and curled up for a long ten-count, oblivious to the ear-shattering pandemonium that rent the heavens.

Within six months both Joe Louis and Billy Conn would be buck privates in the U.S. Army, their heroism untarnished.

In October, Louis faced his nineteenth crown-challenger, this one rated to be more serious than any of the others, a chap who claimed to have a "cosmic punch," who proclaimed himself to be the "Man of Destiny" and who was an acknowledged expert in the ring, as well as a practitioner of yoga, an unsettling revelation. His name was Lou Nova, and he was twenty-six, two years younger than the champ, brawny, fast, smart, confident, unafraid.

It had already been announced that this would probably be Joe Louis' last fight because his Chicago draft board had classified him 1-A. Nova desperately wanted to wrest the world championship from Louis before he donned that uniform.

Probably no fight in history had received such a dedicated press build-up. For good reason: aside from President Roosevelt's last two fireside chats, Louis, when he was in the ring, commanded the biggest radio audience of all time. It was estimated that more than 50 million people would listen to the fight. Because of the headlines, hardly an American was unaware of the impending bout; extremely few were uninterested. Because of his Boy Scoutish, gentlemanly image Joe Louis had as many fans among the ladies as he did among fellow males.

An early October chill brought unseasonable discomfort to the Polo Grounds as 60,000 fans balanced on hard, narrow seats and hoped to get full value for their highest-price-in-history tickets. (Scalpers, it was said, got up to $500 for a good ringside seat.)

Graham McNamee, Ted Husing and other sportscaster notables were as close to the ring as the rules allowed.

Nova was the forty-sixth man to stand up to Joe Louis. His forty-five predecessors had all bitten dust, but to the appraisers in the crowd, Nova did seem to have something different about him, some class, perhaps, but also some—well—*je ne sais quoi*, a style, a manner.

In a breathless hush, they touched gloves and Nova danced off to one side. The champ began his inimitable shuffle, right glove cocked up beside his nose, the left shielding the area just under his chin, imperturbable, measuring eyes glaring over the mounded leather mitts.

Around and around they went, for five long rounds, with

Nova darting in to try, usually unsuccessfully, to land his Sunday punch, and Louis popping one off now and again, whenever the yogaman got in range, with many of them missing the mark.

In the sixth Nova changed his pace and attempted to throw a right hook. It was a dreadful mistake.

Before it was completely unleashed, Louis fired a cannonball right just abaft Nova's jaw. It was the famous much-photographed Joe Louis knock-out punch, a lethal weapon all by itself, and it was just as effective as it had always been. Nova lay at the champ's feet, sound asleep.

It was, indeed, the end for Joe Louis in the ring.

In January, 1942, he risked his title for charity, donating his purse to the New York Auxiliary of the Navy Relief Society. He confronted Buddy Baer again, a stronger, healthier, wiser Baby Baer, but he knocked him out in the first round.

That night, after the charity fight, Louis was notified that he had been drafted into the Army. Beating the draft, he enlisted as a private. He held his heavyweight title until his retirement in 1948, when, beset by tax suits filed by the government and legal actions by creditors, he confessed that he was too old to fight again. He was thirty-five.

In the fall of 1942 some promoters—among them both Army men and civilians—decided it would be a morale-boosting event, and perhaps a profitable one, if Private Joe Louis Barrow and Corporal William Conn squared off for a decision on the world heavyweight championship held by Louis and shelved by circumstances.

The matter was argued up through the ranks of the military and finally got to Secretary of War Henry L. Stimson, who seemed shocked by the whole idea. There was a war on. No, he said. Definitely not. Louis was to return to Fort Riley, Kansas, forthwith, and Conn to Fort Wadsworth, New York.

The great hero of 1938-41 was no more. There's only one way to be a hero in the Army.

There were other heroes a-making.

But Joe Louis, gentleman, endured. His fans never really forgot him, and those who saw him fight have measured all latter-day pugilists against him, to their disadvantage.

3

The First American Czars
1941

Because of unsettled world conditions, President Roosevelt did not want to delay his inauguration as the nation's first third-term president. He scheduled it for the third Tuesday in January. It was pointed out that there was no rule saying a president *had* to be inaugurated in March, though that was the custom

Before the historic day arrived, however, he had taken three occasions to warn the 132 million Americans whom he led, that the war was intensifying and coming closer than ever to forcing the involvement of the United States. The first such occasion was his fifteenth fireside chat—just after the New Year. The second was his opening address to the new Seventy-seventh Congress, which he called his State of the Union message, setting a precedent that has endured. The third was his submission of a bill to Congress that shocked even the most loyal New Dealers, the lend-lease bill, propitiously numbered House Resolution No. 1776.

Roosevelt's New Deal measures had made him highly unpopular with growing numbers of American businessmen and even with some hardliners in his own Democratic party. His thumping defeat of the very popular Wendell Willkie in the elections the preceding fall, however, had given him a mandate. He believed it was to lead America away from its traditional insularity and isolationism and to align the nation with Great Britain—and, if necessary, Russia—in the terrible war against Nazi Germany.

Roosevelt, in fact, itched to go to war against Germany. He was convinced that Hitler must be stopped as soon as possible. He wanted to launch an invasion against the Continent, a wish that would not be fulfilled for several years.

It was not until thirty-one years later, in January, 1972, when the British released a summary of papers and comments left by Winston Churchill, that Americans learned for certain that President Roosevelt had wanted to go to war actively long before Pearl Harbor. Churchill said FDR had complained that there was no way he could think of to get Congress to declare war. Even in the early months of 1941, however, he did not hide his impatience, both with the Nazi aggressors, and with the war-resisting element of the American public.

His fireside chat, broadcast to 500 radio stations from the little Oval Room in the White House—and attended by his mother, Sara Roosevelt; the dour secretary of state, Cordell Hull; and actor Clark Cable and his actress wife, Carole Lombard—was when he launched his first salvo.

"Never before . . . has our American civilization been in such danger as now," emphasized the President. He refreshed American memories about the tripartite agreement between Germany, Italy and Japan in which the Axis powers declared that if the United States interfered with or blocked their program "aimed at world control," they would unite in ultimate action against the United States.

Having a little difficulty getting his verbs into agreement, Mr. Roosevelt said:

"If Great Britain goes down, all of us in the Americas would [will] be living at the point of a gun. The vast resources and wealth of this Hemisphere constitute the most tempting loot in the world."

The solution, declared America's President, was to provide more and more planes, tanks, guns, freighters for the British.

To do this, he cautioned, Americans might be required soon to ration themselves on consumer and luxury goods. He concluded:

"We must be the great arsenal of democracy."

A few days later, addressing the opening session of Congress, he was even more direct, stating his belief that war was necessary. His great head thrown back, his lightly tanned features reflecting only serious sincerity and lacking the customary glimmer of humor, Roosevelt pointed out that "Armed defense of democratic existence is now being gallantly waged on four continents." Then he warned: "No realistic American can expect from a dictator's peace, international generosity. Such a peace would bring no security for us or for our neighbors."

Then he outlined, with exceeding brevity, the historic Four Freedoms, destined to mean so much to Americans in the dark

days ahead and, indeed, to the people of the defeated democracies of Europe and to the beleaguered British:

> In the future days, which we seek to make secure, we look
> forward to a world founded upon four essential freedoms.
> The first is freedom of speech and expres-
> sion—everywhere in the world.
> The second is freedom of every person to worship God
> in his own way—everywhere in the world.
> The third is freedom from want—everywhere in the
> world.
> The fourth is freedom from fear—anywhere in the
> world.
> *To that high concept there can be no end save victory.*

There could be no question of what he meant by that. Yet,
doggedly, vast numbers of Americans refused to believe that the
United States would—or should—get into the war.

Blocking Roosevelt's path was the Neutrality Act. It forbade
military assistance to nations at war. Under it there was no way
that FDR could keep his pledge to turn the United States into
the arsenal of democracy. Whatever war goods were to be made
could not be sold or given to the United Kingdom, and certainly
not to Russia, which had a nonaggression pact with Germany.

Needed was some device to get around the Neutrality Act,
avoiding the necessity of lengthy congressional wrangling over
its appeal.

That device was forthcoming a week before Roosevelt's
Inauguration Day. It was the lend-lease bill, a measure whose
wide-ranging, awesome powers made the crisis unmistakable.
Roosevelt asked for a blank check from Congress with permission to spend it as he pleased. He demanded power to obtain
and to transfer war supplies to "Britain and her allies."

This was to spark a debate that was to rage in the sanctuaries
of Congress for two months while lawmakers from both sides
of the aisle raised anew the fears expressed in the third-term
campaign, that Roosevelt would become a dictator and lead the
nation into some form of collectivism.

Even as the congressmen debated, the war worsened. Hitler
invaded Yugoslavia; the Japanese moved on to Indochina.

The lend-lease bill passed both House and Senate on the same day in March, within twenty minutes it was rushed to the White House, and before ten minutes more elapsed, the President had signed it into law.

Waiting on the President's desk was a list of articles designated to be shipped abroad immediately. Most of them would start on their way that very night. Roosevelt wrote his okay on the list and handed it to his aide, Harry Hopkins. What was on the list and to whom the articles were consigned, he would not say. He sat back and awaited reports and learned, within an hour, that cheering Britons had decorated their blasted and shattered streets in London with American flags. FDR knew that the news of the lend-lease signing had sped around the world and that its great import was being assessed in Berlin, Rome, Tokyo and even in mysterious Moscow.

The President now had the power to make war without actually fighting. It was great power in the hands of the strong leader of the mightiest nation on earth—and that nation was mobilizing its manpower.

At a dinner of the White House Correspondents Association later that night, Roosevelt declared: "Let not the dictators of Europe or Asia doubt our unanimity now. May it be said of us in the days to come that our children and our children's children rise up and call us blessed." It was now a holy war, but for Americans, so far, it was bloodless.

Lend-lease was to affect more than the nations already in contact with the enemy. In the United States, procurement in the name of lend-lease was to strain to the utmost all facilities of production and agriculture. The war was an insatiable maw into which the arsenal of democracy must pour all of its resources, save those most urgently needed at home.

Belts were tightened on the home front, but in Washington the mobilizers knew that there were several notches yet to go. Americans didn't mind much, for along with the tightened belts came much fatter wallets, as crop limitations were removed from farms, and as bombed-out British industries moved their patents, designs and skilled foremen into safe American plants and recruited American labor to work 'round the clock, seven days a week.

Those who were not yet drafted, and those others who were not yet absorbed by one of the defense industries, trooped off to the hiring offices whistling "Chattanooga Choo Choo" and

"Deep in the Heart of Texas," and soon it was a "workers' market." There were more jobs available than there were people to fill them, possibly for the first time since America was an infant nation.

The pulse, the heartbeat of the land quickened. People walked faster, thought faster, worked harder.

Recruiters began to call for women to leave their homes, even if only for part-time work, or to fill the night shifts while the kiddies were sleeping. Thus was born "Rosie the Riveter," whose caricature on posters was a long-lashed, snub-nosed, rosy-mouthed, buxom lass wearing coveralls and with a blue bandanna on her head. To a generation that had practically worshiped the nude, long-legged Petty girls in *Esquire* and other publications Rosie was an over-practical wartime shock.

To manage the titanic lend-lease program, the President appointed his best friend and fellow New Dealer, Harry Hopkins, as executive secretary of the War Cabinet. Since the War Cabinet consisted of the secretaries of state, war, navy and treasury, this made Harry Hopkins virtually the assistant president of the United States.

A quick, slim man of enormous resources and energy, an obvious "doer," Hopkins wasted no time in cultivating friends. He didn't need to; he had a direct, unimpeded line to the office of the most important man in the world, FDR.

Roosevelt dispatched Harry Hopkins to the pristine, marbled Federal Reserve building, where a couple of dozen rooms were hastily cleared and refurbished, and with an original staff of thirty-five people, the executive secretary of the War Cabinet settled down to rearm the democracies, spend $7 billion under the Lend-Lease Act and try to stop Hitler with arms and food. Before his incoming mail could be opened, Hopkins was off to London to confer with Winston Churchill.

The prime minister informed Hopkins of his immediate needs —food and ships. England was hungry. Britannia continued to rule the waves, though barely, but the ships were bringing the hard supplies of war, rather than food. In addition, enormous amounts of shipping had gone to the bottom, victim of the marauding Nazi U-boat wolf packs.

Not just any food would do. There was a great scarcity of refrigerated cargo space in England. Unprocessed food would spoil on the docks and in the warehouses. Worse, the nightly bombing of Britain had destroyed a high proportion of the gas mains so that it was impossible for many people to cook, or even *heat*, food. This put a premium on canned and processed goods.

At that time the United States was not accustomed to packing meat in cans. Its processed foods consisted mostly of cereals, soups, vegetables and a few varieties of fruits.

These things would be fine and welcome in England, Churchill told Hopkins, but Britain also needed condensed or powdered milk, dried and frozen eggs, dried fruits and dried vegetables and every kind of cheese. The British needed proteins.

In short order, Hopkins had arranged for significant shipments of a new canned and processed meat, Spam, far superior to the British Army's "tinned willie," the corned beef from Argentina. It was an instant hit on the besieged island, and was destined to go on and become a staple in the diet of American GI's in years to come.

Under Hopkins' direction, American producers also began to package dehydrated meats, vegetables, fruits and soups, which needed only water to make them succulent and nutritious. Powdered milk, powdered eggs and processed cheese began to flow into Canada to be put aboard British cargo ships and convoyed across the U-boat-infested North Atlantic. England was not so hungry after Harry Hopkins' visit with Churchill, nor would it be again. The British came to acquire a fondness for beans and soya flour. In time even a "joint of beef" (standing rib roast) was no longer an extreme luxury. One development of the "Food for Britain" campaign was corned beef hash canned in combination with powdered eggs, a staple that the British liked and which also had a bright future with American GI's in their field rations.

The new processed foods such as dehydrated soups began to appear on the shelves of American groceries as the big soup-makers, Campbell, Heinz, Hormel and others, felt the shortage of steel and tinplate for their cans. Americans also liked these soups and felt better about the fare being sent to the battling British.

Canners were not the only ones feeling the pinch of raw materials. All metals were being diverted to defense. A system of priorities was growing up in Washington and was beginning to be formalized in the Interior Department under the aegis of the outwardly grumpiest and most acidulous of all cabinet members, Secretary Harold Ickes, known affectionately to the White House coterie as "Irritable Harold." Ickes predicted that under the sprawling, mindless gobbling of the defense effort, the United States would soon run out of just about everything, including electricity and oil.

(Although Ickes was proved correct in his forecasts, as reward for his outspoken and unwelcome advice, he was virtually boxed out of the War Cabinet, later in the year, by executive decree and reorganization.)

On the home front, Americans heard reports of upcoming rationing and were told that there would be no more aluminum ware in the housewares departments of their stores, and they awaited further word from the sources of power and command in Washington.

Philip K. Wrigley, head of the gum empire and owner of the Chicago Cubs, garnered headlines throughout the nation by selling to the Office of Production Management his remaining half-million pounds of aluminum foil, previously used for wrapping his gum, thereby jumping the gun on an inevitable conversion to cellophane, a wartime product developed as a substitute. Wrigley didn't add that his cellophane was superior to the foil.

Envious of Wrigley's publicity, officials at American Tobacco Company took another look at their green-colored packages of Lucky Strike cigarettes with the red bull's-eye circle in the center, decided that the green ink contained precious metals needed in the defense effort, and launched a new, highly effective campaign: "Lucky Strike green has gone to war." It had a patriotic ring; the new white packages with the same old bull's-eye sold well. The aromatic, toasted Lucky Strikes were as good as prewar.

Because of the shortages of basic materials, however, Americans were treated in the early months of 1941 to the spectacle of the birth of a new era—the Age of Plastics. It was hailed as evidence of that old Yankee ingenuity again coming to the aid of a nation in need. Indeed, this is precisely what happened.

Plastics started out replacing hard rubber after the Japanese cut off the source of supply of raw rubber in the Far East and a huge inventory of the semiprocessed latex was destroyed by a fire in the Firestone mills in Fall River, Massachusetts, that started under mysterious circumstances and was fought under

41

what appeared to have been deliberately engineered confusion and obstruction.

Plastics were originally used as a replacement for rubber in such things as steering wheels, fountain pens and hand telephones.

In short order, though, plastics began to show up in a wide variety of items—as kitchen utensils, replacing aluminum and steel pots and pans; as clothes pins, replacing wood; as bottles and jars, replacing glass; as bulk food containers, replacing cardboard; as agitators in washing machines, as paneling and shelves in refrigerators, saving metals; and as casings for radios, clocks and phonographs, replacing a variety of scarce products. Plastic was used to make covers for thermos bottles, soles for shoes, fobs for key chains. The Army used it for underliners for its new skull-conforming steel helmets, which replaced the wash-basin variety worn by the World War I doughboy, and was experimenting with using it in a fuse cap. Plastic was everywhere, and that was fitting for its raw materials came from everywhere—from air, milk, soybeans, wood, coal, petroleum. Du Pont was experimenting with thread made from plastics and had had success with a new stocking made from a thread called nylon, a continuous filament fiber made in the laboratory. Women liked the looks and feel of these hose, but they were saggy and baggy at the knees, and grew somewhat stiff when cold. Du Pont researchers acknowledged this fault and went back to the labs seeking improvements. They were forthcoming in short order. The market was assured, however, for silk stockings had become just about nonexistent. The owners of silk mills were busy making parachutes and didn't mind the intrusion into their civilian market.

What bothered the ladies more than the shortage of silk stockings, however, was the consistent increase in the prices of just about everything they bought. It also bothered FDR, who had told White House confidants, "If we are to keep this New Deal war, we have to keep prices from skyrocketing the way they did in the last war." In the early spring of 1941, prices may not have been skyrocketing, but they had taken giant leaps.

What was needed, Roosevelt decided, was a "Price Czar" with indisputable powers and the authority to broaden those powers when, as and if needed. It had to be a man of enormous ability and with sufficient dedication to ignore the fact that inevitably he would become known as America's premier First-Class Bastard, who would anger equally the consumers of the land and the leaders of business, finance and industry.

Roosevelt didn't have to look far for the man ideally suited for the job. Already serving as a member of the Priorities Committee of the Office of Production Management, a Wharton School-trained economist, an expert on consumer credit and consumer spending, a man who had already served with distinction as a consultant to the WPA and as executive secretary of the Temporary National Economic Committee.

The man was Leon Henderson, big, burly, dynamic, blunt but soft-spoken, and, at forty-six, an indefatigable bear for work. Roosevelt called the new agency the Office of Price Administration and Civilian Supply: OPACS. Into Henderson's hands he placed almost unlimited power to fix priorities on *all* civilian supplies—everything from hairpins to hams, from perambulators to parasols, from tea to toilet tissue—and to withhold supplies at his discretion from uncooperating industries, to have absolute priority on all transportation, to fix and publish maximum price schedules and enforce their compliance, and to commandeer plants in the name of the President, if deemed advisable.

Alarmed businessmen cried that not even Hitler in Germany had such dictatorial powers, and it may have been true. Leon Henderson was by far the most important man on the home front. The entire economy of the nation, the welfare of its citizens, the jobs, the lives of all, resided almost exclusively in his restless hands.

The resisters of Roosevelt's "collectivism" finally had a *cause célèbre*. Here was the hand of the tyrannical dictator, exposed at last.

Henderson did not relieve any of the tensions when, at his first press conference after his appointment was announced, he said: "You can name anything and I would say that prices are already too high. . . . All prices ought to come down."

The entire business community shuddered.

Before the first day's work was ended, Henderson had started plans for building an empire of price and supply policemen with regional and local offices throughout the land that would, in time, outnumber those of the Internal Revenue Service. By the next day the first of tens of thousands of regulations began to flow into what was to become the OPACS's legal department.

This was the ammunition with which Leon Henderson would fight the war against inflation. He began stockpiling it immediately.

On the beaches of both coasts, but primarily along the Atlantic, there began to appear great blotches of black, sticky oil. In the early spring of 1941, in Florida, bathers were bothered by this and they began to glower at the almost endless and constant procession of tankers and cargo vessels steaming hull down along the horizon. They thought the oil came from pumping ballast from the tankers.

Not until burning ships were sighted off Cape Cod and again off Cape Hatteras was it realized that the oil spills came from British tankers that had been sunk by U-boats not far from shore. The war was coming closer to the U.S. beaches, though as yet no American shipping had been hit.

In the first three months of 1941 Nazi warships and U-boats had sunk more than a million tons of shipping. Ships were being torpedoed much faster than they could be launched.

Shipbuilding was booming throughout America, from New England to the West Coast, along the Gulf of Mexico, up the Mississippi and around the Great Lakes, but even so, no more than one million tons of new shipping was scheduled to go down the ways in the entire year of 1941. That much and more had been sunk in the first three months of 1941.

Before he left the OPM for the OPACS, Leon Henderson, foreseeing the shortage of shipping, had given the Maritime Commission a list of "essential" and "nonessential" imports that would soon be listed in cargo priorities. Listed as essential were such strategic and critical materials as tin, rubber, leather, wool, coffee, sugar and cocoa.

Deemed to be nonessential were, among other items, spices, wine, tea, palm oil and burlap. Sage, which had been picked by Greek and Yugoslavian goatherders, came from areas now occupied by the Germans. A wild California sage was tried, but the spice-packagers found that when ground, it tasted of turpentine.

Thyme, which had come from France, was being trampled under uncaring German boots. The French did not harvest it.

Paprika came from Hungary, a land now gobbled up by the Hitler expansion. A tiny bit filtered through from Portugal, but was bought up long before it could reach regular store shelves.

Spanish saffron simply didn't exist any longer. Under the victorious Franco, Spaniards were too preoccupied to harvest it. U.S. growers wouldn't try to produce it, since 14,000 tiny stigmata from the bloom of the plant are needed to make one ounce of saffron.

Government officials were reluctant to admit it, but the greatest shortage shaping up was in oil. Supplies were running desperately low, both in Britain and in the United States. Clearly more "bottoms" were needed from shipyards around the country. Oil moves by sea.

To the rescue came the man destined to become the industrial hero of the war. He set about immediately to solve the problem. His bald head gleaming, when not covered by his omnipresent slouch hat, his lips pressed tight from perpetual inner tension, Henry J. Kaiser viewed the shortage of ships and said it could be ended, and soon.

An engineer who had been awesomely successful in myriad projects, such as building the San Francisco-Oakland bridge, longest in the world, and the Grand Coulee Dam, largest in the world, Kaiser was president of fifteen companies and a director of twenty additional corporations. Other engineers said that if you had a problem all you had to do was take it to Henry Kaiser. When, for instance, slides threatened to delay work on the Coulee Dam, he froze a whole mountainside solid to keep it in place while work was completed and the mountain shored up.

Henry Kaiser was now at work, he revealed, on sixty new cargo ships for Britain, eighty-seven freighters, and a fleet of destroyers for the U.S. Navy. The word was received with a sigh of relief on both sides of the Atlantic.

When he had turned fifty, Henry Kaiser started counting his birthdays backwards until everyone but members of his immediate family lost count. None but they knew his right age. He was not young. He refused to be old.

In time Kaiser would design and build the Liberty cargo ship, and speed up schedules so that he could launch one a day. He applied mass production and prefabrication techniques to a highly skilled industry that had worked from individual draftsmen's plans since the time of the ancient Norsemen.

Wall Street's financiers, speculators and investors watched the burgeoning American industrial scene with keen interest, but they had their own problems right at home on Manhattan's nether tip. It looked as though the first paid president of the New York Stock Exchange, William McChesney Martin, Jr., salary $48,000 a year, was going to be drafted. Worse, it appeared that the happiest potential draftee in America, eager to be called, was William McChesney Martin.

The thirty-one-year-old bachelor, a bookish mathematics genius, who shunned the lush clubs of the area and ate in the Automat, who violated tradition by wearing no hat, who, instead of reading market reports, wrote plays, was also a New Dealer, rather enthusiastic in a polite way about the reforms, social and otherwise, attributed to Roosevelt. Despite it all, he was well liked in the financial community where he he had won his spurs. The trouble was, Martin did not really reciprocate the feeling toward the financial community. He wanted to get out of it.

Right from the beginning, Martin had been the center of strenuous tugging and hauling by factions in the community. The Stock Exchange had previously had "honorary" presidents until the conviction of Richard Whitney in 1938 for grand larceny. Whitney had been the vice president who, with the committed resources of New York's five largest banks, had tried to stem the avalanche of the market crash on October 24, 1929. He had served five terms as president of the exchange until his personal improvidence in handling the affairs of his own brokerage firm resulted in his arrest, conviction and expulsion from the exchange. In 1941, Whitney was in Sing Sing serving an eight-year sentence, a model prisoner.

Martin, as the first paid president, a former governor of the exchange, was pulled in one direction by the Old Guard, which wanted to mount some resistance against newfangled government regulations, in another direction by the Young Turks, who wanted to set up a system of self-policing, and in yet another direction by the Securities and Exchange Commission, getting now to feel its oats after several tests of the new Banking and Exchange laws of 1933-34. (The drafting of the laws had been the work of a committee headed by Joseph P. Kennedy, who had gone on to become ambassador to the Court of St. James in England.)

Now, in 1941, Wall Street's Boy Wonder of 1939 was looking forward to a reprieve from his monstrous headache by responding to the beckoning finger of the stern chairman of his draft board. He was drafted on April 16, 1941, as a buck private,

46

and after progressing steadily through the ranks of the infantry, he was promoted to a full colonel on August 4, 1945. Later, of course, in 1951, Martin was to become chairman of the Federal Reserve Board, a post in which he would serve with honor, never far away from the headache he left in Wall Street, until 1971.

Farther uptown in New York an interesting merchandising experiment was undertaken in early 1941 by the brothers Gimbel, Bernard Gimbel of Gimbel Brothers department store, and Adam Gimbel of Saks Fifth Avenue. They tried to dispose of a large part of the $50 million worth of *objets d'art* that had been accumulated by William Randolph Hearst, now "broke" and employed as editorial director of his own newspapers at $100,000 per year. (The condition of being broke, gentle reader, is relative.)

For years Hearst had purchased more than a million dollars' worth of art treasures per year, stuff ranging from Egyptian mummies to gold candelabra, amphoras and urns, and death masks as well as priceless paintings and beautiful statuary.

Now his twenty-five newspapers and the profits from the mines he had inherited from his father could no longer pay the interest on their debts and his. He had mortgaged for $600,000 his enormous and breathtaking showplace, his San Simeon estate in California, to get walking-around money, and ultimately he decided to offer his accumulation of art back to the art market.

He found it was one market where it may not pay to have a "corner." Art dealers couldn't or wouldn't take it back. They were afraid their price structure—an fragile prop at best —would collapse under the weight of so much art.

Thus it wound up on the counters of the Manhattan stores of the Gimbels'. One item, a medieval cannon, sold almost immediately, buyer not recorded. By the end of the year, most of the collection had been sold, much of it to housewives.

Meanwhile, the literary world was saddened. It suffered one of its most sorrowful times in the early months of 1941. It lost, through tragic coincidence, four of the greatest authors of the period, F. Scott Fitzgerald, James Joyce, Sherwood Anderson and Virginia Woolf.

The "lost generation" died with Francis Scott Key Fitzgerald. He had postponed a visit from his doctor because he was racing time to finish a novel he was writing, still festooned with a gag title, *The Love of the Last Tycoon—A Western*. It was a story about

Hollywood. He was struck down by heart failure and an alcohol-weakened liver, though he had not had a drink in several years. Gone was the great journalist-author of *The Great Gatsby, All the Sad Young Men, This Side of Paradise, The Beautiful and the Damned* and *Tales of the Jazz Age*. Fitzgerald *was* the Jazz Age—gone now, forever.

The author of *Ulysses* and *Finnegans Wake*, James Joyce, the puzzling, compelling Irish writer, died in Zürich, an expatriate from France, where he had lived as an expatriate from Ireland. For a dozen years he had been bothered by stomach pains, belatedly diagnosed, when he finally reached Zürich, as a malignancy in the duodenum. Joyce, his wife Nora and his son Giorgio had fled to Vichy before the Nazi invasion of Paris, and from Vichy to Switzerland, under German military and bureaucratic harassment all the way. Deeply in debt, stone broke, unable to raise money, almost blind, Joyce died worrying about his daughter Lucia, suffering from a mental disorder, who was in a sanitarium near incessantly bombed St. Nazaire, where the Germans and cowed French officials held her, refusing her an exit visa to Switzerland—and about his persistent, leechlike creditors, including some bankers, who, despite the war, hounded him to the very end.

Sherwood Anderson, paint manufacturer, ad man, unparalleled story teller and novelist, died in Colón, in the Panama Canal Zone, where he had been carried from a cruise ship after being stricken with an abdominal obstruction and peritonitis. He was sent home to be buried in Virginia, distant but not too far from the small-town mid-America that he had chronicled in *Winesburg, Ohio* and many other stories, peeking with sharp focus behind the unpainted false-fronts lining the main streets of small-town America.

Mrs. Dalloway and *To the Lighthouse* had enshrined Virginia Woolf as a great British novelist. On a morning in March she sat down at her desk, as was her custom, wrote a note to her sister saying "Farewell to the world," wrote another to her husband, and taking a walking cane, set out across the Sussex Downs to the River Ouse. Later, searchers found her stick lying on the bank. They found no body. She was declared a suicide by a coroner's jury.

Many Americans were appalled at such a great cumulative loss to the literary world in such a short span of time, but they were consoled, somewhat, in that dreary spring of 1941, by the book of a new and powerful writer, one who called himself Jan Valtin, an obvious *non de plume*, whose work *Out of the Night* revealed him to be an ex-German Communist, and an ex-agent and prisoner of the OGPU, the Soviet secret police, and an escaped prisoner of the Gestapo. He provided safe and secure Americans with an insight into what it was like to be a political activist in Europe at that time.

Soon afterward, another European, Arthur Koestler, almost as unidentifiable as Valtin, released his book *Darkness at Noon*, which revealed the other side—the horrors of an OGPU prison in Russia. It became an instant bestseller.

Before spring was over, however, readers in America had something they could sink their teeth into. It was William L. Shirer's *Berlin Diary*, the most complete news report to come out of Germany. It told Americans who hadn't bothered to read *Mein Kampf* what they needed to know about Hitler. It confirmed their suspicions of his unbelievable ruthlessness and bestiality. It revealed the Fuehrer to be a Barnumesque pretender, backed by powerful armed forces and a fanatical police force.

Nearly every American was reading a syndicated column. It was "My Day," written by Eleanor Roosevelt. The nation's foremost housekeeper, and likely the busiest, had started out jotting down the comings, goings and doings around the White House, the great people she met, how they impressed her and what she said to them and they to her, but lately she had been expressing some of her own opinions, impudent or refreshing, depending on how one looked at them.

In the spring, however, she had taken to writing occasionally about domestic matters pertaining to the economy or the home front. In a piece in early March she had warned housewives to start thinking about doing without new kitchen utensils and new automobiles and new washing machines. The *Wall Street Journal* alerted its readers: "Watch her for tips on policy." Thus, "My Day" became *must* reading on Wall Street. Even the most ardent Roosevelt-haters, if they were in a business of any size, took up the habit of reading Eleanor Roosevelt's chitchat. She was the most widely read writer in America.

As spring drew to a close there were brief headlines about the biggest hero of the late 1920s, Colonel Charles A. Lindbergh. People read that he had resigned his commission in the Army.

Some may have wondered why, at this particular time, the man who had flown solo across the Atlantic in a single-engine monoplane, would choose to become a civilian. Some, but not those who had been following the news closely.

Lindbergh was an ardent America-Firster, a top speaker for the America First Committee, a group denying vehemently any Fascist leanings, that nevertheless wanted to keep America out of the war, even at the cost of some kind of appeasement with Germany. Lindbergh learned then what many other Americans had learned earlier and many more have discovered since, that it is dangerous to embrace an opinion opposed to the reigning power and the public majority.

At a Madison Square Rally of the America First Committee, Lindbergh had said that the majority of Americans were opposed to U.S. participation in the war—which was probably true, at the time. He had added that the United States could not alone win the war for England—which was undoubtedly true, at the time. He had also said that the United States had an independent destiny and should keep out of the war. "I have constantly advocated a negotiated peace" he said.

Next day a reporter, possibly prodded by someone in the administration, asked President Roosevelt why Colonel Lindbergh hadn't been called up in the general mobilization.

Well, pondered the President, didn't the reporter recall reading that during the Civil War numerous people fought on both sides of the conflict, and at the same time, both sides refused to call into service certain people who were known as Copperheads?

This was printed in most of the newspapers.

Flabbergasted and heartbroken that his peace efforts should be so callously linked with a semitreasonable attitude, or Copperheadism, Colonel Lindbergh submitted his resignation to the Army and plunged deeper into the shy man's secluded retirement, from which, to this day, he has rarely emerged.

It was cruel and cavalier treatment to administer to a heretofore uninvolved folk hero. It was a lesson, however, to other prominent people who may have had questions about the direction the nation was taking, the sharp tilt toward war. They learned from the experience of Charles Augustus Lindbergh, ex-hero, that one couldn't successfully oppose Franklin Delano Roosevelt on this issue. He meant to enter this war.

The opposition was silenced.

The truth was, Lindbergh was an isolationist, and he lent his name to several "isolationist" groups that proved to have questionable political motivations. At an America First rally in Chicago in April, Lindbergh noted that England was in a desperate situation, that her shipping losses were serious, and her "cities devastated by bombs," and stood silent amid the cheers of 10,000, who were obviously pleased to hear of England's travail.

4

Our Ships at Sea
1941

In mid-June the American public learned of the first sinking of an American ship by a German U-boat. There came with it the awkward awareness that possibly Britannia no longer ruled the waves and that the free world's maritime pipeline would have to be maintained by the United States. The vessel destroyed was the 4,999-ton freighter *Robin Moor*, bound from New York to Capetown. The incident took place in the South Atlantic on May 21.

Surprisingly to many, and certainly to the nation's chief executive, Americans were not aroused by the incident. The reason for this unexpected apathy, pulse-takers said, was that there had been no lives lost.

It was near four o'clock in the morning when the officer on watch in the *Robin Moor* wheelhouse spotted the blinking signal lights. "Send over a boat," they said. He aroused the captain, who came up to the bridge in his pajamas and verified the signal. The *Robin Moor* signalman was ordered to acknowledge the signal and confirm that a boat was being launched.

The lifeboat was lowered and four seamen rowed the executive officer toward the signal light, now barely discernible in the faint dawn as belonging to a long, low shape lying awash in the sea, about a mile and a half away. As they got closer, the men could see that it was, as they had feared, a Nazi U-boat.

There was a carefree picture of a laughing cow painted on her conning tower. Under the cow was the vessel's name—*Lorricke*.

The *Robin Moor* exec scrambled aboard and confronted the U-boat captain on deck. He rendered an unmilitary salute. A few minutes later he vaulted back into the lifeboat and bade the hands make for the *Robin Moor* as fast as possible.

"They're going to let us have it," he said. The submarine's captain, speaking impeccable Oxonian English tinged with a German accent, had given them a half-hour to abandon ship. He would brook no discussion of the matter.

Roused from their sleep were the *Robin Moor's* eight passengers, including three women and a child in arms. Three more lifeboats were lowered to join the one that had been used by the executive officer. He and the four seamen remained in their boat to supervise the launching of the others. All were equipped with emergency supplies, including food, water, first aid kit, flashlights and fishing gear, the latter being useless, it turned out, that far from the feeding and spawning grounds of the coastal waters. Hastily, with supplies from ship's stores, the crews added other foods and such necessities as blankets and rain gear.

The *Lorricke* had been circling the *Robin Moor*, running her big diesels to charge her batteries, as the captain, in the conning tower, watched the proceedings aboard his victim through his glasses.

Precisely within the time limit, the four lifeboats pulled away from the *Robin Moor*. When they were clear, the submarine launched a torpedo, which blasted into her amidships, sending flames belching through her hold and shooting from her stacks. Then, methodically, as if at target practice, the submarine's gunners shelled her for twenty-three minutes until she was practically porous, and she sank wearily, stern down, into the rose-tinged water. The sun had just appeared above the horizon. It shown brightly on the large American flag painted on the *Robin Moor's* hull as it slipped beneath the surface.

The submarine circled the lifeboat carrying the *Robin Moor's* captain. A Nazi sailor handed the lifeboat crew four cans of Germany's much-discussed "ersatz" bread (Hitler said it was superior to bread made of wheat flour) and a couple of cans of butter.

"I am sorry," shouted the U-boat's commander, "but you were carrying supplies to my country's enemy." He promised that he would radio a distress call and give the *Robin Moor* position. He waved a salute toward the captain in the lifeboat, turned and disappeared down the conning tower, and the sub headed into the sun and disappeared beneath the coiling surface of the water. If he did radio the position, it was not heard. It is unlikely that he did, for it would also have revealed his general position.

The equatorial sun beat down onto the lifeboats all of the first day. The next day brought torrential rains followed by enormous, bone-cracking seas.

For five days with each sunrise and each sunset heralding its own measure of special torment, the four lifeboats stayed together. Then a strong wind sprang up, separating them, and they headed off, out of sight of each other, toward what they surmised would be the Brazilian coast. They had been 750 miles out of Freetown, Sierra Leona, when sunk, but the navigators huddled on the little craft knew that the set of the tides as well as the direction of the winds had carried them westward.

In late afternoon of the eighteenth day after the *Robin Moor* went down, one of the lifeboats sighted a ship on the distant horizon. The eastern sky behind them was dark, so the men broke out their flashlights and signaled. After what may have been five prayerful minutes a light on the big ship signaled back, "Sending help." The big vessel slowed and stopped. A boat was lowered. The lifeboat was picked up. News of the rescue was flashed back to the United States. But prolonged radio messages revealed a position, so only the bare-bones facts were given. It was the first news Washington had received of the *Robin Moor* fate. Even then, the news was woefully skimpy. Not until the big ship, whose name was not revealed, put into a port, which was never identified (it was probably Rio de Janeiro), was an adequate message sent back to the States.

For the next seven days it was believed that the other three lifeboats had been lost in the vicious storms that had beset the South Atlantic in recent days. Then, from Capetown, South Africa, came word that all three boats had been picked up by a British ship bound for that port.

Though they had been out of sight of each other, the three lifeboats were really not so far apart, and after the British ship picked up the first one, it cruised the area until it had found the other two.

The story of the *Robin Moor*, now complete, was released to the world press.

In Berlin an official announcement was issued stating that the Nazis would enforce their campaign against American ships carrying cargoes of war supplies to the British.

The stories printed in American newspapers, however, revealed that the *Robin Moor* carried no ammunition or war supplies. Her cargo had been mostly equipment for South African mining companies. There was also some ballast.

Thus unfolded the saga of the first sea disaster for an Ameri-

54

can ship and crew and American passengers in World War II. It caused only the mildest reaction with the American public. The "plot" of the *Robin Moor* was destined to be picked up by Hollywood and used over and again during the next few years, but this most modern sea yarn carried little significance beyond that. It sparked little if any belligerence in America.

Nine more times between June and October the Nazi U-boats sank American merchant vessels in almost exactly the same way. They would signal the ship to stop, order the evacuation of all hands and then either torpedo or shell it until it sank. The U-boats usually fired only one torpedo, if any, and did the fatal damage to the victim ship with surface shelling. They conserved their torpedoes for undersea attacks against armed ships.

Almost universally the Germans were polite, respectful and somewhat solicitous, offering food and drink to the men in the lifeboats before resuming their undersea prowls. Only a handful of men were lost and that was because of bad weather. Most of the survivors were picked up within a few days' time, for the shipping lanes were extremely busy.

Many of the ships were on the U.S.-to-Africa route, assigned to bring precious manganese ore back to the United States. Most of these were sunk before they had a chance to get the ore, and were carrying supplies for nonwarring Africans, or relatively worthless ballast such as sand, trap rock or run-of-bank gravel.

On July 7, President Roosevelt, acting as commander in chief of the armed forces, landed a contingent of marines and a "substantial" naval force at Reykjavik, Iceland, without having consulted anyone in advance in the congressional leadership. That night he admitted to seven leaders of Congress in a supersecret meeting at the White House that he had taken a serious step. He wasn't asking for approval, though, He said simply that it was necessary to occupy a base in Iceland in order properly to defend the United States.

This wasn't exactly unprecedented. Earlier, American troops, planes and ships had been sent to Greenland, with the consent of the Danish government in exile, to protect the North Atlantic shipping lanes. This was ostensibly another move to guard the shipping of the North Atlantic. But from Reykjavik, Iceland, American bombers would be 1,100 miles closer to Berlin than if they were based on the Eastern American shore.

Since that time, some historians have suggested that the landing was at the request of the Iceland government, which welcomed the protection of the American base.

There could be no doubt in the minds of careful observers back home, however, that Roosevelt had taken a giant step closer to war.

Particularly sensitive to the move were those left in the remnants of the isolationist movement. Roosevelt, they said, was "looking for an *incident*." FDR didn't bother to answer such charges. That is, he didn't deny them.

The nation learned of "Roosevelt's incident" on September 11, barely two months after the Navy forces had been deployed to Iceland.

Two hundred miles southwest of Reykjavik, the destroyer U.S.S. *Greer* was carving through the high, gray waves in the frigid North Atlantic, en route to Iceland, when the lookout spotted the white wake of a torpedo slashing toward the ship. His chilling cry of alarm resulted in immediate evasive action, and as the helm was put over as far as it would go, careening the "tin can" onto its side, the torpedo raced past, a near miss. For several hours the *Greer* worked out a grid defense of the area, dropping depth charges at the mere suggestion of some underwater object. Apparently the U-boat had escaped. At least no oil slick appeared.

The original announcement had it that the *Greer* was innocently carrying mail to Iceland, bringing word from home to lonely boys in an icy, foreign country. Later the Navy amended this, admitting that the *Greer* was aiding a British air patrol against the U-boat when it was attacked. The U-boat had been detected earlier and the *Greer* had enlisted to help the British find it. She was not a neutral vessel.

The President, who as commander in chief must have known the truth about the *Greer*'s involvement with the British air patrol, used the incident to *commit* the United States to war against Germany and Italy without having Congress *declare* war.

In an ensuing speech he said: "The time has now come to tell the Nazi government: 'You shall go no further.' If German or Italian vessels *enter the waters* the protection of which is necessary for American defense, they do so at their own peril."

Thereby he declared the whole North Atlantic to be "American territory" under American protection. It meant that the British maritime supply line from St. John's, Newfoundland (then a British territory and not a province of Canada), and Halifax, Nova Scotia, would be under American protection.

Though unnoted by many at the time, thus did America enter its eighth war, though still without the declaration of Congress as required by the Constitution.

FDR had told the Navy to start shooting.

It did not do so immediately. It wasn't being panicked.

By mid-October, Speaker of the House Sam Rayburn was trying desperately to marshal forces behind an administration bill that would repeal Section 6 of the Neutrality Act, which forbade U.S. merchant ships to carry any armament greater than the captain's sidearm pistol or a harpoon gun for whales or other large sea creatures.

Congress, heretofore resolutely isolationist despite the fact that it was controlled by Democrats, had taken a month's vacation in September and had returned, as Rayburn predicted, more attuned to FDR's foreign policies after talking to the folks back home. Rayburn thought this proved there was more isolationism in Washington than in the hustings.

Less isolationist they might be, but a large number of congressmen still could not tolerate the notion of arming merchant ships to go out against arms-bristling submarines or the heavy weapons emplaced on Nazi ships of the line. It was inviting suicide for our brave merchant seamen, they argued. Unarmed, the crews of merchant vessels at least stood a chance of survival by being evacuated from their ships before they were shelled. Armed, they were likely to be outgunned and destroyed. So the argument went. It did not contemplate naval escorts for *American* merchant ships in convoy. Congress seemed to be unaware that U.S. naval vessels were already on convoy duty in the North Atlantic.

Shiny-pated, wily Sam Rayburn wheedled and persuaded and steered and engineered his bill toward a vote, strongly supported by the Navy, which was ready, spokesmen said, to install gun crews and fine, modern weapons on all transoceanic merchant ships.

On the morning the bill came up for vote, October 23, Sam Rayburn was still unsure of the outcome. As he was about to call it up, there arrived word of the latest Nazi assault against the United States on the high seas. This time it appeared that there had been a loss of American lives. This time it was an aggressive act of war.

The report said that a Nazi U-boat had attacked and torpedoed an American destroyer, the U.S.S. *Kearney* on patrol duty in the North Atlantic. After one day of debate the bill was passed 359-138; it went immediately to the Senate, where the entire Neutrality Act was repealed. Smilin' Sam Rayburn chalked up another victory for his chief.

First news of the *Kearney* was brief. The skipper didn't want the radio message to reveal his position to Germans. It said only that the *Kearney* was proceeding to port after having been torpedoed 350 miles southwest of Iceland, and that there were casualties aboard. Two days later, a terse dispatch added the horrible facts about losses. Eleven of the crew were "missing," said the message, and ten more were injured, two of them very seriously. Navy men in Washington figured that the "missing" men had been trapped in a watertight compartment and were dead.

Within a few days Americans read the first casualty list of the war, all next of kin having been notified.

The story seeped from Iceland with glacierlike slowness due to highly intensified censorship, but soon the details of the torpedoing of the *Kearney* were pieced 'together.

The *Kearney* had been on escort duty, presumably for a fleet of tankers and merchantmen, westbound to Canada. She received a signal to leave her convoy and go to the assistance of another convoy in the same waters, which was being attacked by Nazi U-boats.

The *Kearney* complied and the second convoy reformed and proceeded westward into "as black a night as I've ever seen," according to wounded Ensign Henry Lyman of Ponkapog, Massachusetts, interviewed on his hospital cot in Iceland.

Out of the blackness came the second submarine assault, launched by a wolfpack of U-boats. The *Kearney* began an evasive pattern and dropped depth charges to drive them off. Sonar stations could not hear the subs and it was surmised that they were on the surface out in the darkness, decks awash, engines silenced, lurking safely in the black night and firing at ships silhouetted dimly against the sky.

Off to the port side a tanker exploded with a billow of flame and immediately began to sink. The flames lit up the area.

A U-boat maneuvered between the convoy and the *Kearney* and loosed three torpedoes at her. The third struck the year-old destroyer at the forward engine room on the starboard side.

The explosion killed seven men stationed in the forward boiler room. The force blasted up through the deck, knocking the forward stack back and blowing four men overboard to their deaths. The falling stack severed the siren cord and its shrill scream rent the hellish night. It could not be shut off, so that on the bridge no orders could be heard or issued. The compass was smashed.

With men battling the roaring blaze in her hold, her siren screaming her agony to other ships, the *Kearney* cut away from the convoy, dropping more depth charges as she went, and pulled aside to do battle alone, if need be. She searched for her attacker. It was gone. So, apparently, were the other subs.

In the morning's first light the helmsman learned that by watching the flag to see which way the wind was blowing he could navigate to Reykjavik. There was power enough to limp slowly to port. Smoking, taking some water, the *Kearney* presented a prime target to the subs lurking somewhere beneath the surface of the pitching sea.

Two days later, the *Kearney*, flag flying, her wounded men responding to emergency treatment in sick bay, warped into the dock at Iceland's safe harbor. The captain brought ashore the list of eleven dead men, the first to die in the war not yet declared.

Now it was official. The United States was at war with Germany. A war is when opposing forces do battle with each other. Each side was doing that, even if Congress did not acknowledge it officially.

The attack on the *Kearney*, said President Roosevelt, was no chance encounter. It was part of the long-range Nazi plan to drive U.S. shipping from the seas, then to dominate *all* of the Americas.

"We have wished to avoid shooting," he said. "But the shooting has started. And history has recorded who fired the first shot. . . ." All that will matter," promised the President, "is who fires the last shot. We Americans have cleared our decks and taken our battle stations. We stand ready in the defense of our nation."

This was said six weeks before Pearl Harbor was attacked by

the Japanese. It was surprising how many Americans persisted in the belief that the United States was at peace.

War was raging on the high seas.

In most places at home, it was business as usual. There was even a question as to whether Congress should continue the selective service draft.

5

Private Lockard Goes to Breakfast
1941

The fields on the flatlands of Russia were adorned with a verdancy that promised a bumper grain crop. In the Kremlin, however, worried officials pored over reports that showed the industrial revolution was not going well. With Europe at war and America preoccupied, Russia was all but being boycotted. Few ships came to Leningrad, on the Baltic, Odessa, on the Black Sea, or Vladivostok, on the Pacific, except for Nazi vessels, which brought nothing but ballast and wanted precious raw materials and scarce food supplies in return.

A fortnight before, Premier Josef Stalin had faced a horrible reality: His nonaggression pact with Hitler, which he had thought would keep Russia safe from the war, was not a good idea. He had discussed it at length and in many all-night sessions with leaders of the Party and of the government. Stalin's displeasure had been conveyed to Adolf Hitler, and there had been no response.

Suddenly Hitler replied. He declared war on Russia. It was the strangest and most significant development of World War II. It gave Franklin Roosevelt and the United States of America the time needed—a few precious weeks—to speed up the arming and the training of military forces. As Roosevelt was said to have confided to friends later, it was even more of a break than he had been hoping for.

Without the Moscow-Berlin Pact, Hitler would have been unable to start his European war with such confidence. He had gobbled up Czechoslovakia and Poland, charged up into Scandinavia, overrun the Low Countries and France, and spread his armies south and east into Greece and Yugoslavia. When Mussolini's forces had bogged down in Greece, Hitler had sent special troops, and had gone right on through, ending, ultimately, and with great speed, in Croatia.

Most of Europe was now Hitler's. He could turn full force on Great Britain, except for the enigma of Russia. Hitler chose to take on Russia first, thus revealing, irrevocably and for the first time, that his real intent was to conquer the entire world.

It was not merely in the White House that Hitler's declaration of war against Russia caused surprise and consternation. In Ankara, New Delhi and Chungking it was instantly realized that, if Hitler conquered Russia, he could not only turn maximum attention to the British Isles, he could also sweep through Turkey, take over the Middle East, command the Suez Canal, pick off a virtually unarmed India and Burma, establish German control in Africa and effectively confront and isolate China, a China that was already bleeding heavily from Japanese assault and occupation. Only the Americas would be left, their economic, much less their military, survival would have been in grave doubt.

Hitler had taken on the biggest army in the world (10 million Russian troops, compared to 9 million German)—and it possibly might be among the best-equipped armies in the world; that no one knew for certain. What *was* certain was that when the war was over, either Stalin or Hitler would no longer be in power: only one could emerge victorious—whichever it was would be the greatest dictator in mankind's history.

In those capitals where there was still a choice left—in Washington, London, Ankara, New Delhi, Mexico City, Rio de Janeiro—it was deemed wisest to support Stalin and let him become a full-fledged ally of Great Britain. There seemed no other choice.

Thus it was that on June 22, 120 German divisions began the biggest attack in the history of warfare, launching an assault along a 2,000-mile front stretching from Finland to Bessarabia. It was a traditional Nazi attack; the Luftwaffe bombed and strafed Russian troop concentrations, blew up ammunition and supply dumps, bombed out all communications. Long-range bombers dropped high-explosive and fire bombs on the cities, blitzing even into the suburbs. The engineers built bridges and highways and the German infantry advanced behind fast-moving armored divisions. It was a familiar strategy by now, but always effective.

As Napoleon had discovered, the size of Russia will wear down an invader, and Moscow, defended by superb Russian generals, can seem like a million bloody miles away from the tiny provinces and cantonments of Western Europe.

The task of out-generaling the seasoned, hardened, well-schooled generals of the Nazi Army fell to Marshal Semion Timoshenko, a hero of the Soviet invasion of Finland. Timoshenko knew the Germans. He had first fought against them as a draftee in the Czar's army in 1915.

Tough and hard-headed, peasant-born and possessing a peasant's instincts, bowling-ball-bald Timoshenko had early captured Stalin's favor and had risen rapidly in the Russian Army, displacing numerous generals, many of whom had been executed on orders from Stalin. He had become a textbook general, but a smooth and wily one. The German General Staff had a dossier on him that rated him as the most formidable opponent the Russians could put up.

Two things the Germans hadn't counted on—the number of heavily armored tanks in the Russian Army and the fanatical defense put up by the Russian foot soldiers.

From a point near Jassy, Rumania, the Nazis swept into Bessarabia, threatening Odessa in the south and crossing the Dniester River at a dozen places. They smashed into Galicia and plunged as far eastward as Zhitomir, and were even threatening Kiev and the Dnieper River. From Poland they slogged into the Pripet Marshes and bogged down, before forging north toward Minsk. From East Prussia they launched the Panzer attack that was to go charging to Smolensk, only a few score miles west of Moscow. From East Prussia also went another German armored column, followed by infantry, up through Lithuania, Latvia and Estonia to Ostrov.

It was blitzkrieg, as only the Germans could execute it.

"In occupied regions, conditions must be made unbearable for the enemy," Stalin instructed his troops. "In case of a forced retreat [of Red Army units], all rolling stock must be evacuated. To the enemy must not be left a single milligram of grain or a liter of fuel."

If the Germans meant to fight their way to Moscow, they would do it over hundreds of miles of scorched, barren earth. Their trains would be blown up, their troops ambushed, their supplies burned, their rear echelons harassed. And at the fronts, Timoshenko assembled thick, tough walls of soldiers to defend the homeland, bulwarked them with thick-skinned tanks and armored vehicles, supported them with the finest artillery in the world and equipped them with high-powered infantry weapons, including, later, the new rocket guns.

The Germans complained in the Berlin press that the Russians fought with "stupid Asiatic courage," but what was apparent in the war offices in London and Washington was that Hitler, like Napoleon, had found he could bite off chunks of Russian territory, but couldn't digest them. It took as many troops to occupy what had been won as it did to move ahead to conquer more.

For 1,500 miles, the Russian front was ablaze.

The air attacks on Britain eased somewhat.

In Washington, FDR swung the full force of lend-lease behind the Russian effort, and intensified the preparations at home for war. America had its breathing spell; he intended to make full use of it. The Russian sacrifice would not be wasted.

Throughout America the factories were lighted all night, as were the shipyards and the rail-humping yards, and all day and all night trains sped across the face of the land to marshaling depots, and the goods of war, now, were also for Russia. The "Arsenal of Democracy" revised its production schedules upward almost daily. At no time in mankind's history had so many labored so hard and at such high speed to make the machines and necessities of destruction.

The mood of America was changing now, growing more somber as the tempo of the land quickened. The reminders of war were everywhere. The draft had been accelerated, and soldiers, sailors, marines and coast guardsmen were seen on the streets of every community in the land, and they filled every bus terminal and railroad depot. Every public building had posters urging young men to enlist, and now there were posters urging young women, too, to get into the nursing corps or to join the Army's WACs or the Navy's WAVES or the Coast Guard's SPARS.

Finally the government announced what women had known for many months—there was no more silk coming from Japan and there would be no more stockings or sleek undergarments, and not even any pongee, for the Chinese manufacturers of that blend of silk and cotton had been overrun by the Jap armies. Women didn't care much; they were busy with other things, either filling in for men on nonessential jobs, or actively engaged in war work themselves. Besides, the new nylons seemed to be working out fine; that is, when they could be found on the store shelves.

The giant industries of the Midwest, from Chicago and Detroit, right down through the center of heartland America to New Orleans and Houston, cried out for workers, more workers, as their production facilities were strained to capacity. From the farms and plantations and pine tree country of the South whole families responded, white and black alike, leaving some sons on the way at the Army and Navy reception centers. They crowded into the already jammed cities, sending rents skyrocketing and straining housing facilities beyond all imagined capacity. The nation could not spare wood, bricks and mortar for additional housing. Garages, chicken coops, old warehouses were pressed into service. In the more amiable climate of California, tent and tarpaper cities sprung up around Los Angeles and San Francisco. Rawwood shacks sheltered workers from the rains in Washington and Oregon. In the East, old, once-abandoned "mill houses" were shored up and refurbished and pressed into use. Outside of busy Hartford, unused tobacco barns became temporary barracks.

Nobody cared where he slept. There was almost a war on. The money flowed like never before in man's memory. There was work for all. There came a great pressure on the automobile market, and the 1941 models were snapped up fast, not always at the listed prices, and soon even the used car lots were emptied of all but the most unrepairable old models. The enterprising lot owners converted to businesses that engaged in tire recapping and retreading, a process that at first used melted down rubber from irreparable old tires mixed with a new chemical, butol, that served to recap tires that still had good sidewalls.

The gin mills and juke joints, running low on the scotch and gin imported from Britain and even on the bourbon and blends made at home (imbibing Americans discovered to their chagrin that alcohol is used in making gunpowder) did a booming business, limited only by the local laws. Beer became the national drink for those who insisted on alcohol in their beverages, and Congress decreed that even soldiers at American posts could drink beer in their Post Exchanges, though PX beer would have to be limited to 3.2 percent alcohol by volume, compared to the standard 12 percent by volume for any malt beverages served off the post. GI's said it tasted like a blend of kerosene and dishwater and wouldn't raise the spirits of an aging caterpillar. Nevertheless they drank it in copious quantities.

The jukes blared from as early in the morning until as late at night as the law allowed. In most places there was a wartime curfew of 1 A.M. when all bars closed and when New Yorkers, accustomed to a 3 or 4 A.M. cutoff time, complained to restaurateur Toots Shor, he said, "Hell, if you can't get drunk by 1 A.M., you ain't trying."

Swing, which had threatened to peter out with the thirties, was revived, mostly because it was favored by the big-name bands. Glenn Miller was beyond doubt the all-time favorite, but ranking close were the Dorsey brothers—Tommy and Jimmy, Benny Goodman, Duke Ellington, Harry James, Charley Spivak, Horace Heidt, Sammy Kaye, Larry Clinton, Hal McIntyre and many others.

Two of the new top dance tunes in late 1941 were "Jersey Bounce" and "Music Makers," the latter written by Harry James.

Vocalists were popular on the records, too. The newcomer, Frank Sinatra, had a hit with "This Love of Mine." Two of the most popular vocalists with Glenn Miller were Ray Eberle and Marion Hutton, sister of film actress Betty Hutton, who was rising to stardom as the all-American dumb blonde sexpot. Making it big with recordings were the Andrews Sisters, the Mills Brothers, Ozzie Nelson and Harriett Hilliard, the Four Modernaires and Nat King Cole.

A bit of culture crept into the music, incongruous in the wartime atmosphere, but modified by the addition of rhythm tempo to the venerable old strains. "I Think of You," with up-to-date words and musical arrangements, was based on Rachmaninov's Second Piano Concerto. "Concerto for Two," likewise streamlined, was a revision of Tchaikovsky's First Piano Concerto. It was so popular that Freddy Martin, the admired arranger and bandleader, dipped into another part of Tchaikovsky's same concerto, and came up with an exceedingly successful version called "Tonight We Love."

Schmaltz was also admired on the jukes, with such tunes as "The Anniversary Waltz," "Don't Take Your Love From Me," "How About You?," "I Don't Want to Set the World on Fire" and, of course, "The White Cliffs of Dover." Latin music made some inroads in the juke sales with "Flamingo" and "My Adobe Hacienda." The Australian "Waltzing Matilda" was introduced, but was not to reach its great popularity until the following year.

"Blues in the Night" set some sort of record as the most universally sung blues song—"Mah Momma done tole me . . . "

Several instrumentalists in the big-name bands also acquired reputations of their own. Not the least were trumpeter Bunny Berrigan, tenor saxophonist Tex Beneke and drummer Gene Krupa.

For many months the American Society of Composers, Authors and Publishers (ASCAP) warred with the networks over the royalty payments to be made for the broadcasting of recordings of music or of live musical numbers, and as a result, for a long time only non-ASCAP tunes were heard on the airwaves. This, too, enhanced the volume at the jukeboxes.

The ASCAP dispute was resolved on October 29, and on the next night, Thursday, when the Glenn Miller band played its "Chesterfield Show" on CBS from 10 to 10:15, this was on the agenda: "Moonlight Serenade" (Theme), "Star Dust," "Chattanooga Choo Choo," "This Is No Laughing Matter," "One O'clock Jump" and "Slumber Song" (Theme).

It was the first broadcast of "Chattanooga Choo Choo" since it had been recorded on May 7, and Miller was swamped with requests to repeat the song on following shows. The tune began its spectacular rise from that date on, and the following year became a million-copy seller.

The Nazis pushed on into Russia's vastness, leaving bloody and burnt earth behind them. Kiev fell. Leningrad was under siege. Smolensk fell, 260 miles from Moscow. But American newsmen radioed stories of incredible stolidity. The Muscovites, they said, were going about work as usual, doing what they always did. They were not worried. They were merely determined. Military experts, however, knew that Russia was desperate. But winter was coming.

Josef Stalin, who was noted for disposing of his Russian opponents by simply shooting them, and who had never before been known to speak kindly of the United States, threw a state dinner, inviting some American diplomats. He startled everyone by drinking a toast to Franklin Roosevelt and saying, "May God help him in his task." Could the old atheist have found God in his hour of travail? One diplomat described him as a "nice old gentleman." This was after a seven-hour, ten-course meal in which thirty-two "bottoms up" toasts in vodka and cognac had

67

been drunk, though some guests, having difficulty with arithmetic, thought it might have been thirty-seven toasts.

In Vichy France, Marshal Pétain and Admiral Darlan found that it suited their political beliefs to get along with Hitler and his occupying forces. They seemed willing collaborators. The French Naval fleet was in a variety of ports and had not been turned over, but most of the merchant shipping had fallen into German hands and the tri-color on many hulls had been painted over with a swastika.

The hope of France abided in two widely separated headquarters, one in London and one in French Equatorial Africa, the headquarters of tall (six-foot-four) ungainly General Charles Andre Joseph Marie de Gaulle, Free French Commander of an army of 40,000 men, an air force of 1,000 and a navy of seventeen ships of line.

General de Gaulle's forces had joined the British in Syria to guard the northern approaches to the Suez Canal, through which poured a continuous stream of British, American and Russian ships, along with some merchantmen that flew the flags of Belgium, the Netherlands, Sweden and Norway. The lean General de Gaulle dreamed of the day when he would help liberate France as a trustee of the French Republic and return *la belle patrie* to free Frenchmen.

In England, the talk, when not of the war, was of Rudolf Hess, third-ranking man in the leadership of Nazi Germany. He was in England, and no one seemed to know why.

Hess had taken off from Augsburg in a new type of Messerschmitt reconnaissance plane on a fine summer Saturday evening, wearing a gold wrist watch, a gold wrist compass and an expensively tailored uniform. He carried several photographs of himself, several bottles of medicine and a chart showing the course from Augsburg to the flat grounds of Dungavel Castle, family seat of the Duke of Hamilton.

Hess circled low over the Dungavel grounds, then bailed out. A tenant saw the plane crash and watched the white parachute drift down. Arming himself with a pitchfork he approached Hess gingerly and found him lying on the ground with a fractured ankle. In cultured English Hess asked: "Will you take me to Dungavel to see the Duke of Hamilton?" However, the thirty-eight-year-old duke, a Wing Commander, was on active service.

Instead the tenant called the Home Guard and Hess disappeared into British officialdom, and jail.

Did he carry secret peace plans from Hitler? Speculation ran throughout the British Isles. Prime Minister Churchill promised Parliament that he would clear up the mystery. He never did. Hess remained in jail.

Across the Pacific, Japan, which (thanks to the Vichy government) had strong military bases in French Indochina, had taken advantage of a border dispute to become "mediator" in Thailand. When the war between Thailand and Indochina ended, Japan was the victor.

Japan's "New Order in Asia" was being pushed by Foreign Minister Yosuka Matsuoka, who suddenly broadened its scope from northern China only to all of China, and added, "We Japanese have a heaven-sent right to settle in some part of the United States . . . "

With Chungking under constant bombardment by Japanese planes, and with Japanese armies threatening the city from two sides Generalissimo Chiang Kai-shek fought valiantly but precariously against the invaders, trying to establish a working agreement between his Nationalist government and the Communists. But it didn't work, and the Nationalists had to fight the Reds as well as the Japanese.

Onto the scene came a colonel from the U.S. Army Air Corps, Claire Chennault, who set about organizing a volunteer (mercenary) group of American airmen to be equipped with planes spared from the American forces. His superiors in Washington promoted Chennault to the rank of general, a gesture he barely took time to acknowledge, as he whipped into shape the first American air squadron to go into battle in World War II. The Flying Tigers soon became legendary, and after Pearl Harbor, flew on to great glory, the subject of stories, films and songs.

At the same time, however, and virtually unnoticed by the home front public in America, U.S. fighter planes were in almost daily contact with the dreaded Japanese Zeros. They "scouted" each other, flew past each other in formations, but had, so far, exchanged no fire. They were Chennault's Flying Tigers, and came from secret bases in China.

The reason for this was the existence of the Burma Road, China's only unblockaded supply line, the only source of goods from the United States. Since Japan now occupied French Indochina, her fighter airfields were within easy range of the Burma Road. The only solution was to fly air patrols over the long truck convoys. Since China's own fighter force was virtually wiped out, the task fell to U.S. fighter planes manned by U.S. pilots.

Twenty thousand miles from home port American-made goods were roaring over the Burma Road into China in American-made vehicles, while American-made planes scouted overhead and kept the Japs away.

American-made goods and American-grown foodstuffs were literally pouring around the world, to Murmansk, to Vladivostok, to Liverpool, to London, to Dundee, to Cairo, to New Delhi, to Rangoon.

To maintain this pace, American factories, American mines, American railroads, American shipyards, American processing plants had to be worked around the clock, seven days a week.

The one thing America could not—would not—tolerate was industrial strikes.

Yet 1941 was one of the worst years for strikes. In the spring the CIO's Steel Workers' Organizing Committee had struck the giant Lackawanna plant in Buffalo of Bethlehem Steel Company and threatened to close down all Bethlehem plants, where $1.5 billion in defense orders was being processed. The steel workers won their contract with Beth, wresting for the first time a labor agreement from tough, labor-resisting Eugene W. Grace, America's highest-paid industrialist, who had received $600,000 a year in salary for twenty-three years up to that time.

Hardly had that been settled than the CIO's United Auto Workers struck Ford Motor Company plants, all of which were totally engaged in war production. The biggest contracts were for airplane engines and plane fuselages. Ultimately Henry Ford, for the first time in his long career, negotiated with a labor union. Now every major auto manufacturer was organized under the CIO-UAW.

Worriedly, Roosevelt, hailed as the Friend of Labor, appointed a National Defense Mediation Board, and ordered that strikes be called off so that the new board might arbitrate them. It didn't work. The San Francisco shipyards were shut down by strikes. North American Aviation's huge plant in Inglewood, California, was struck and closed. The logging camps in the

Northwest were sealed off. All were under the direction of unions that were affiliated with the CIO.

Then the other shoe fell, dropped by the gruff, rasp-voiced labor giant John Llewellyn Lewis, president of the United Mine Workers Union. He decreed a strike by 53,000 miners in the soft coal fields.

Lewis made no secret of the fact that he hated Roosevelt and despised the New Deal. He said often that he did not think Hitler posed a great threat to the United States, and he had remarked to friends that he believed the Russians would whip Hitler before long. In short, he could see no reason for the great "Roosevelt emergency" on the home front.

The issue was, to him, simple. The mine workers union had a closed shop for the 350,000 miners in the commercial soft coal mines, but it had no closed shop in what Lewis described as the "captive" mines, those owned by the steel companies to produce coal for their own use. Though they were 95 percent unionized, the 53,000 workers at captive mines did not enjoy the closed shop privileges of other bituminous miners.

For weeks the captive mines were struck, then, when Lewis made no progress against the big steel companies, all of the other mines were struck too, closing down one by one. America's giant steel industry, hope of the rest of the free world, was closed down.

Then, suddenly, Lewis unexpectedly agreed to submit the dispute to arbitration in the strong belief that the arbitration board would decide in his favor, since he, himself, was a member. The miners went back to work.

On the night of December 7, 1941, the arbitration board did, indeed, rule in Lewis' favor.

For other reasons, as well as for the decision, John L. Lewis stated: "When the nation is attacked, every American must rally to its support. All other considerations become insignificant."

There were other distractions at home. One was the continuing argument, waged throughout much of the late summer and fall, as to whether you agreed or disagreed with the stern, leathery discipline of Lieutenant General Ben Lear. He was known as "Yoo-Hoo" Ben Lear.

The story started on a hot midsummer Sunday afternoon in Memphis, Tennessee, with a convoy of eighty trucks of the 110th Quartermaster Regiment, bearing 350 tired, steamy soldiers, returning from more than a month's hard bivouac and maneuvers. As soldiers had done since the hordes of Genghis Khan, they were whistling and shouting at girls who passed by on the sidewalks.

Hampered by heavy Sunday traffic, the convoy crept slowly past the first tee of the Memphis Country Club. A group of lovely southern belles in shorts was strolling along the walk. From the trucks came a fusillade of shouts—"Yoo-hoo-o-o-o" and "Hey there, baby"—and a shrill chorus of wolf whistles.

On the first tee, a golfer who was getting ready to tee off, glanced up at the convoy with a scowl, then returned to address himself to the shot. As he prepared to swing, a soldier shouted "Fore!" and the golfer missed. Other GI's called, "Hey, buddy do you need a caddy?"

The golfer threw down his club, vaulted a three-foot fence and stalked up to the convoy. A command car jerked to a lurching stop. The officers piled out and came face to face with a horrible truth. The golfer was Lieutenant General Ben Lear, commander of the Second Army and director of the maneuvers from which the 110th was returning.

Lear, an old sergeant from the ranks, knew the language of the GI's. He spread it thick and blue, then told the convoy to move on to its quarters at Camp Robinson, 145 miles away, and to stand by for further orders. When they got to camp, the general's order was awaiting them. They were to turn around and go back to Memphis, where they were to bivouac at the airport and await mass punishment, the innocent and guilty alike.

The trucks were reloaded and the return to Memphis was begun. Three hours out on the road, the convoy was stopped so the weary, vision-blurred drivers could rest. At dawn they filed into the airport and pitched tents. Soon Lear showed up, still angry, still snarling out an old sergeant's invective. They could rest up for the day and the night, he said, and next day they would go back to Camp Robinson, but on the way, each man, soldiers and officers alike, would march a full fifteen miles with full field packs, rifles and steel helmets.

Next day, in 97-degree heat, the trucks rumbled off with plans to leapfrog along the route until each man had received his punishment. The soldiers took it all cheerfully, singing an improvisation of the World War I song: "Old Ben Lear—he missed his putt, Parley Voo—." Sympathetic townsfolk along the way re-filled canteens with icewater as the sweaty marchers plodded past. The heat-stricken were treated by a dentist and a sanitary officer who were also being disciplined.

Such a public display of Army discipline made the newspapers, however, and soon the issue was roaring in Congress.

Angry parents from throughout the country wrote to their Washington representatives demanding that General Lear be discharged or horsewhipped or made to march thirty miles, or turned over to his troops for retaliatory discipline. Senator Bennett Champ Clark, the Missouri isolationist, roared that Ben Lear was a "superannuated old goat, who ought to retire."

Worse, wherever the Army went in convoys, throughout the remainder of summer and most of the fall, civilians would line the streets and shout, "Yoo--Hoo-o-o!"

Ben Lear said nothing. In the Army, a general is always right.

The harder Americans worked, the harder they played, and from soaring box-office receipts it became evident that Hollywood couldn't turn out new movies fast enough to meet the demand. It was the day of double features, and there had to be as many B-grade and C-grade movies as there were top-notch productions. Fortunately there was the war on in Europe and in the Orient, which provided great opportunity for low-budget "intrigue" fare. Then there were westerns, with some marvelously popular singing stars such as Gene Autry and Roy Rogers. And there was an endless supply of who-dun-its. In 1941, Hollywood hadn't gotten into producing real war dramas with fighting scenes. After all, America wasn't yet at war.

Playing in movie theatres throughout the year was the ultrasophisticated, marvelously upper-crust Katharine Hepburn film, *The Philadelphia Story*, which also starred the youthful, skinny Jimmy Stewart, soon to enlist as a pilot in the Air Force, and the debonaire Cary Grant, whose acting fee of $137,500 was paid directly to British War Relief.

An equally long run, after a turbulent launching, went to the film ultimately voted Best Picture of the Year—*Citizen Kane*, starring Orson Welles. When columnist Louella Parsons saw the preview of the movie, depicting a corrupt and all-powerful newspaper publisher who collected art objects from Europe's repositories, it reminded her of her boss, William Randolph

Hearst. Indeed, the story line seemed quite similar to his professional career, at least, even if it did seem to exaggerate his other proclivities.

Lolly Parsons appealed personally to RKO to withhold the picture. No mention of RKO appeared in any of the eighteen Hearst papers while RKO pondered the powerful Parsons' request. Finally it was decided to go ahead and release the picture anyway. At first, RKO had difficulty finding theatres willing to challenge Hearst's wrath, but soon it was showing to applauding audiences throughout the nation.

Great and glorious nonsense filled the screen and packed the theatres with *Road to Zanzibar*, starring Bing Crosby and Bob Hope. Neither was new to the business, but for each it was his most successful role, and it helped continue the long series of *Road* pictures, which established Hope as the comedian of the day and Crosby as the "groaner" without parallel. "Crosby," said *Time* magazine, "sings every song—whether *Mexicali Rose* or *Silent Night*—as though he felt it was the best song ever written."

One of the most splendid comedies of all time emerged in the film *Major Barbara*, personally revised and restructured for the screen by its author, the eighty-four-year-old George Bernard Shaw. One of the all-time treats, it offered Wendy Hiller as the lassie from the mission, and also starred Rex Harrison, Robert Morley and Robert Newton. Untold to the public was the harrowing story of its filming in London, where the set was repeatedly bombed out and the cast and crew, as well as the world-celebrated author, lived in almost daily danger.

And then, unexpectedly, and without particularly strong reviews, there burst on the movie scene one of those quiet sleepers that set the entire nation talking and singing its praises. For a long while the movie-going public had admired the quiet, lanky, Montana-born Gary Cooper, then forty years old. Earlier in the year they had enjoyed his portrayal of a gawky bush-league baseball pitcher who wound up writing a column for the lovelorn, in the movie, *Meet John Doe*. With Barbara Stanwyck he turned in such a performance that he became the best-known actor of the time and, nudging out Gable, the biggest box-office draw.

At the peak of his popularity, he outdid himself with his performance in what ranks as one of the screen's most memorable and enduring biographies: *Sergeant York*. In the Tennessee hills, on the farm which his grateful countrymen had bought him, Sergeant Alvin Cullum York, now fifty-three, agreed to let his Congressional Medal of Honor-winning exploits be Hollywoodized only if Gary Cooper would impersonate him in the title role. He also demanded that the picture be an honest-to-God account of what happened, with no frills, and that Hollywood refrain from casting an "oomphy" girl as his wife.

Joan Leslie was selected as the shy but very female sweetheart for Alvin York. The result was one of the most pleasing screen presentations ever made up to that time. The real Sergeant York, who had passed up a fortune in commercial ventures as America's No. 1 hero, passed his laurels on to a Hollywood Sergeant York who was equally shy and retiring and universally known as just a "great guy."

In the course of the 1941 movie season a new star was born. She was a lady named Margarita Carmen Cansino, who took her Irish mother's maiden name of Hayworth and shortened her first name to Rita. Her big chance came with a role as Fred Astaire's dancing partner in *You'll Never Get Rich*. Americans accepted the film as a happy blending of two great talents.

Superb movie treats were also offered in *The Little Foxes*, starring Betty Davis as Regina Giddens in the Lillian Hellman drama; *The Maltese Falcon*, starring Humphrey Bogart, Sydney Greenstreet and Peter Lorre—Bogart's best performance and the first movie appearance of veteran Broadway actor Greenstreet, in a slippery, slithery role that was to become his Hollywood hallmark; *One Foot in Heaven*, a delightful and inspiring story of a Methodist minister, starring Frederic March and Martha Scott; and Walt Disney's greatest cartoon movie to date, *Dumbo*, starring a flap-eared little elephant, so humanlike he stole into every heart.

In the dark days of early December, movie-goers drenched their handkerchieves and filled their hearts in the glorious simplicity of ordinary, awkwardly-speaking working people portrayed magnificently in celluloid poetry in *How Green Was My Valley*.

Beautifully underplayed performances were turned in by Roddy McDowall, Maureen O'Hara, Donald Crisp and Walter Pidgeon. The picture's brilliant director, John Ford, couldn't see it right away. He was on active duty in the U.S. Navy.

The $58 million Queens-to-Manhattan tunnel under the East

River, later to be known as the Queens Midtown Tunnel, had been opened with appropriate fanfare, though autoists complained that after speeding under the river from 40th Street and 1st Avenue, they were unceremoniously dumped into the horrendous traffic of Queens Boulevard. Progressing rapidly was construction on the East River Drive, later to be known in part as Franklin D. Roosevelt Drive, though much of the fill under the highway was not native to New York. It came from Bristol, England, where the rubble from bombed-out buildings was scooped up and put into British ships for ballast before sailing for New York and American supplies.

Since early fall, the Japanese ambassador to the United States, Admiral Kichisaburo Nomura, had been pleading with the U.S. government to find some way to ship oil to now embargoed Japan. "Human being[s] must be able to make [reach] some formula," he said plaintively.

He was joined in November by a newcomer, Saburo Kurusu, a personal envoy of U.S.-hating Premier Tojo, who had taken over the Japanese government a month before after the fall of the cabinet of Premier Prince Konoye. That Kurusu was coming to the United States was interpreted by Asia-watchers as a sure sign that Japan's warlike language would remain just talk and nothing else.

Japan continued to pour troops into Indochina, where 100,000 men were now poised to attack the Burma road, and formations of planes conducted bombing raids over much of China and machine-gunned convoys on the Burma Road.

On Saturday, December 6, President Roosevelt sent a message to Emperor Hirohito asking him to please consider further discussions in negotiating a peace in Indochina. As a consequence Envoy Kurusu and Ambassador Nomura scheduled a noontime meeting with Roosevelt for Sunday, December 7.

At 7:30 A.M. in Honolulu on Sunday, December 7, 1941, Private Joseph L. Lockard, a radar operator from Williamsport, Pennsylvania, detected some planes approaching Pearl Harbor. He reported the appearance of the blips on his radar screen to his superior officers. Assuming that the planes must be friendly, the officers told Joe to go and eat breakfast. He didn't get his breakfast that day.

There were 360 Japanese planes in the air armada that swept in from the southeast over Diamond Head. They snarled over

Waikiki, dropped tons of bombs on Hickam and Wheeler Fields, and loosed the fury of hell on the silent, cable-riding hulls of the Pacific fleet.

Not for years would the military toll be known. That first day it was revealed that of the 200,000 civilian inhabitants of Oahu, 1,500 had been killed and 1,500 had been injured. Later it was thought that the civilian casualty figures had been exaggerated, though the exact statistics were not recorded.

Five battleships were sunk or beached; eleven smaller warships were destroyed or so heavily damaged they were out of the war; three more battleships were so badly damaged they would be out of service for many months; and the planes and facilities at Hickam and Wheeler fields were wiped out.

The battleship *Arizona* lay on the bottom with all hands.

The navy lost 91 officers, with 20 more wounded, and 2,638 enlisted men killed and 636 wounded. Army losses were 168 killed in action, 223 wounded, 26 missing.

The government and people of the United States of America declared war on the Japanese Empire at 4:10 o'clock on the afternoon of Monday, December 8, 1941.

The peace that had been won in World War I had lasted for twenty-two years and twenty-five days.

As allies of Japan, Nazi Germany and Fascist Italy declared war on the United States of America on December 11, 1941.

The preliminaries were over.

6

"I Came Through and I Shall Return"
1942

New Year's Day, 1942, was set aside by Presidential Proclamation as a National Day of Prayer. Men, women and children of every persuasion and faith, in every part of the nation bowed their heads and implored divine help and guidance. The President led the nation in prayer:

> The new year of 1942 calls for the courage and the resolution of old and young to help win a world struggle in order that we may preserve all we hold dear. We are confident in our devotion to our country, in our love of freedom, in our inheritance of courage. But our strength, as the strength of all men everywhere, is of greater avail as God upholds us.
>
> Therefore I, Franklin D. Roosevelt, President of the United States of America, do hereby appoint the first day of the year 1942 as a day of prayer, of asking forgiveness for our shortcomings of the past, of consecration to the task of the present, of asking God's help in the days to come.

Roosevelt, an Episcopalian, had not been thought of as an especially religious man, and his earnest message, given over all radio stations and front-paged by most newspapers, went directly to the hearts of the American people. Thus it was that they rang out the old and rang in the new year in an attitude of deep reverence.

The old year had waned with Americans in deep shock, only slowly recovering from the disaster of Pearl Harbor. With the United States now at war, the only American army that was fighting was in the distant Philippines and it was losing the battle. Looming was a defeat as serious and costly as the fall of

78

France earlier—the possible loss of strategic parts of the Far East.

And then, a few days before Christmas, as surprising and mysterious as a visit from Santa Claus, Winston Churchill dropped out of the sky into Washington. It was the first time a wartime prime minister of Great Britain had ever visited the United States. He was the war-scarred, seasoned commander in chief, come to bolster the spirit of the fledgling commander in chief of a newly warring sister democracy. So tight was the censorship on his travel plans that only President Roosevelt knew he was coming.

Next day Churchill, puffing his long black cigar, sat beside Roosevelt at the famous desk in the Oval Room of the White House and met more than 200 newsmen. He didn't say much, other than that he and the President were conferring on plans. When photographers in the rear of the crowd of news-gatherers shouted that they couldn't see him, Churchill obligingly stood on a chair, waved his cigar and made the V-for-Victory sign.

On Christmas Eve, Churchill stood beside Franklin Roosevelt as the President observed the annual ceremony of turning on the outdoor Christmas lights, and then joined the President in broadcasting felicitations to the nation.

With typical Churchillian simplicity he sent tingles through the nation's spine, saying only: "I spend this anniversary and festival far from my family, and yet I cannot truthfully say that I feel far from home. In God's mercy, a happy Christmas to you all."

Between Christmas and New Year, representatives and senators who had returned home for the holidays shuttled back to Washington en masse and turned out in full force, with no absentees, at a joint session of Congress, to hear the British prime minister. The standing ovation they accorded him lasted on and on, great and roaring, from isolationist and interventionist alike. It was so emotion-packed that newsmen who clock such things, forgot to time the length of the cheering and applause. It eased only when it was seen that tears had come to Winston Spencer Churchill's eyes and he was obliged to push back his utilitarian horn-rimmed glasses.

His pudgy hands clutching the lapels of his waistcoat, referring only infrequently to his hand-written notes, the man who was considered by many experts and scholars to be one of the reigning masters of the English language spoke in his gravelly voice, heaping scathing scorn on his enemies in satisfying syllables, and praising his friends in eloquent and royal terms.

"I avow my hope and faith, sure and inviolate, that in the days to come the British and American people will for their own safety and for the good of all, walk together in majesty, in justice and in peace," he said.

Right after the first of the year the various new wartime agencies in Washington began to exhort Americans to cut back on their high and prosperous style of living. The prodigious announcements filled the newspapers and the airwaves. Don't hoard sugar, they said. Cut back on sweets and desserts. The White House is on a dessertless regimen, the bulletins advised. Don't use up tires or gasoline needlessly. Don't overbuy meats and fresh produce. Search your home again for items made of tin and aluminum, they said, and turn them in, at the nearest fire station. Don't spend your money foolishly, warned the treasury, implying that higher taxes were coming; save it by buying war bonds or defense stamps.

This was confusing the public. Worse, the myriad orders flowing out from Washington to the industrial, business and financial world were so obscure, poorly written and conflicting that leaders were inundating the White House with complaints. Roosevelt was reluctant to admit it, but red tape was threatening to hobble if not trip up the war effort. To the Oval Room was ushered a waspish, gray-haired little man, a senator from Missouri and chairman of the Senate's Special Committee to investigate the National Defense Program. Senator Harry Truman laid it on the line: unless the President put in a single director, he would blow the lid on the whole affair and disclose a horrifying mess. On his heels came Wendell Willkie, top spokesman for the Republican National Committee, with precisely the same request and a more politely veiled threat of exposure if something were not done immediately about putting in one all-powerful executive to head the war effort.

Grudgingly admitting that the time had come to act, Roosevelt knew exactly where to go for the man for the job. He sent a note to the executive director of the Supply, Priorities and Allocations Board, bidding him come to the White House immediately. He responded, accompanied by Vice President Henry A. Wallace.

When Donald Marr Nelson emerged from that meeting in the Oval Room, he was head of the War Production Board, a brand new agency, and possessed more authority than any citizen, with the exception of the President himself. Harry Hopkins had been displaced as No. 2 man in the hierarchy.

Don Nelson was an able man with a reputation for getting things done and a penchant for being both decisive and incisive. The son of a locomotive engineer from Hannibal, Missouri, he had been, before being called to government as a dollar-a-year man the $70,000-a-year manager of Sears, Roebuck and Company, and as such was the country's foremost purchasing agent. He was admirably trained for the job the President handed him.

One of the first things Nelson did was to "freeze" commercial airplane seats. The fact that many Americans had no cars and no tires and no gasoline made no difference. Henceforth, ruled Nelson, private citizens wishing to fly would have to stand in line behind government personnel, the Army, Navy and Marine Corps, and businessmen with priorities traveling on government business.

Would-be travelers without credentials who turned to the railroads found no solution there. Already jammed by defense travel, the railroads had been strained beyond capacity since Pearl Harbor. In the sixteen days after December 7, the railroads moved 600,000 troops, three-quarters of them in Pullmans, the remainder in coaches.

Nelson was busy, it was said, with plans to order buses off scenic routes and give them to cities with no streetcars. Seats would be ripped out and replaced by poles and straps for the sardinelike accommodation of standees.

It wasn't long before the press and the public were having fun with the intense, no-time-for-humor Don Nelson, reciting limericks, singing parodies and generally lampooning the enormous number of alphabetized committees, commissions and agencies he was creating within the structure of the WPB. The niftiest one of all was: PWPGSJSISIACWPB. It was easy to see why it was alphabetized, for the proper name of the outfit was Pipe Wire Product and Galvanized Steel Jobbers Subcommittee of the Iron and Steel Industry Advisory Committee of the War

81

Production Board. Not to be overlooked, of course, was the BCPSBIDIOWPB—the Biscuit, Cracker and Pretzel Subcommittee of the Baking Industry of the Division of Industry Operations of the War Production Board.

Ignoring the barbs, Nelson plowed onward, using his exhaustive knowledge of the intricacies of industry and business to plug wasteful leaks, eliminate profiteering and channel and steer the entire productive machine of the United States into the war effort.

He had no control over the people, but he had absolute power over their jobs, and just about every material thing that they used. And sometimes more than the war effort was served. The BCPSBIDIOWPB, for instance, learned that by adding cracker dust to canned soups, it made them thicker, so that they stretched further, were more nourishing and were "home style," a process that endures today.

Thus did Donald Nelson embark on his wartime odyssey, which would take him over many bumpy roads, evoke the snarls and protestations of many of those who felt his authority, but bring him in the end to the successful completion of what was one of the hardest jobs ever undertaken by any executive anywhere at any time.

The war was not yet two months old when a newsman at a press conference asked the commander in chief if the United States could be attacked.

"Enemy ships could swoop in and shell New York; enemy planes could drop bombs on war plants in Detroit; enemy troops could attack Alaska," replied Franklin Roosevelt.

"But," persisted the newsman, "aren't the Army and Navy and the Air Force strong enough to deal with anything like that?"

"Certainly not," said the President.

Shortly thereafter came the first attack on the continental United States. About seven miles north of Santa Barbara, California, a submarine surfaced and glided gently toward the shore.

For the next twenty minutes it lobbed shell after shell at an oil refinery, turned around, submerged and disappeared from U.S. view. The refinery was damaged but no one was injured. No fires had been started. Nearly twenty-five shells exploded in a nearby open field, frightening some horses that had been pastured there. One shell whined over traffic-crowded Highway 101 and smashed into the low hills.

California felt that its 3,250 miles of exposed shoreline was not sufficiently guarded and nervous residents of the coastal areas began to report frightened "sightings" that were relayed to military officials. Such alarms proliferated throughout the year.

As oil slicks washed up on the beaches on the Atlantic and Gulf of Mexico sides of the continent, it became apparent that the war was on in dead earnest. Fishermen off Cape Cod and Long Island, hugging as close to shore as possible, reported seeing surfaced submarines with the big *U* of the Nazi U-boats (*Unterseebooten*) painted on their conning towers. Naval authorities who received the reports told the fishermen to keep quiet about what they saw.

The California shelling couldn't be hushed up, however, and suddenly the citizens living behind that long, curving coast line looked at their lifetime neighbors, realizing that many of them were Japanese. As they looked, the once-friendly faces became inscrutable. Some imagined that Oriental savagery lurked behind those dark, slanty eyes.

Los Angeles District Attorney John Dockweiler made public a map showing that Japanese-Americans held leases on land adjoining nearly every strategic spot in Los Angeles County, including power lines, railways, highways, aircraft plants, airports, oil fields, refineries and aqueducts.

Moreover, the map showed that Japs held in lease a flat tract of land covering more than a square mile just outside Los Angeles that could, said Dockweiler, be turned into a landing field for bombers in only a couple of hours.

He pointed to the Palos Verdes peninsula right next to the war-vital San Pedro harbor and observed that landing parties could sneak in on a number of good beaches. Palos Verdes is foggy a good deal of the time, especially at night.

Not long after that the FBI broke into the beachfront home of George Makamura in Santa Cruz and found sixty-nine crates of colored flares and signal rockets.

It made no difference that Makamura was an alien, a *real* Japanese, and that most of the others were Japanese-Americans, native-born in California, who called themselves Nisei and were mostly farmers, keepers of small shops and fishermen. California became frightened of its Nisei neighbors.

Under orders of the Western Defense Command, 70,000 Nisei living along the coast and the Mexican border were rounded up and told they must go to an "encampment" for the duration—America's first concentration camp.

When word got around that even the kids in school and college would be yanked out and sent off to the encampment with their parents, some Californians took a second look. It was only then that they discovered that a great many Nisei had been in America for more generations than they had, and they remembered that a large number of Nisei sons were already serving in the military forces. And then they discovered something else: The Nisei actually *wanted* to be segregated into the concentration camps. The reason: They also suspected that some among them might try to bring aid or comfort to the enemy, and to avoid suspicion for all, they wanted all to be placed under surveillance. (This was reported in the newspapers at the time, and it was confirmed by the author when he was serving as training cadre for Nisei troops at Camp Blanding, Florida, troops that later distinguished themselves in Italy.)

So on a chilly dawn in March those Japanese-Americans of the Los Angeles area who owned cars or trucks assembled in Pasadena's Rose Bowl. In swaying, sagging, battered vehicles, the teetery trucks piled high with furniture, hoes and rakes and boxes of keepsakes, they formed up under the command of an Army sergeant. Then, with a motorcycle cop leading the way, they headed for the forbidding mountains to the east.

Their destination was Manzanar, in California's bleak Owens Valley. At the Santa Fe station those without cars or trucks boarded a special train to take them to Manzanar. And so it was in every city from Phoenix in the south to Seattle in the north that the Nisei of the western United States were rounded up so they could cause no harm.

It wasn't long before residents along both coasts were well aware of the fact that the Japanese sub's appearance off Santa Barbara was not an isolated incident, but nowhere was it more vividly realized than on the East Coast. From Halifax to Key West and New Orleans, shipping was brought to a virtual standstill. Axis submarines, some of them believed to be Japanese, but most of them Nazi, ranged from Newfoundland to Buenos Aires in wolf packs, sinking everything found afloat.

Between Pearl Harbor and mid-May it was estimated that 213 Allied vessels had gone to the bottom, many of them within sight of land. Nearly a dozen ships had been sunk in the Gulf of Mexico, so close to shore that survivors swam to land or rowed ashore in lifeboats. Southern bayou Louisianians grew almost accustomed to seeing military ambulances hauling the dead and wounded from the beaches.

Bodies floated ashore all along the Atlantic coast. Thick oil slicks came in with the rising tides. Wherever a promontory of land stuck out into the ocean, the Navy quickly sealed it off with cyclone fencing in an effort to keep out the curious and to prevent the horrible truth from reaching the public. With coastguardsmen patroling with dogs it was impossible for an unauthorized person to get to the Atlanticside beaches on Cape Cod, or at Westport Point or at Montauk, or along the Jersey shore, or at Cape Hatteras—or on any jutting high land where it would be possible to see the disaster at sea, or to signal any enemy craft.

Even with the full support of the U.S. Navy, it was clear that Britannia no longer ruled the waves. As facts about the sinkings and carnage filtered through the cyclone fencing, it became apparent to all that the United States was being defeated at sea all along its own eastern seaboard.

Appeals to the White House to bring back the Navy to protect American shores were in vain. Roosevelt had made his position clear earlier: "We must all understand that our job now is to fight at distances which extend all around the globe."

No matter what was going on at home, the Navy had its assignment, and that was to blast through the enemy defenses and escort the ever-larger convoys through to Ireland, Russia, England and Eritrea. The Navy was doing that, valiantly, successfully. *That* battle was *not* being lost. The Navy was also rebuilding its fleet in the Pacific at several locations. It was enlarging its tonnage and manpower in the Mediterranean. The Navy had shipyards operating all along both coasts and in the Great Lakes ports as well.

Some of the great steel companies were directly involved in turning out cargo ships and tankers—U.S. Steel, Bethlehem, Republic, among others—and so was the West Coast engineering genius Henry J. Kaiser. In New Orleans, boat-designer and builder A. J. Higgins had landed a contract to build 200 cargo vessels—Liberty ships, they were being called by then—under a new mass-production technique. Higgins was already hard at work making the Eureka landing boats and motor torpedo boats, both of his own design. The Eureka was a thirty-six foot motor-boat with a spoonbill bow and a half-pipe-like projection protecting the propeller so that it could land on a beach without being damaged. The torpedo boats (called "mosquito boats" by the British, who used them for patrol in the English Channel) came in seventy- to eighty-foot lengths and carried formidable armament—two antiaircraft guns, an armor-piercing gun, four torpedo tubes and eight depth charges. They skimmed the water at speeds over forty-five miles an hour.

(In July, without explanation, the Higgins contract for Liberty ships was canceled, after 10,000 workmen had been hired at the shipyard and $10 million had already been spent and the first ship was nearing completion, ready to be launched in early September.)

The new 1942 models of cars that came onto the market in the fall of 1941 were the last to be produced for the duration. In early January the Office of Price Administration issued an order forbidding the purchase of any new cars, and at the same time notified Detroit that by the end of the month all automobile production lines had to come to a stop and be converted to war production.

Those who had relatives in the car agency business and counted on getting one of the 1942 models were to be disappointed. The government issued an order impounding all new cars on showroom floors or in transit. They were needed in the war effort. A few assembly lines were kept in operation to turn out "staff cars," four-door sedans of every major manufacturer, painted olive drab, for use by staff officers of the military. They came equipped with flag brackets and a little piece of metal on the front bumper to which was attached the letter *O* in white on a blue field, designating "officer" to enlisted men, so they would salute the vehicle.

GI's who had been taught that what they saluted was not the man but the uniform, or more precisely, the insignia of rank, raged at the notion of saluting dung-colored cars, and around bivouac areas it was said that this gave rise to the strictly military

term "chickenshit," which denoted any purposeless or nonsensi-
cal order or regulation imposed merely to drill the lower ranks
in military courtesy and discipline. The term in no way cir-
cumscribed the older expletive "bullshit," which in military usage
described the speech of a senior officer who said one thing but
meant another; e.g., "If I don't get perfect scores from every
one of you guys on the rifle range today, not one of youse will
get a weekend pass."

With the end of new cars came tire and gasoline rationing.
Rubber was becoming the scarcest commodity in America,
though the public was not to learn the gravity of the situation
until later in the year. Then it would learn that the rubber shortage was virtually paralyzing the war effort.

Within a few days of the ban on auto production, President
Roosevelt addressed the nation and revealed his plans—the biggest production schedule in world history. For 1942 he
demanded the completion of 60,000 airplanes, 45,000 tanks,
20,000 antiaircraft guns, and 8 million deadweight tons of
merchant shipping. For 1943, he said, he wanted 125,000 planes,
75,000 tanks, 35,000 antiaircraft guns and 10 million deadweight
tons of merchant shipping.

"Let no man say it cannot be done," said the President. "It
must be done and we have undertaken to do it."

Oldtimers blinked their disbelief. In World War I, the United
States had managed to produce fifty tanks, but not one airplane.
American aces had flown in either French or British planes.
Supplies to Britain and France had gone mostly in British and
French convoys. The British even convoyed supplies to Ameri-
can ground troops in World War I.

The burden for this massive production, it became obvious,
was to fall on Detroit, Michigan, home of the mass assembly
technique. Detroit was to become, for the duration at least, the
capital of the whole world.

Now and again a story began to appear in newspapers around
the country explaining something about the "new" Detroit,
which was now, even more than Washington, the boomingest city
in America.

"Willow Run" became a magic phrase. Willow Run was the
most gigantic industrial operation in the history of man. It
dwarfed every other effort, including, perhaps, the construction
of the Great Wall of China.

Only a year before Willow Run had been a sluggish little creek just west of Detroit, surrounded by some farmhouses and a couple of country schools. The area was lush Michigan flatland, with the kind of rich, well-drained soil that had attracted settlers for nearly three hundred years, since its value was first praised by such explorers as Pere Marquette and Louis Joliet.

By the spring of 1942 Willow Run was an enormous single-roomed building more than a half-mile long and nearly a quarter of a mile wide. Rail sidings and loading ramps were located at one end, the source of all of the raw material that poured into the huge shed. A half-mile away, out the other end, came one four-engined Consolidated bomber each hour, twenty-four hours a day, seven days a week. The bombers ran out onto the ramp of a giant airstrip. As soon as work on each one was finished, it was taken up on a test flight. If it checked out, the test pilot was relieved by an Air Force pilot and crew who took it up and headed right for a base where it was soon made ready for action. Not a minute was wasted. Besides, production was so great that there would have been no room to store the giant birds.

Inside Willow Run, where those working at one end of the line could not see as far as the other end, where messages were delivered by automobile and motorcycle, Henry Ford employed thousands, probably tens of thousands, but the number was not disclosed for security reasons. No sense in tempting enemy bombers, was the thinking.

Elsewhere in Detroit the machines and weapons of war spewed forth at the same tempo. General Motors, the biggest auto-maker, was producing arms of all kinds on contracts totaling a billion dollars a year. Nash was making engines and propellers. Hudson was making antiaircraft guns. Packard and Studebaker were both making airplane engines. Chrysler was producing tanks on three assembly lines and was shipping a trainload of tanks each day. Willys was making Jeeps.

Workers flocked to Detroit from all over the country. There was just one requisite: they must be draft-exempt. Even the very young and the very old were put to work. In Detroit and all of its suburbs, by the spring of 1942, not a room was to be found, nor an apartment. Families from the same towns in the South, who might have hardly known each other back home, doubled up, and then tripled up. Beds were used twenty-four hours a day, their schedules coinciding with the shifts at the factories.

All day and all night trucks and trains streamed into Detroit bringing raw materials for the plants and food and necessities for the workers. Stores ran out of comfort items like cigarettes and toothpaste and toilet paper, retailers having underestimated the enormous demand that grew daily. Most restaurants catering to workers refused to post menus because food kept running out. People surging back and forth from plants to homes jammed the buses until they groaned on their axles. Local breweries and soft-drink makers and candy manufacturers got special permission from the government to expand their facilities to meet the great demand for their products. Because they helped keep up the morale of the workers who made the tools of war, they were deemed essential.

Shortly after a rather cheerless St. Patrick's Day, the long-expected happened: The Office of Price Administration announced that sugar was to be rationed. Citizens had plenty of warning. During the week of April 27, said OPA, no sugar at all would be sold. After that, sugar would be sold only upon presentation of sugar-rationing books, from which coupons would be detached. People who did their own canning, it was promised, would be given extra ration coupons when the time came.

After the hiatus in the last week of April, Americans poured forth at the government's bidding and lined up at their local elementary schools, where 1 million schoolteachers took depositions as to the amount of sugar each one had at home, copied down copious statistics and issued ration books with coupons to provide a fifty-two week supply of sugar. One member of each household was supposed to show up and register his name, address, height, weight, color of eyes and hair, number and relationship of others in the household.

When the day was over, 122,604,000 Americans had their first ration cards. The registration went well, despite the fact that many did not know their height or the color of their eyes or hair, and plump ladies were prone to shave the weight figure a bit. At their first taste of regimentation, the people of the United States responded with docility.

Still worried about sugar shortages, the Agriculture Department urged beekeepers to increase their swarms to effect a 50

89

percent increase in the 206,591,000 pounds of honey produced in 1941.

The WPB moved in, with its top priorities over everything, and assured owners of apiaries that bees could have at least 80 percent of the amount of the raw sugar they had eaten in 1941. To confused consumers it was explained that bees have to be sustained sometimes before the orchards and groves bloom, and each ten pounds of sugar would insure the production of as much as 200 pounds of honey after the nectar-gathering season.

Along with this announcement, WPB ordered that the apiarists allow their bees to build more combs instead of having them refill old combs from which the honey had been removed. The Army and Navy, it was explained, needed thousands of pounds more beeswax for waterproofing for shells, gaskets, canvases and even airplane surfaces.

The war in the first half of 1942 was as discouraging as anything ever faced on the battlefield by Americans.

The Japanese had been met in the Philippines. The United States Army was small, underprovisioned, unsupported after the attacks of December 7 and 8, and consisted largely of semi-trained Filipinos.

There was one redeeming factor: the troops were under the command of General Douglas MacArthur, regarded by most top professional soldiers in the U.S. Army as the most able leader in uniform.

But MacArthur knew, and he so warned his superiors, that without planes, munitions, men and strong U.S. naval intervention, the Japs could not be be held off. The Japs were willing to pay the price for the Philippines, no matter what it might be. MacArthur's army had withdrawn from Manila and had holed up on a small peninsula called Bataan. Across two miles of water, guarding Manila Bay, was the fortress, Corregidor, whose 12-inch guns kept the Japs from steaming into the city's harbor.

Down the island onto the peninsula swept the Japs, inching forward, grinding, bloodying every inch as they forced the men toward the tip of Bataan peninsula. Once, in a surprise raid, MacArthur mustered an assault squadron of patched-up P-40s to go on a mission for which they were not constructed or intended, and the Japs were sent reeling back into the jungles. The planes peeled off over Subic Bay and sank three large Jap transports—30,000 tons in all—killing thousands of Japanese troops en route to Bataan.

But it was only a brief respite. The siege of Bataan was fifty-three days old on February 22 when the commander in chief ordered MacArthur to leave. MacArthur went to Australia, turning his command over to Major General Jonathan Mayhew ("Skinny") Wainwright.

After a harrowing escape from Corregidor, details of which were not disclosed at the time, MacArthur wrote from Australia: "The President of the United States ordered me to break through the Japanese lines and proceed from Corregidor to Australia for the purpose, as I understand it, of organizing the American offensive against Japan, primary object of which is the relief of the Philippines. I came through and I shall return."

The message was delivered to the desperate men on Bataan and Corregidor. If MacArthur said it, MacArthur would do it, of this they were certain. Sooner or later he would return. The question was: when.

When he did, it was too late for most of those who had received his message.

Two months later, Bataan fell: the white flag was hoisted in probably the most humiliating defeat in American history. Some 76,000 troops, 31,000 of them Americans and 45,000 Filipinos beaten, ragged, hungry, and outgunned, if not outnumbered, surrendered to the Japanese.

Some—a few—swam the shark-teeming waters to the temporary safety of Corregidor. A few boatloads of nurses were also brought to the rock fortress.

A month later the ammunition ran out on Corregidor. An army of 10,000 American soldiers, nearly starving, burning with malaria, disconsolate in the knowledge that there was no hope for relief, could not stop the Japs from storming the beaches and seizing the rock.

Early in the morning of May 5, 1942, Corregidor fell.

The Battle of the Philippines was over.

Japan now controlled the seas and the skies of the entire South Pacific.

The American public turned on its Congress. Increasingly regarded as not much more than a clubhouse for bumbling privilege-seekers, Congress became the target of an angry and frustrated people, infuriated over the events at Bataan and Corregidor.

The mail was blistering, filled with the four-letter words that home-fronters had learned were in common usage in the services.

"Why in hell were you so God-damned stupid as to vote against fortifying Guam when the Navy asked for it back in 1939 and 1940?" was a typical query. There was, of course, no answer. Congress *had* been stupid.

Some letters bore scores of signatures, indicating that home-town forums had sprung up for the purpose of criticizing their representatives.

Congressmen had reason to worry. The public was filled with disgust over all of the windy talk on Capitol Hill.

It wanted action.

It didn't want another Bataan, another Corregidor.

7

A Little Time for Heroes
1942

In looking back on the early days of the war, many people are prone to recall that Army Captain Colin Kelly was the conflict's first Medal of Honor winner. He wasn't. He didn't receive the Congressional Medal. Colin Kelly was a hero, though—the first to be lionized in the press and he was awarded the Distinguished Service Cross—posthumously.

On December 12, 1941, over the sea somewhere in the vicinity of the Philippines, Colin Kelly flew his B-17 bomber over a large Japanese warship, came in at pagoda-mast level and dropped three bombs into her; one was thought to have gone down her stack, and the vessel burst into flames and went to the bottom. Kelly was shot down by a Zero while returning to base. Originally it was thought Kelly had sunk the *Haruna*, keystone battlewagon of the Japanese fleet. In truth, however, it was a Jap transport. The *Haruna* was nailed by U.S. bombers in 1945.

It wasn't until 1942 that Americans learned the name of the first winner of the Congressional Medal of Honor, the nation's highest military award for bravery. He was Second Lieutenant Alexander R. Nininger, Jr., a Gainesville, Georgia, boy who had grown up in Fort Lauderdale, Florida, and had graduated in June, 1941, from West Point.

After a brief assignment at the Infantry School at Fort Benning, Georgia, Lieutenant Nininger was reassigned to the 57th Infantry, Philippine Scouts—MacArthur's pride and joy—and sent to Manila.

Lieutenant Nininger was in the army that was bottled up on Bataan.

On January 12, 1942, one month and one week after Pearl Harbor, Lieutenant Nininger was near Abucay, on Bataan. Though his own company was not in combat at the time, he assigned himself to Company K, which was under heavy attack by Japanese forces with superior firepower.

The Japs had pushed Company K away from its primary dug-in position at the perimeter of the combat area, and when Nininger joined the company the enemy snipers in trees and foxholes were successfully repelling a counterattack.

In hand-to-hand fighting, Lieutenant Nininger repeatedly forced his way into the hostile position. Though exposed to a literal hail of enemy fire, he pressed his personal attack with rifle and hand grenades, knocking out several enemy groups in foxholes as well as a half-dozen snipers in the trees.

Wounded three times, he crawled deep into the enemy position, spewing his rifle fire at anything that moved and tossing grenades ahead of himself.

When his body was found, after recapture of the position, one enemy officer and two enemy soldiers lay dead beside him.

After the great losses on land and sea, morale both at home and at the many fronts needed a boost. What Americans needed was some heroes. They took a little time off to honor a few.

In April, the most daring attack of the war was carried out successfully. In bright noonday a squadron of American bombers came in low over the sprawling city of Tokyo, dropped bombs in a wide and destructive pattern, and flew on home to a base which President Roosevelt, in response to a reporter's query, identified as Shangri-La. In monitoring enemy radio broadcasts, American observers were amused to learn that neither Axis Sally nor Tokyo Rose had caught onto the fact that Roosevelt was kidding, and had used the name of the Utopian city in James Hilton's novel, *Lost Horizon*.

A month later, just before Memorial Day, Americans learned who had conducted that raid when the hero returned home to go to the White House and receive the Congressional Medal of Honor. He was Brigadier General James Harold Doolittle, forty-five years old.

The two-engined B-25s had skimmed the housetops, eluding detection until it was too late for the city to mount strong defenses. A hornet's nest of Jap Zeros took to the air and nine attacked Doolittle's plane, but most were quickly outdistanced and held at bay by the B-25s' powerful armament. The raiders swooped right over Hirohito's palace, but Doolittle had given orders not to bomb it. It remained an untouched shrine in the center of incredible devastation.

The success of the raid exceeded our most optimistic expectations," said Doolittle after receiving his Medal of Honor. "It appeared to us that practically every bomb reached the target for which it was intended. About 25 or 30 miles at sea the rear gunners reported seeing columns of smoke rising thousands of feet into the air."

After Pearl Harbor, Bataan, Corregidor and the losses in the ongoing Battle of the Atlantic, it was cheering news for Americans, a fresh, cooling liquid for their parched egos.

After the war it became known that the base Shangri-La was, in fact, the aircraft carrier *Hornet*. It also became known that after the raid on Tokyo the sixteen bombers had flown on to a planned rendezvous in China, but that because of bad weather all sixteen of them either crash-landed or were abandoned in the air by crews after running out of gas. Of the eighty men involved, all volunteers, three were killed on landing, five landed in Siberia and were interned by the Russians and eight were captured in Japanese-held territory. All, including Doolittle, were nominated for the Distinguished Service Cross.

One of the most dramatic stories developed over a period of a month in the late fall of 1942 and involved a man who was already a much-beloved hero, Captain Eddie Rickenbacker, the ace of aces of World War I, and possessor of a multitude of friends who regarded him as one of the nicest guys ever to wear a smile, something he did a great deal of the time.

Late in the afternoon of October 21, a four-engined bomber carrying Captain Eddie Rickenbacker and seven others had radioed from somewhere in the Southwest Pacific that it had only an hour's supply of gasoline left. A week later the Army simply announced this fact, and added that nothing had been heard of the aircraft since. It said that Army and Navy patrol planes had conducted wide-ranging searches of the areas to no avail.

The communiqué said only that Rickenbacker had been on a special mission for the secretary of war, flying from Hawaii to one of the Pacific combat areas.

Edward Vernon Rickenbacker, who had turned fifty-two on October 8, was an American idol, one of the few men who had made the transition from dashing war hero to solid business tycoon. Moreover, he was the personification of the Horatio

Alger hero who, by diligent work and sheer courage, had made it from rags to riches. That such a man should be lost seemed impossible and sent the nation into mourning.

Eddie Rickenbacker had gone to work at the age of twelve, progressing successively through a glass works, a brewery, a steel mill, a monument works, a shoe factory and a bicycle shop. The latter also had a garage. Eddie learned to drive and landed a job in an automobile factory. He studied engineering via an International Correspondence Schools course. It was the automobile's speed that interested him, and by 1910 he had gained a following and a reputation at the race tracks as the "daredevil with the heavy foot."

Eddie was twenty-seven years old when the United States entered the war against Germany in 1917. He had already enlisted and went to France with General Pershing as a member of the Motor Car Staff. He was assigned as chauffeur to Colonel Billy Mitchell of the Army Air Service but pestered Mitchell until he was assigned to the flying school. Soon he was flying and in a matter of weeks he became commanding officer of the 94th Aero Pursuit Squadron, the first American air unit to go into combat in a wide area on the Western Front.

Eddie's outfit, the 94th, soon became a dreaded sight to German fighter planes and bombers. It was easily identifiable by its gallant insignia of a star-spangled top hat in a ring with a cane superimposed on it. By the war's end the 94th had been credited with sixty-nine victories, more than any American unit, and Eddie Rickenbacker, with twenty-six victories to his personal credit, led everyone. No American flyer in that war topped his record of twenty-two German planes and four balloons.

When he returned he became the popular operator of the Indianapolis Speedway and even took a short-lived venture as an automobile manufacturer, turning out the Rickenbacker motor car, replete with the top-hat insignia. It was a good car, owners said, but the competition was murderous and richer. In 1938 Eddie Rickenbacker found his real place in civilian life as the gutsy, two-fisted president of Eastern Air Lines.

When his wife, Adelaide, was notified that Eddie was down in the Pacific, she said, "He's not reckless and he knows the air. He always said he was the darling of Lady Luck." The newspapers, however, reflecting the glum attitude at GHQ in Hawaii, printed Eddie's obituary.

But the Navy had orders to keep up the search. The big Catalina flying boats criss-crossed the area where it was thought the Rickenbacker bomber might have gone down. Then, on the twenty-third day after the ditching, one of the Catalinas spotted a tiny yellow raft. On it was the bomber's pilot, Captain William T. Cherry, Jr., alive, but emaciated and barely able to communicate.

The Navy intensified its efforts and next day the good news was radioed back to Hawaii and out to the world: Rickenbacker had been found.

After twenty-four days afloat on rafts, Captain Eddie and two of his crew were picked up some 600 miles north of Samoa. Three other crew members were on a tiny island, said the communiqué. One crewman, Sergeant Alexander Kaczmarczyk of Torrington, Connecticut, had died and had been buried at sea. The Navy said that Rickenbacker's condition was good and that he and the others had been rushed to a base hospital.

More than a month later, the military allowed newsmen to talk to Captain Eddie V. Rickenbacker on his hospital cot. The ordeal showed in his gaunt, deep-lined face and the way he moved his pain-wracked body. He told the story of how the Flying Fortress had taken off on October 21, just after midnight and how, next morning, it was discovered that the compass was out of commission and the radio was not working. Running low on gas, they had ditched the giant plane and Eddie, with seven Army officers and enlisted men, had scrambled aboard three rubber life rafts. Soon the plane sank, leaving them as three infinitesimal dots on a vast, endless ocean.

His eyes sunk deep into his skull, Captain Eddie spoke to the newsmen almost as if he were in hypnotic sleep. "We organized little prayer meetings in the evening and morning," he said. "Frankly and humbly we prayed for deliverance. Then we prayed for food. If it wasn't for the fact that I have seven witnesses, I wouldn't dare tell this story because it seems so fantastic. But within an hour after praying, a sea gull came in and landed on my head."

They ate the gull raw and saved his entrails for bait. With the innards they caught two fish. They ate them raw, too.

Eddie told of the death of Sergeant Kaczmarczyk, age twenty-two. When his raft overturned, he inadvertently swallowed salt water. This caused him to become crazed with thirst, so he drank more of it later. He died of salt-water poisoning and starvation.

"For two nights I cuddled him like a mother would hold a child, trying to give him warmth from my body. At 3 A.M. I heard his final gasp."

For all but Sergeant Kaczmarczyk, the prayers had been answered.

For the folks back home, Eddie had a message: "If people only knew that the saving of one old rubber tire makes it possible to produce one of those rafts, they might not worry whether they have their automobiles on weekends."

The heroes in the fall of 1942 were not all prominent men. There was the story, for instance, of "the toughest marine in the corps," which was told and retold throughout the country. It was the saga of Marine Private Eugene Moore, twenty-two, in civilian life a checker in a San Francisco grocery store, who liked to bake chocolate cakes, who played football for his high school.

A marine for a year, Private Moore was one of the leathernecks who landed on one of the little islands in the Solomons. His tank went on up the beach ahead of the infantry. The driver spotted a Jap pillbox and stopped so Moore could fire at it. Out of a nearby bomb shelter, which neither Moore nor his driver had seen, poured a platoon of Japs. They piled over the tank, jamming a crowbar into the track and immobilizing it.

One of the Japs stuck his head inside the turret. Moore shot him between the eyes. Suddenly there was a roaring explosion and a burning, searing pain shot up Moore's back and neck. The Japs had tossed a grenade down the turret. Moments later they set fire to the tank. Believing it was better to get out and be shot than to burn to death, Moore and the driver planned how to exit from the tank. The driver stuck his head out of the forward hatch and was instantly killed by a hail of bullets.

Moore figured it was safer to come out feet first. He thrust his feet out and the Japs shot them. He vaulted clear, and fired point blank into the assembled enemy soldiers.

Counting the ones he had shot from the tank, Moore killed thirty-one Japs that day before they grabbed him.

When the Japs yanked his weapon from him, they kicked him in the face and stomach, they pulled his hair out in fistfuls, they smashed him with their fists, they stuck him with a knife, they jabbed him with a pitchfork, and then, with one holding him by the arms and another by the legs, they bashed him again and again against the side of the tank.

The Japs left him for dead. The Navy believed he was dead, too, and reported him killed in action. Marines picked him up, though, and Navy doctors patched him up and sent him home to San Francisco.

His father, who used to kid him about his cake-baking hobby, shook his head proudly and said, "I don't see how we could have raised such a fellow."

The Marine Corps also was proud of Private Moore. But so was all of America. He was a hero right out of the best of movies, and here he was a real live soldier, come home from his noble duty on the far-off islands of the South Pacific.

This was the time for heroes, as America gathered her strength. There were to be many more—thousands more—but at this time they were very important to the lacerated morale of a country new at a war that wasn't going too well.

8

Raids, Landings and Shortages
1942

Suddenly the war was no longer a matter of flags and bands and heroes. It was death and hunger and fear and shortages of familiar items and stories of atrocities and massacres. It was the telegram announcing the loss of their son to the wonderful couple who lived next door. It was the pretty girl down the street who became a widow at age twenty. It was the high school football team canceling its game because last year's star quarterback had been killed in action. It was the corner druggist going about his chores as usual, though his son was reported missing over France.

As the draft took bigger and bigger bites into the young male population, America's home front discovered faith. Never before had the churches of the country been so popular, so well and consistently attended. Clergymen felt the intensified responsibility and spoke thoughtfully and selected their texts with great care: "For whosoever believeth in me . . . " "My Father's house has many mansions . . . " "I go to prepare a place for you . . . " "If it were not so I would have told you so . . . "

Service flags hung in millions of windows, a star for each son at war, and there were, in 1942, nearly 8 million sons at war, with 4 million more to go in the next two years. In 1942 the maximum draft age was twenty-six for a married man, and thirty-five for a single man. Everyone over eighteen was subject to military duty.

The service flag in the White House window contained four stars. The Roosevelts had four sons at war. Marine Major James Roosevelt, thirty-four, having served in the Middle East, came under fire at the Battle of Midway. Lieutenant Colonel Elliott Roosevelt, thirty-one, of the Air Corps, had seen action in Africa in the spring and was now, after surgery, in charge of an aerial photography unit in Colorado. Lieutenant (junior grade) Franklin Roosevelt, Jr., twenty-eight, was aboard a destroyer on convoy duty in the North Atlantic Patrol. Ensign John Roosevelt, twenty-six, had last been heard from on the West Coast, but was now away somewhere, his parents didn't know where, though it was presumed he had sea duty.

Dreadful stories began to filter into the U.S. press of the incredible famine in Greece, where no food at all was to be found under the occupation of Italian troops. In Athens alone, 2,000 people were dying each day, the reports said. The cemeteries were so full the dead could not be interred there. Those who owned any property at all, buried their dead in the lawns and garden plots to give them some security against grave robbers, who ransacked nightly to steal jewelry from the corpses to trade to Italian soldiers for bread.

Greece, Americans reminded themselves, was where democracy was born. It was where, in the enlightened twentieth century, it was being humbled, tortured and put to agonizing death. Cholera, typhoid, typhus, dysentery and tuberculosis joined forces with Mussolini's "overseers of hunger" to torture and kill the mainland Greeks and the Aegean Islanders.

Horror stories began to mount. Among the most horrible was the one from Czechoslovakia, freely admitted by the Germans, indeed boasted about on Nazi radio. Late in May, on a road outside Pilsen, two assassins tossed a bomb into the touring car of Reinhard ("Hangman") Heydrich. It exploded directly into the stomach of the hated Nazi governor of Bohemia and Moravia, a top SS commander. He died of his wounds a week later.

No one knew who threw the bomb. It was later "leaked" in London that the assassins were Czech parachutists who had been dropped from British planes, but at the time of the death of the Third Reich's No. 2 SS leader, it was thought to be the work of local patriots.

For four days Heydrich's body lay in state in famed old Prague Castle, while outside could be heard the cracking of angry rifles as, even during the nights by torchlight, the Black Shirts of the SS rampaged through Prague's streets, exacting vengeance for the death of their chief. By the time Heydrich's casket was borne to a train to be shipped to Berlin for a high state funeral ordered by Adolf Hitler, 216 Czechs had been killed.

It was not the end.

Two weeks later the small town of Lidice (pronounced Lid-a-chee), not far from Prague, was expunged from the map, wiped out, burned, all humans either killed or sent to concentration camps, as "reprisal" for Heydrich's death. The name of the little village was seared into the minds of free people around the world.

Lidice was clustered around its church, St. Martin's, which had stood for 500 years. Many of the 1,200 villagers worked their own small farms. Others were coal miners and woodworkers. A number walked to work daily to the munitions plant at Kladno.

As the sun went down, the German soldiers surrounded the village. They moved in and picked out all adult males. After forcing them to dig their own graves, they killed them all, first by firing with machine guns, and then by administering the *coup de grace* with a pistol bullet in each head.

The women were rounded up. The young were sent to special camps for prostitutes. The older ones were sent off to die slower deaths in concentration camps. The children, those under twelve, were put into trucks and, according to the Nazis, were sent to "educational institutions," though no child was ever heard from again. No living soul remained in Lidice.

Then the Germans, methodically, machinelike, burned Lidice to the ground. When they had finished, nothing remained, not even the old stone walls of historic St. Martin's. Lidice was just a big, black memory.

It had been a cool, precise, military operation against unarmed men, women and children and an old, weathered village. The Germans had not plundered or raped or looted. They had not shouted or jeered or cheered. They had killed and burned, exactly by the textbook. Lidice was no more. Gone were Lidice's people.

Aside from the 1,200 in Lidice, the Germans shot 400 Czechs in reprisal for Heydrich's death.

Why Lidice? asked the world. Why?

Because, responded the Nazi radio in Berlin and Prague, someone in Lidice had sheltered the two assassins who threw the bomb at Heydrich.

Not a month later, the Nazis staged another massacre in Zagreb, Yugoslavia. It was for the same reason.

This time the victim was Major Helm, the Gestapo chief for the puppet state of Croatia. On market day in Zagreb, when the square was filled with peasants trying to sell their wares and produce and the tables of the sidewalk cafes were jammed with relaxing townspeople, Major Helm swaggered across the square. From somewhere, a rifle's muzzle was poked through a window. A shot snapped out. Helm fell dead in the square.

Responding, Helm's bodyguards turned their pistols at the crowd and began to shoot. They unhooked grenades from their belts and lobbed them at the tables and vegetable stalls.

When it was over, more than 700 persons were dead and other hundreds had been wounded.

The Nazis broadcast the story as a lesson to those in other occupied countries.

These stories of atrocities disturbed Americans on the home front, but somehow they failed to slow down the Yankee drive for fun and pleasure under even the most adverse circumstances.

Americans in 1942 bought a record number of books and records, drank a record-shattering amount of alcohol, set new attendance figures at movie theatres and baseball parks, but the thing they seemed to like to do most was drive their cars.

Highways were jammed each weekend as war workers sought beaches, parks, mountains and woodlands, or just a drive through the countryside. They didn't know how long the war might last, but they put their faith in their cars to see them through. They didn't know, most of them, how much gasoline it took to fly one of the big B-29 bombers, or how little rubber there was in the national stockpile.

Gasoline rationing had been in effect on the East Coast since spring, but it had not been necessary elsewhere. The war-planners thought they could reduce the use of rubber by voluntary restraints—by cajoling people on radio and in the press.

When this didn't seem to work too well, President Roosevelt himself took to the airwaves to ask Americans to search their attics and cellars and hall closets for old rubber products and turn them over to the government.

He patiently explained that 92 percent of the nation's normal supply of rubber had been cut off by the Japanese. The shortage would be even more serious if the nation had not built up a huge stockpile, but the needs of the war were eating into that stockpile, he said. The government, with the rubber industry, was building new synthetic rubber facilities, but they were not yet completed.

What he did not say was that on the night of October 11, 1941, five huge mills of the Firestone Tire and Rubber Company in Fall River, Massachusetts, had burned to the ground, taking one-eighth of the nation's reserve supply of rubber with them. Nor did he say that the Navy, which had played a custodial role at the mills, suspected sabotage.

The unknown factor, said Mr. Roosevelt, was rubber scrap. We simply did not know how much rubber scrap there was in the country. Therefore he designated a two-week period in which he asked all Americans to scout up all the old rubber scrap around their homes and take it to the nearest garage or filling station. The gas station operators would pay 1 cent a pound for it, promised the President, and would themselves be reimbursed by a grateful Uncle Sam.

Through this method, said Mr. Roosevelt, "we are going to see to it that there is enough rubber to build the planes to bomb Tokyo and Berlin—enough rubber to build the tanks to crush the enemy wherever we may find him—enough rubber to win the war."

The trouble, as Mr. Roosevelt would learn, was that Americans had been through the exercise before. They had given up all of their aluminum and tin utensils and accessories and had turned them into the government's "scrap piles," only to see them sit there, the tinware rustihg, because the head of that drive, New York's Mayor Fiorello LaGuardia, couldn't reach a bargain with the scrap dealers. Americans had been fooled by the junkmen only a few months earlier. The search for scrap rubber fizzled out.

Even so, most American kids continued to save tinfoil and aluminum foil and to roll it into big, shiny balls, which, when turned in at City Hall or Town Hall, yielded them 50 cents a pound. They also continued, as a labor of love, to cut the ends off tin cans and stamp them flat and tie them into bundles for the junkman.

When Harold Ickes announced that the rubber drive had been a failure, he accused the American public of hoarding rubber. The public shrugged off the charge. Truth is, it wasn't hoarding, it was simply indifferent to the drive. People hadn't bothered to check their attics, cellars and garages for the stuff.

Knowing that something would have to be done, Roosevelt appointed a distinguished committee to probe the rubber crisis and come up with suggestions. Heading it were Bernard M. Baruch (invariably referred to in the press by the empty title of "elder statesman," since Roosevelt had once called him that), Harvard President James B. Conant and MIT President Karl T. Compton.

In little more than a month the committee handed in its report. It went directly to the point:

"We find the existing situation to be so dangerous that unless corrective measures are taken immediately this country will face both military and civilian collapse."

The committee also had three "urgent and specific" recommendations:

1. Nationwide gas rationing to force a reduction in tire use.
2. A national highway speed limit of thirty-five miles per hour.
3. Intensification of the synthetic rubber program.

Within a short time national gas rationing was in effect. The machinery was already in existence for the East Coast, so it required only an expansion. The driver of every car was assigned a windshield sticker *A, B, C* or *E,* denoting the kind of ration book he would possess and how many stamps he'd have.

The *A* sticker was for cars used for pleasure only and entitled the driver to one stamp, worth five gallons of gas, per week. *B* stickers were for vehicles used to commute to work, but not used on the job. *C* stickers denoted cars used in the line of work (e.g., salesmen, deliverers, etc.). The *E* stickers were for "emergency vehicles," and went to police, firemen, motor vehicle inspectors, clergymen, press photographers and reporters, highway tow trucks, and the like, including, in some instances, assorted politicians. *E* sticker owners had to use stamps, but they could get as many as they wanted. In truth, so could the holders of *C* stickers, though the need would have to be explained to a bureaucrat at the ration board. The holders of *B* stickers had to report exactly how far it was from job to home and the mileage was computed and stamps awarded accordingly. The holders of *B* stickers also had their *A* stickers for a bit of pleasure driving.

It was shortly after the issuance of so many stamp books and the filing of so many forms and the proliferation of paper work in Washington and at federal offices everywhere in the country

105

that the shortage of newsprint began to be felt. As much pulp as ever was being produced, but it was going into paper for forms and other government documents.

For a while all major American newspapers, the biggest users of newsprint, slimmed down their size, and printed fewer pages. But costs were mounting and it hurt to limit advertising. News was mounting, too, with the war, and more space was needed to print it all.

Some publishers increased the width of their papers slightly so they could print nine columns across the page, in this way adding the equivalent of a page with every eight pages in the paper, so that a forty-eight-page paper actually carried six additional pages of space. Others shrunk their borders, eliminating "white space" at the sides and on top and bottom of the pages. Still others began printing five columns to a page instead of eight, eliminating the extra column rules that took up space. Some newspapers, such as the *Wall Street Journal*, retain the five-column page to the present time. Classical in its way is the Bridgeport (Connecticut) *Post-Telegram*, which still retains its wartime nine-column page.

It may have been the failure of the rubber scrap drive that forced President Roosevelt to the realization that there was simply too much "news" flowing to the public for it to digest and understand. "News" came from the war fronts, from foreign capitals, from Washington, from regional and local federal offices, from the OPA, the WPB and myriad other agencies and, of course, from local sources. The public was bemused by it all.

Needed was a new superpress bureau, and for months he had been considering it and delaying appointing the man to head it. Finally, in June, he called to his office the calm, unpretentious, unruffleable radio commentator for CBS, Elmer Davis. He told Davis he was to head the new Office of War Information and that his task was to tell the United States as much about the war as possible, as fast as possible, and with as few contradictions as possible.

"Sure," said Davis, and next night made his last broadcast.

To make way for the Indiana-born, somewhat nasal-sounding Elmer Davis and his new agency, Roosevelt abolished a number of conflicting agencies, among them the Office of Facts and Figures headed by Archhibald MacLeish, the Office of Government Reports, headed by Lowell Mellett, the Office of the Coordinator of Information, headed by "Wild Bill" Donovan, and the Office of Emergency Management, headed by Robert Horton.

(Donovan's outfit was reorganized into a special combined espionage-infiltration-commando-type unit, and its name changed to Office of Strategic Services; it was put under the general staffs of the Army and Navy. The OSS was to perform brilliantly during the war and later changed its name again to CIA—Central Intelligence Agency.)

Within days after Davis took over his duties, Americans began learning more genuine facts about their war and the war of their allies and enemies than had been available to them previously. The reports were not exactly stripped of all emotion, but they were believable, detailed, accurate and frequent. Fewer dispatches from the front carried the word "delayed". News of combat began to flow in from the battle scene while the fighting was still going on. The home front drew closer to the men doing the dirty work of killing.

At about this time President Roosevelt got a personal fill-in on the war in the Pacific in a White House visit from a young congressman, an event that would have been more widely reported had newsmen been gifted with prescience. As it was, it got passing notice. The visitor was tall, lanky Congressman Lyndon Baines Johnson of Texas, who was a lieutenant commander in the Navy and had been on duty in Perth, Melbourne, Sydney, Darwin and Port Moresby. He had asked for a commission and active duty one hour after he had voted to go to war against the Axis powers. The Navy had obliged.

Ordered home with all other congressmen to be demobilized, he had returned to Washington nearly thirty pounds lighter as the result of a pneumonia attack. He was invited to brief the President about the war. Roosevelt must have thought he looked hungry, for he invited Johnson to breakfast, a meal that lasted four hours.

In a soft Texas accent he told reporters: "There is one thing they are not short on out there, and that is courage and guts and fighting spirit. They've got plenty of that."

After months of squabbling Congress finally got around to passing the "Petticoat Army" Act, which created the Women's Army Auxiliary Corps, the WAAC, for which recruiting had been going on for months. The purpose was to free men for combat by giving women the lesser jobs such as chauffeurs, laundresses, cooks, switchboard operators, clerks, typists, hospital and dispensary attendants, administrative workers and even public relations writers.

Secretary of War Stimson appointed as director a busy Texas socialite and glittering star on the Washington scene, Mrs. Oveta Culp Hobby, thirty-seven, mother of two, wife of former Texas governor William P. Hobby, and at the time of her appointment, an official in the War Department Bureau of Public Relations.

Mrs. Hobby's rank was that of major. Her first statement answered many questions: The WAAC personnel could wear light makeup; they could wear civilian clothes while on leave, they would not be disciplined by confinement to Army guardhouses.

Later, many anxious young ladies were cheered to learn that the Army would not design their uniforms, but that the delicate task had been turned over to the expert Miss Dorothy Shaver of Manhattan's Lord and Taylor. Further good news came with the announcement that each recruit would be issued three brassieres and two girdles.

A few weeks later the Women's Naval Reserve came into existence, known as the WAVES. Inducted as commandant with rank of lieutenant commander was Mildred McAfee, forty-two, president of Wellesley College. Impressed with the response of young ladies to the auxiliaries of the Army and Navy, the Army Air Forces (like the Air Corps which preceded it, still not a separate branch of the service) decided to use female pilots to fly planes from the factories to the air fields. They wouldn't be inducted, but would be civil service employees, known as WAFS—members of the Women's Auxiliary Ferrying Squadron.

Soon the other service branches followed suit. The Coast Guard, mobilized as a branch of the Navy, inducted young girls as SPARS, and the Marine Corps went recruiting for Lady Marines.

The young womanhood of America was involved, either in war plants or directly in the services, or in the essential jobs connected with the American Red Cross or the United Service Organization (USO Clubs) or the hard-working Salvation Army.

Then, suddenly, on the busy, busy home front, came a chilling reminder that the war was still close at hand, as well as in the remote lands datelined in the news releases. As Americans prepared to observe the Fourth of July weekend, the Federal Bureau of Investigation announced the capture of eight German saboteurs, who had been landed by a U-boat with enough equipment to destroy hundreds of industrial plants and cause thousands of deaths.

How they were captured, FBI head J. Edgar Hoover didn't reveal. All he said was that they had enough explosives to wage a two-year campaign of destruction. Six had been seized within ten days of their arrival on U.S. soil; the other two were captured four days later en route to a mission in Chicago. They had had no time to cause any damage.

Four of them had come in first, brought by submarine and landed in a large, black rubber boat. They came ashore under fog on Long Island's South Shore near Amagansett, sheltered by rolling dunes and tall dune grass. They dug a hole, buried several large wooden crates and then buried the collapsible boat itself. They mounded it over with sand. Then they headed for the nearest Long Island Railroad station and bought tickets for New York.

Four days later, apparently from the same U-boat, four more men, again using a rubber boat, landed in the dark of night at Ponte Vedra Beach, just south of Jacksonville, Florida. Again they brought huge wooden boxes with them and buried them in the sand. Then the men headed north.

Among them, the eight men possessed more than $170,000 in genuine U.S. currency. They were cleancut "average Joes." They spoke excellent "American." In the boxes they had buried were bombs shaped to look like lumps of coal. In addition there were timing devices, incendiary pistols and shells, acid sticks, fountain pens that burst into magnesium fires.

From two of the saboteurs who turned informer, it was learned that the list of primary targets of the "invaders" included factories, bridges, railroads, terminals, power plants, reservoirs, canals and department stores. Their prime objectives were the light metal plants making airplane parts.

All had been in the United States for years, at an earlier time, working at various jobs. One was a naturalized citizen. All had been members of the German-American Bund. Between 1939

109

and 1941 they had returned to Germany, their passage paid by German diplomats or American sympathizers. They had gone to espionage school in Berlin.

The superb undercover work of the FBI was never fully explained. It was not known how the men were located and rounded up. Arrested with them were fourteen American men and women who had given them food, shelter and cover.

The saboteurs were tried by a military tribunal and found guilty. Six were sentenced to die in the electric chair. The two informers were given life imprisonment.

Exactly two months after the first spies landed on Long Island, the six who were sentenced to death were electrocuted in the District of Columbia's antebellum red brick prison. They were buried nearby in unmarked graves. Four different official executioners had been employed. The executions took one hour and twenty minutes. The two remaining began lifetime sentences.

In rapid succession the home front received glorious news from the Pacific, news of a major naval victory in the Coral Sea, and then news of another near Midway Island. Soon word began to filter back about a fierce battle raging on a small island with a funny name, Guadalcanal. After the loss of Wake Island following the disaster of Pearl Harbor and then the defeat in the Philippines (Bataan and Corregidor), the Battle of the Coral Sea and the Battle of Midway provided morale-inspiring headlines.

For five days a mighty U.S. naval force supported by Army bombers from nearby land bases engaged a powerful Japanese task force, invasion-bound against Port Moresby in southeastern New Guinea. If the U.S. defenders failed, it was likely that Australia would be attacked also, and the greatest U.S. base in the South Pacific would be endangered.

The Coral Sea situated northeast of Australia, rocked with the thunder of bombs and heavy naval gunfire. Again and again carrier-based bombers supported by fighter planes ripped their way through Jap fighters to shower bombs and launch torpedoes on the Japanese armada. Suddenly it was over, with billows of smoke hugging the turbulent water. The Japanese were in retreat.

In the shambles it seemed as if the Nip fleet was disorganized, acting without orders, scurrying out of the area as fast as possible. It was the first significant U.S. victory of the war. The early announcements said only that the Japs had lost twenty-one ships, either sunk or disabled. Later the Navy, reassessing the damage, announced that the Battle of the Coral Sea had caused Japan to lose much of her naval striking power.

The Navy was wrong about that.

Only later was it reported that the giant U.S. carrier *Lexington* had also been lost at the Battle of the Coral Sea.

The victory in the Battle of the Coral Sea had been won by two of the Navy's largest aircraft carriers, the *Lexington* and the *Yorktown*, both protected by a force of cruisers and destroyers.

During the first two days of the assault on the Japanese fleet every U.S. plane returned to its assigned carrier. On the third morning reconnaissance planes spotted what appeared to be the main body of the Jap assault force, including three carriers accompanied by cruisers and destroyers. It was the most luscious plum so far in the war. The planes were ordered off the *Lex* and the *Yorktown* into history's first carrier-versus-carrier combat.

When American fighters roared in over the fleet and attacked the 14,000-ton 45-plane *Shoho*, it was noted that her decks were empty of planes. She was bombed, torpedoed and sunk.

The *Shoho* planes, joined by those from two other Jap carriers, were attacking the *Lexington*. Forty of them were shot down by the inverted rain of steel and lead from the decks of the carrier. Nine torpedoes were fired at the *Lexington* and she gracefully dodged each one. Two more could not be avoided. One of them struck amidships. Two bombs also hit her.

Returning from their own raid the *Lexington* aircraft attacked the Japanese planes, ultimately driving them off after repeated dogfights, and returned to the deck of the *Lex*. The valiant crew had three fires under control and another just about extinguished when the last of the planes had landed. Then an internal explosion, apparently caused by leaking gasoline fumes from the aviation storage tanks, ripped through the carrier. The men were ordered overboard to be picked up by the cruisers and destroyers. Later a destroyer torpedoed the flaming hulk until she sank, lest she fall into Jap hands and be used as precious scrap in the making of new enemy carriers.

The carrier *Yorktown*, after engaging in her supporting role with the *Lexington* in the Coral Sea, steamed northward to Midway for the biggest naval battle of the war. There she met her end, a bloody one, but the public was not to know of it for three months.

It was with the *Yorktown* at the Battle of Midway that American sailors learned about the Japanese *Kamikaze*—hell-divers on suicide missions, who didn't care whether or not they survived so long as they hit their target.

Planes from the mighty *York* had scored heavily on the Japanese at Midway. They had sunk three Jap carriers and were hammering at a fourth when the Japanese planes discovered the *Yorktown*. They shaped up into formation and came in at 18,000 feet, tiny specks in the sky. Then they began a long formation dive, directly toward the *Yorktown*'s vitals.

Every gun on the *York* and her fleet of escorting cruisers and destroyers opened up, sending up a solid wall of steel. Some forty Japanese planes burst into flame and smoke and smashed into the sea. A few kept coming on. Bombs slashed through the carrier's decks, hitting into fuel tanks and ammunition magazines.

Then came double waves of Jap torpedo planes and bombers. There may have been sixteen torpedo planes, possibly more. At least half were shot down before they could reach the carrier, but eight got through, streaking in fifty feet above the water's surface. The first torpedo hit directly amidships, right into the magazines. The second seemed to strike into the same target.

All 19,900 tons of the *Yorktown* leaped out of the water. When she settled, she was listing badly, appearing about to capsize.

Reports did not reveal how many died on the *Yorktown*. Survivors said it was a large number.

After Coral Sea and Midway Allies seized their advantage and moved against the Solomon Islands, a string of exotic volcanic peaks strung for 600 miles marking the northern limits of the Coral Sea, including the island of Guadalcanal. The first of the Solomons to fall to the U.S. Marines was Tulagi, an island with the finest harbor in the chain. From it the other attacks were launched.

Hardly had the news of the *Yorktown* been assimilated on the home front than the Navy announced the loss of the U.S. carrier *Wasp*. She went down in September near Guadalcanal. Again, the Japanese had used the *Kamikaze* technique with dive-bombers and surface-skimming torpedo planes.

The one difference in the outcome was reported almost defensively: Escort craft had saved 90 percent of the *Wasp*'s crew.

The United States was winning back the South Pacific, island by island, but it was clear that the cost was high. Between July Fourth and the first snowfall at home, four of the biggest carriers in the U.S. fleet had gone to the bottom. The *Dorset* was such in October.

It was necessary for Elmer Davis's Office of War Information to remind the home folks: The war *was* being won. Losses *must* be expected.

Civilians took some comfort from the satisfied and knowing smiles of confidence worn by military men those days, the direct result, they said, of the arrival in England of Brigadier General Dwight David Eisenhower to take over a new command: U.S. forces in the European Theatre.

The fifty-one-year-old Texas-born West Pointer had been promoted to colonel only nine months earlier. He had made lieutenant colonel in 1918, but had been dropped back to major after the war. Eisenhower had made a reputation for himself as Douglas MacArthur's assistant in the Philippines. He had done such an excellent job as chief of staff of the Third Army during the Louisiana maneuvers in 1941 that he had been appointed as head of the Operations Division of the General Staff.

Now Commander-in-Chief Roosevelt and the General Staff had selected him to head up U.S. forces in the European theatre. He was a superb strategist and tactician, said professional military men. He would be the ideal man to assume the mantle of John J. "Black Jack" Pershing.

In the fall of 1942 Americans learned a new word. It was supposedly taken from an old word—the English verb "greme" meaning "to vex." RAF pilots put it back into use as a noun, usually a plural noun—gremlins. These were little creatures about a foot high, dressed very much like elves or, depending on which part of the British Isles you came from, possibly like leprechauns. Gremlins can get into compasses and cant them off a few degrees. They can cause spatters of rain to fall on a plane's windshields when there is not a cloud in the sky. They delight in making a sound like a knock in an engine when it is running perfectly smoothly. A favorite trick for a gremlin is to climb into gun barrels and deflect bullets from their targets.

Possibly coming over as stowaways aboard British merchant

ships loading at U.S. ports, the gremlins had soon invaded America, too, and were gleefully at work not only at all of the airfields, but in thousands of defense plants and aboard U.S. ships. Student pilots flying a straight course with a perfect compass, would hear a little whisper in their ear—"You're off by five degrees north." They had to be cautioned to pay no heed to the gremlins, and to rely, instead, on their more trustworthy instruments. Female gremlins were called finellas, and gremlin children were widgets. Widgets were equally vexatious.

The Nazis' smartest general was in North Africa, Erwin Rommel, head of the Afrika Korps, an autocratic militarist of the old school. The Nazi press called him the "Desert Fox," and the British, who opposed him, found out why. Like Eisenhower, the American commander in London, whose dossier Rommel had memorized, the Desert Fox was a superb strategist and tactician. His troops had been honed to fine sharpness for their warfare in the sands of North Africa.

The British had marched against Rommel under General Sir Claude John Auchinleck. Attacking out of Egypt they relentlessly drove Rommel farther and farther west. As they did so, their lines of supply and communication stretched thinner and ever thinner. The Desert Fox knew what was happening to the British and he waited.

Then, unexpectedly, Rommel turned and struck back. In a humiliating defeat, Britain's stronghold at Tobruk fell to the Germans. Rommel took 28,000 Allied prisoners. Then, as relentlessly as the British had driven him back, Rommel turned the British around and sent them inching eastward, defending every mile. After being driven back 300 miles, with their lines of supply now shortened, the British dug in at El Alamein. To bolster the dam they had placed across the desert to stem Rommel's tide, the British sent General Sir Harold Alexander, at fifty the youngest general in the British Army, and said to be one of its cleverest, to take command of their forces in the Middle East, and a brilliant commander, Lieutenant General Bernard Law Montgomery, to head the Eighth Army, which was facing Rommel.

To the west stretched the vast area of French North Africa.

"Vichy North Africa," the Allied maps designated it, since it was controlled by collaborating Frenchmen who had taken up arms with the Germans, headed by a man who at times had seemed reluctant to play his role, French Admiral Jean François Darlan.

In the early dawn of November 8 a great Anglo-American armada stood off the North African coast at Algiers, laden with U.S. and British troops. The first bombers to sweep over the city bore leaflets from Lieutenant General Dwight Eisenhower, asking the quarter million people of Algiers not to resist the Allied invasion. Soon a destroyer warped into one of the docks and a small force of U.S. Rangers went ashore, expecting some resistance but meeting none.

Simultaneously, other landings took place elsewhere in that theatre. The objective was the seizure of Algiers and Oran on the Mediterranean and Casablanca and Rabat on the Atlantic, giving the Allies control of French Morocco and Algeria. From there the U.S forces could do two things: First, they could join forces with the British in Libya to lick Rommel, and second they could set up bases from which to assault southern Europe, across the Mediterranean. Early the next morning, a Sunday, sixteen hours after U.S. troops had landed, General Alfonse Juin, Vichy's military commander in North Africa, and Admiral Darlan, agreed to surrender Algiers. It was the second surrender of the war for the French—first to the Germans, now to the Americans.

Then it developed that General Eisenhower had made a deal with Darlan: if Darlan would surrender and persuade the French to actually help the Americans, Darlan would be recognized as chief of state of French Africa.

A great outcry arose on the home front. Eisenhower was dealing with the devil, the critics said, a traitor, another Quisling. It was the Army commander's first brush with public opinion. It would not be his last.

There was bitter fighting at Oran, 130 miles west of Algiers. U.S. pilots, under the command of Brigadier General James H. Doolittle, hammered at the French. Besides bombs, the planes dropped leaflets from General Henri Giraud urging Frenchmen to save their bullets for the *Boche*.

In Morocco, Major General George S. Patton encountered the toughest resistance of all. The defense of Casablanca was heated and it was not until Patton's tank columns had surrounded the city that the French gave up. By that time, all the rest of Morocco had been taken by the Yanks.

The Americans turned east and began the long march toward Bizerte, then on to Rommel and the British, singing an improvised spicy ditty called "Dirty Gerty from Bizerte."

Rommel's African days were drawing to a close.

The war was stepping up.

The war made itself felt on Broadway. Shows opened, fizzled and died. Not even revivals seemed to make it, with the exception of *Porgy and Bess*. It was the worst "season" in many years.

Then, in the fall Maxwell Anderson's *Eve of St. Mark* broke the spell. It was the first successful war play. A month later the new season was assured with the opening of Thornton Wilder's *Skin of Our Teeth*, with Tallulah Bankhead, Frederic March, Florence Eldridge and Montgomery Clift.

The theatre lost two of its greats, one to dissipation, the other to age.

First to go was John Barrymore, the "Great Profile," scion of a family of great theatre people for more than a century. He had been *the* Barrymore of the current generation, which included his sister Ethel and his brother Lionel. He had forsaken the stage for the movie set and in' the soft sunlight of the Hollywood Hills had succumbed to alcohol.

With his health shattered (liver and kidneys, among other things), he had tried a comeback on Rudy Vallee's radio show, but simply could not continue. With his brother Lionel at his side, he had died at age sixty.

Broadway mourned the untimely passing in early November of one of its greatest and most versatile showmen, the star-spangled kid himself, George M. Cohan. Cohan, as his song "Yankee Doodle Boy" revealed, had been born on the Fourth of July—just sixty-five years earlier in Providence, Rhode Island. He was the son of troupers, and in a lifetime on the stage he had been a song writer, actor, dancer, vaudevillian, playwright, producer, director and entrepreneur, and had been successful at all of them.

The records show that there were years when Cohan had produced six or seven shows, writing one, rehearsing another and acting in a third. He was immortalized by some of his patriotic songs, such as "Grand Old Flag," "Give My Regards to Broadway" and "Yankee Doodle Boy," but he also achieved honors for serious acting—in Eugene O'Neill's *Ah Wilderness*! He impersonated President Roosevelt so successfully in *I'd Rather Be Right*, that when he went to the White House in 1940 to receive a medal, the President greeted him by saying, "Well, how's my double?"

Variety, reporting that Nelson Eddy was paid $7,000 for a single concert, also revealed that he had earned more than any other singer in the past year—$200,000. Runner-up was coloratura Lily Pons, who received an average of $3,000 an appearance.

The report on Nelson Eddy's earnings was not unexpected. America was finding something precious in music in its first full year of war, something that it needed.

There were many lilting dance tunes—"Be Careful It's My Heart," "Don't Get Around Much Anymore," "I Left My Heart at the Stage Door Canteen," "Jingle, Jangle, Jingle," "The Lamplighter's Serenade," "Paper Doll," "Serenade in Blue," "That Old Black Magic" and "You'd Be So Nice to Come Home To," among others.

During the spring and summer the two most popular tunes were strangely unalike. Standing neck and neck for tops in U.S. popularity were "Deep In the Heart of Texas" and the Harold Arlen-Johnny Mercer song, the raunchy "Blues in the Night."

Then in the fall, the song hit of that year, and of the next year or two, came to the silver screen and in short order broke all records for the sale of discs and sheetmusic. Especially tailor-made by Irving Berlin for the baritone of Bing Crosby for Paramount's *Holiday Inn*, it became the first big sentimental hit of World War II.

White Christmas washed over the nation in a vast musical wave, and came ashore in USO jukeboxes on hot, arid patches of land from North Africa to the Solomons where millions of homesick American boys were facing snowless Christmases.

All over America fans were also clamoring for the records of two new instrumentalists—trumpeter Harry James and pianist Hazel Scott, the former cool, the latter hot.

Harry James had started out hot; he had not made it very well with the fans. Then he decided that in wartime, music lovers wanted their heartstrings touched a little, and he soared into the big time with a revival of Al Jolson's 1914 hit, "You Made Me

Love You." Glenn Miller had gone into the Army. Harry James filled the great gap that he left.

Hazel Scott was hard to describe in 1942 and is even more so thirty years later. "Impish" is a word that might fit. She played as an accomplished classicist, enchanting her audience with a flawless rendition of something European—say, from Beethoven. Then, with just a flicker in her impudent eyes, there would be a breath of a hot lick on the keys, sounding at first like a mistake. Then there'd be another; next a dash of Count Basie; then back to Beethoven . . . but was that now a Dixieland beat on Beethoven? Or was it—no—it couldn't be—it was boogie-woogie! Hazel Scott was no doubt the only pianist in the world who could swing Tchaikovsky and make the devotee of classical music love it. And the fans loved her.

Despite the pressures of work, folks on the home front were reading more. Four books were published that year that won Pulitzer prizes in 1943. They were: *Admiral of the Ocean Sea* by Samuel Eliot Morison, the biography of Columbus; *Paul Revere and the World He Lived In* by Esther Forbes; *A Witness Tree* by Robert Frost; and the novel *Dragon's Teeth* by Upton Sinclair. This was the year that Lloyd C. Douglas brought out his long-time best-selling *The Robe*. *See Here, Private Hargrove*, by Marion Hargrove, also hit the best-seller lists.

Record crowds flocked to movie theatres to see *Mrs. Miniver*, with Greer Garson and Walter Pidgeon (who were to remain "Mr. and Mrs. Miniver" to movie fans for many years thereafter).

There was, all told, splendid fare on the silver screen that year, including *In Which We Serve* with Noel Coward; *One Foot in Heaven* with Frederic March and Martha Scott; *The Pied Piper* with Monte Woolley and Roddy McDowell; *The Pride of the Yankees* with Gary Cooper and Teresa Wright; *Random Harvest* with Ronald Colman and Greer Garson; *Yankee Doodle Dandy* with James Cagney; and *Woman of the Year* with Katharine Hepburn and Spencer Tracy.

On Mount Palomar in southern California, the National Geographic-Palomar Observatory Sky Survey was begun in 1942, a project to photograph 500 million stars. No one knew how many years it would take.

In mid-August, between the games of a war-chest-benefit double-header baseball game at Yankee Stadium, two of baseball's mortal enemies came out of the Hall of Fame to face each other once more for the fans. On the mound was Walter Perry Johnson, fifty-four, who had struck out 3,497 batters in twenty-one years with the Senators. At the plate was George Herman ("Babe") Ruth, forty-seven, who had chalked up 714 home runs in twenty-two years with the Red Sox, Yankees and Braves. Johnson had retired in 1927, and Ruth had tossed down his bat in 1935. Each managed to squeeze into his old uniform.

The good old days came rushing back to the 70,000 paying fans as the Babe stepped up to the plate on those same deceptively spindly legs and Johnson moosed around on the mound, winding up his long right arm for his famous side-arm delivery.

The first pitch was low and inside; the second, a called strike. The third was popped into right field. The fourth was ball two. The next ball was the way the Babe wanted it. He connected. It went up, up, far into the right-field stands. On the eighteenth pitch of the encounter he belted another right into the same place, paced around the bases, holding his elbows back as he always had, and called it a ballgame. In all, Johnson had got only three strikes on him in eighteen tries: Just like the old days.

9

Labor's Lancelot
1943

The thorn in Franklin Roosevelt's side, ever since the defense effort got underway even before Pearl Harbor, was a gargantuan, big-footed, wide-set, lion-maned Iowan of Welsh descent, who emitted volcanic grumblings and spewed forth biblical oaths—the wily king of America's collieries, John Llewellyn Lewis.

A Republican, he mistrusted Roosevelt, and often said so. Pacing the deep-piled carpet in his cavernous, dark-paneled Washington office and tonguing a cigar that seemed as big as a crowbar, he often protested that the war effort was a mismanaged farce that provided unprecedented opportunity for skulduggery and profiteering. He resented the overnight political careers that were born of the war effort, and frequently said so.

Even before the United States entered the war, he didn't really believe that Hitler could win against the Allies, and he implied that Hitler victory in Europe might not be as disastrous as many people feared. Besides, he was certain that the Russians could and would lick Hitler. This, of course, would prove what a reckless fool Roosevelt had been to push the nation ever closer to the brink of war when all the time it was being handled all right without us.

The first concern of the United States, he often said, should be its domestic affairs.

Pearl Harbor removed some of the thunder from Lewis' storm center, but there remained definite rumblings and flickers of angry heat lightning around his horizon.

Lewis had won a solid victory for his United Mine Workers Union in 1941 with a 15 percent wage increase following a strike that terminated with Pearl Harbor. It was far beyond the "reasonable" increases that Roosevelt had said might be tolerated. For many months thereafter, Lewis worked on his own tycoonery in the labor movement, emerging only occasionally to roar at Roosevelt or at flighty Labor Secretary Frances Cora ("Ma") Perkins or at the Wall Street bankers.

In defying President Roosevelt's mild pleas for labor peace in the fall of 1941, Lewis had brought down the wrath of the nation. Leading the Lewis-haters, of course, were the left-wing periodicals, which, with Russia now fighting Hitler instead of standing with him as an ally, were then opposed to isolationism (which Lewis represented) and any impediment to the war effort, which his strike of the so-called captive mines certainly caused. Even the more objective newspapers, however, including those which were prone to be sympathetic to labor, condemned Lewis' arrogance and belligerence in the face of national need. Shrieked the leftist *New Republic*: "The magnificent megalomania of John L. Lewis has reached its apogee." It was, in itself, a Lewisian phrase, and it reflected the thinking on both sides of the ideological aisle, left and right.

There was one segment of the American public, however, where John L. Lewis was admired, respected and even loved, and that was in the ranks of labor. Here was a two-fisted rank-and-filer of the old school, union members said, a man from the mines and pits who wore those giant shoes because his feet had been splayed by standing all day on the rubble in the shaft. Here was no striped-pants labor diplomat who drank tea with the Great White Father at the White House. His giant shovel-shaped hands, with their thick spatulate fingers, were not meant for the tea cup or the thin-stemmed martini glass. They were shaped in the mines for the purpose of pounding on conference tables and demanding and getting the things that workingmen needed. When John L. Lewis snarled about his archenemy, J. P. Morgan, Wall Streeter and member of the board of U.S. Steel, which owned the captive soft coal mines that Lewis ordered struck, the workers could almost see the great Lewis fist smashing into the nose of the correct little banker.

With his silver-gray mane and his huge black eyebrows adorning his giant, erect frame, he was, to many, the personification of the American labor movement, the guardian of all that had been gained, the garnerer of the good that was to come.

Love him or hate him, John Llewellyn Lewis was one of the towering figures on the home front during the war years. He simply could not be ignored.

The admiration for Lewis did not cover the entire labor front. He had pulled the United Mine Workers Union out of the AFL, and then out of the CIO, which had not endeared him to its president, Philip Murray, one-time vice president of the UMW.

And he had for years waged a behind-the-scenes war with the president of the AFL, William Green. The feud between Green and Lewis was the chief obstacle to uniting the labor movement, and for six years, ostensibly because of Lewis, the CIO had gone one way, the AFL another, and the United Mine Workers, yet another. At heart, the public believed, was the fact that Lewis was a Republican and Green a Democrat at a time when the ideological differences seemed broad. The catalyst, of course, was Franklin Roosevelt himself, who personified the Green political and social philosophy and was anathema to Lewis.

In the winter of 1942, like a big bear emerging from his den, Lewis called a conference. and with his rolling, gruff voice modulated as much as he could manage, revealed a proposal for labor peace—an instrument, he said, that would unite all factions into one movement, to work for the good of the country at war.

"It is obvious that if accouplement could be achieved the results would be advantageous and in the public interest," he growled with unaccustomed moderation of expression. The plan itself was not made public, but was turned over to the other labor leaders for study.

Word began to leak, however, that what Mr. Lewis had proposed was that the new president of the "accoupled" labor organization was to be a man named George Meany, who was serving as secretary-treasurer of the AFL. The president of the CIO, Philip Murray, was to replace Meany as secretary-treasurer.

Mr. Lewis, himself, would be a vice president—the only one—in the new labor set-up.

In other words, both the Murray and Green heads would be severed.

Murray, the shrewd Irishman who spoke with a Scottish burr, looked over the plan and said:

"I will not be blitzkrieged."

The battle was on. At stake were the loyalty and dues of 10 million union members. It soon became evident, too, that the gladiators in labor's arena were not to be Lewis vs. Green but Lewis vs. Murray—the lifetime friend of John L. Lewis and the man Lewis had personally chosen to succeed him as president of the CIO in 1940 when he had stepped down. Murray was still an active vice president in Lewis' United Mine Workers Union, an affiliate of the CIO.

The Lewis peace plan for reuniting the AFL and the CIO triggered internecine warring when it became known that Lewis had been collaborating with Big Bill Hutcheson, president of the AFL's Carpenters union. Hutcheson, as giantlike, as tough, as politically wise as Lewis, was also, like the miner, an isolationist and a Republican.

The thought of a Lewis-Hutcheson link-up caused shudders in the White House, where it was still firmly believed that labor delivered a rather solid vote and that it would, with the right leadership, go to Roosevelt and the Democrats.

The President sent for Phil Murray. He wanted a different kind of labor peace, one that John L. Lewis hadn't engineered.

The war effort must come first, the President said. He set up a committee, with Phil Murray's assistance, to consult with him on all questions of labor participation in the war effort, and that, of course, included every enterprise in the country. To sit on the committee, the CIO picked Mr. Murray and R. J. Thomas of the Auto Workers Union. The AFL picked William Green, George Meany and the president of the Brotherhood of Teamsters, Dan Tobin. Neither Lewis nor Hutcheson were on the committee.

Glowering, Lewis retreated to his lair. Murray crowed at a press conference, "This man Lewis never saw the day when he could lick me."

Then Lewis called a meeting of the executive board of the United Mine Workers Union for the sole purpose of firing Murray from the vice presidency he had held for twenty years. Murray and Lewis had been inseparable shoulder-to-shoulder fighters in labor's cause since 1916. Murray had followed Lewis wherever he went. When Lewis pulled his union out of the AFL, and when he had formed and headed the CIO, Murray had been right behind him. Murray had become president of the CIO at Lewis' specific, and, in fact, tearful, request.

As Murray squirmed on the platform beside him, Lewis vilified him, called him his "former" friend and pointed out that Murray had betrayed the mine workers by accepting other offices (he was president of the United Steelworkers of America).

When Murray tried to speak, he was shouted down by Lewis followers. Finally Murray walked from the room.

Winding up his meeting the next day, Lewis declared the office of vice president of the United Mine Workers to be "open." The firing was complete.

It developed later that Lewis had made a tactical error in alienating Murray for he was not only extremely popular throughout the CIO, but also in Lewis' own miners union. The men regarded him, like Lewis, as a fighter, up from the ranks, a man they could trust and admire. But Lewis didn't know that, at the time.

Inklings of this feeling began to reach Lewis, however, and he pondered his next move. In October of 1942, he made it. He disaffiliated the United Mine Workers from the CIO and declared it to be an independent union. It was a repetition of his action in 1935 when he had walked out of the AFL.

Both Murray and Green scoffed at this move toward labor isolationism. All by himself, they thought, Lewis was nowhere near so formidable. But they were wrong about Lewis' abilities as a tactician. Shortly after Pearl Harbor, labor had given a pledge not to strike, and Lewis, as a member of the CIO, had joined in it. Moreover, the labor leaders had generally agreed to stay within the War Labor Board's "Little Steel Formula" in making demands on employers. This limited increases and other benefits to 15 percent. The big labor organizations felt they must abide by this formula. Not so Lewis, who considered himself freed from any agreements the CIO had made in his behalf.

To those who understood Lewis, it seemed that only one shoe had fallen.

In the early spring of 1943, the other shoe fell. Lewis demanded a $2 per day increase for every soft coal miner, believed to number about 600,000 strong. This far exceeded the 15 percent of the "Little Steel Formula." He issued a deadline of April 1, when new contracts were due.

But labor had taken a no-strike pledge, people said. Lewis wouldn't shut down the mines, not in wartime.

As the deadline neared, Lewis revealed his trump card. "Friends, Romans and millionaires," he bellowed at the mine operators, "it is a safe assumption that without a negotiated con-

tract the miners will not *trespass* on your property on April 1."
It was a question of semantics. The miners were not going to
strike for a contract. They simply wouldn't "trespass" on private
property if there were none.

The White House vibrated as administration brain trusters,
advisers and contact-men consulted with the President about
Lewis' bold move. If he succeeded, there was no question that
all of the unions in the AFL and the CIO would have to follow
suit. Otherwise Green and Murray and even Hutcheson would
have to abdicate their prestige and political power to Lewis. His
economic advisers warned Roosevelt: if industry-wide wage
increases were won, it would virtually ruin the nation's economy,
completely jeopardize the war effort and, with soaring inflation,
cause a forced devaluation of the dollar.

Roosevelt stalled for time. He asked Lewis to advance the
deadline to May 1. Lewis complied. What, after all, was another
thirty days?

Lewis relished these games of chess. He licked his chops at
the idea of playing with the great master, Roosevelt.

On May 1 there was still no contract. The miners struck. Four
days later the government, its hand forced, had to take over the
mines, but not until President Roosevelt, personally, had agreed
that it would be for only fifteen days and that during that period
Lewis could continue negotiations—with the government. (The
"government" was Solid Fuels Coordinator Harold L. Ickes.)

The government was a much better adversary for Lewis. It
had unlimited funds. It desperately needed the coal. In one
move on the chessboard, Lewis had checkmated the coal
operators, who legally no longer owned the mines, and the War
Labor Board, which was in no position to grant special concessions to one labor union without opening up a horrendous can
of worms. Lewis wanted a six-day guaranteed work-week with
a rate of $7 per day for the first five days and $10.50 for the
sixth, which would give the miners wages of $45.50 a week, an
increase of $2 a day. He also sought a guaranteed annual wage,
something that Ickes was not wholly against. Later he raised the
demand to $57.50 a week.

Roosevelt wanted the fifteen-day truce for negotiations, and
he had warned Lewis that if he didn't agree to it, he would go
on radio Sunday night with a fireside chat and lay the whole

ugly mess before the public. It is not known exactly what he said to Lewis, but there is indication he implied that Lewis might be tarred and feathered by the time he got through with him.

Lewis evened that score immediately.

Sunday forenoon Lewis and three members of his executive committee huddled with Harold Ickes and worked out the details of a truce. Then he told Ickes he would have to take the plan to his policy committee in New York for approval which, he said, he would do immediately.

Lewis and the three unionists took a train to New York, met with the policy committee and deliberated and debated. The meeting stretched on. Just twenty minutes before the President was scheduled to go on the air, Lewis announced to the press and radio that a truce had been approved and he ordered the miners to go back to work on Tuesday.

Roosevelt got the news all right, but it was too late for him to write his speech over again. He went on the air, blasted Lewis, and pleaded with the miners to go back to work on Monday. He made a feeble attempt to stress the *Monday* return rather than Lewis' order to return on *Tuesday*, but it was a meaningless speech and made the effort seem worthless.

It is not known whether Lewis chuckled over this or merely rolled his big cigar around in his mouth, as was his habit when he was pleased with one of his chess moves.

By the time the period of the truce was up, negotiations were still going on and had not reached a satisfactory conclusion. The War Labor Board had granted a 25-cent-a-day increase to the miners, but that was incidental. Lewis pressed his demands. The War Labor Board issued a statement saying that Lewis' defiance of the government's plea to settle the issue "gives aid and comfort to our enemies." It was an official accusation of treason, but what the WLB wanted was not Lewis' arrest, but an extension of the truce.

Lewis sent out 5,000 telegrams to union officials and ordered them to extend the truce for another thirteen days, until May 31. He implied to the press that he was being very patient with the government, the new owner of the mines.

A week before the May 31 deadline rolled around, Lewis grabbed the cat by the tail, swung it and knocked both organized labor and the White House off balance. It was the kind of move to evoke a great belly laugh in the big bear of the coal pits.

Lewis, who had disrupted the American labor movement by pulling his union out of the American Federation of Labor in 1935 and forming the revolutionary Congress of Industrial Organizations, and who then, within the last year, had pulled the mine workers out of the CIO, now petitioned to have his miners taken back into the older, more conservative AFL.

It was a deal that had been negotiated behind the scenes between Lewis and Big Bill Hutcheson, and it gave the AFL 7 million members, as opposed to the 5 million in the CIO, making it the biggest, strongest voice of labor.

When May 31 came and there was no contract, Lewis had his miners strike. They returned on Lewis' orders, after pleas by the War Labor Board, the War Production Board and Harold Ickes had made Lewis realize how seriously he was harming the war effort.

Less than a month later they struck again, pulled out by Lewis in anger at the failure of the government to negotiate with him.

On President Roosevelt's desk was the Smith-Connally Act, awaiting his signature. It would outlaw strikes for the duration.

With a stroke of the pen, Roosevelt could have ended the problem of John Llewellyn Lewis, but Roosevelt did not sign Smith-Connally. He feared the potential of an angered labor force. Instead, he vetoed it.

Lewis, meanwhile, had added an ingredient to his demands. It was "portal-to-portal" pay. He wanted money for time spent going to and from work. War plants, he explained, were being built near the labor centers, as close to the people as possible. Coal mines couldn't be moved. Miners had to commute to them. It was a whole new dimension in the concept of labor and the government was plainly unequipped to deal with it. Harold Ickes, short-fused at best, harummphed around his office, but could figure no way to suggest a compromise.

In a last-minute attempt to retrieve leadership in the crisis, Roosevelt proposed a law making all men up to sixty-five eligible for the draft so that strikers could be put into uniform. The suggestion shocked everyone, from far left to far right. The press was unanimously horrified with the notion. Newspaper publishers couldn't see themselves as officers in uniform going through channels to non-publishers to do the things that are required to put out a newspaper. Almost all publishers were accustomed to supreme command in their own bailiwicks, answerable to no one and with hand-picked experts to enforce their wishes or set things aright whenever they made poor decisions.

Congress stepped into the breach by passing the Smith-Connally Act over the presidential veto. Smith-Connally not only outlawed strikes for the duration, it authorized the President to seize and operate any facility engaged in war production that was threatened by strike, and it required the unions to furnish thirty days' notice of such strikes.

Congress had measured the temper of the voters more accurately than Roosevelt had. The overriding of the veto was, in effect, a vote of no-confidence in the President in his inept handling of the coal strike situation.

It was also a slap at Labor Secretary Perkins.

Clearly Roosevelt had not expected such action from a Democratic Congress.

Congressmen knew that the public was infuriated with John L. Lewis and would accept almost any legislation that would cut him down to size. His three strikes had cost the country 20 million tons of coal and 100,000 tons of steel, losses that would cause incalculable delays in war production and, indeed, result in the loss of lives on the battlefronts. Also lost was the time—never to be regained. The Middle East edition of the U.S. Army's GI newspaper, *Stars and Stripes*, had carried an editorial: "Speaking for the American soldier—John L. Lewis, damn your coal-black soul." It was widely reprinted throughout the nation and was said to reflect the thinking of the average GI. It was true that the 100,000 tons of steel that Lewis had prevented from going to industry would have eliminated a great many Nazis and Japs, and would have helped shorten the war.

Lewis was angrier at the mine operators than he was at the government, and he kept control of the situation, knowing that if Roosevelt acted under provisions of the Smith-Connally Act and made the miners end their strike, he would also have to seize the mines in the name of the government.

This is exactly what happened. Lewis ordered his miners back to work on the *provision* that the government seize and operate the mines, and he set October 31 as the deadline for negotiating the now long-overdue contract.

Throughout his campaign against the U.S. government—notably the War Labor Board—(and, incidentally, Franklin D. Roosevelt), Lewis had skirted around Fuel Boss Harold L. Ickes. Ickes was as much of a thunderer as Lewis, though in a more waspish way, but never did the two meet head-on. They seemed to obey the law of nature that two great storm centers with equal energy and malevolence cannot collide.

In the final battle of Lewis' eight-month campaign, he won from Harold Ickes, representing the seized mines, a contract giving the miners $1.50 a day for overtime, plus portal-to-portal travel time. With the 25 cents a day granted by the War Labor Board earlier, this was more than Lewis had demanded. He had wanted a weekly wage of $57.50, and wound up with $58.87.

The operators had won one concession. The miners were to cut their lunch hour from thirty minutes to fifteen minutes.

"Well, at least now they can afford to have some food in their lunchpails," Lewis said. The miners didn't seem to mind that they'd have to gulp it down faster.

A few months earlier, in the spring, John L. Lewis had been hailed before the special Senate war-investigating committee headed by Harry S. Truman, to explain why he felt he could call a strike during wartime, and witnesses had been treated to a typical Lewis theatrical production, the kind that angered politicians and delighted rank-and-file miners.

The old actor showed up wearing his black frock coat with its wide, Victorian flare, with two tiny flowers peeping from the lapel button, one white, one blue. He strode with even-paced majesty to the witness stand, bowed twice, as if to thunderous applause, glanced around the silent room and settled his broad beam into the chair. He looked expectantly toward Chairman Truman.

The senator from Missouri, no novice at theatrics, decided on a flanking approach. Would Mr. Lewis comment about absenteeism at the mines? Absenteeism during wartime was a critical problem.

John Lewis cleared his throat. It sounded like the deep rumble of a volcano. "I have been told," he said, "that absenteeism is higher in Congress than it is in industry. I note," he added, sweeping the room with sharp eyes under shaggy brows, "I notice that absenteeism prevails on this committee this morning."

Mr. Truman explained that the absent senators were hard at

work on some other chore connected with the committee. "I thought," he said, forcing a thin smile, "that you might have some concrete statement that would be helpful."

Did he have such a statement?

"Well, yes," said Lewis. His voice fell an octave, underscoring the gravity of what he was to say. "We have to fight this war with human beings. Human beings are subject to all the ills to which the flesh is heir."

Inflation came next. Would Mr. Lewis admit that wage increases were inflationary?

Lewis pretended shock. How could that be? How could wage increases be inflationary when they represented such a paltry part of the total economy? Quite the contrary, declared Lewis, the greatest danger from inflation was the "government's excessive rewards to industry for producing war commodities."

High payments to war contractors was something the Truman committee had been studying. No one on the committee could very well refute Lewis.

Maine's Senator Ralph O. Brewster told Lewis, however, that there were safeguards against industrial profiteering. One device for keeping profits down, he pointed out, was the excess profits tax. "We still hope the rich will not get richer out of this war," he said.

"Hope deferred maketh the heart sick," growled John Lewis.

"Mr. Lewis, you are a disciple of discontent with things as they are," retorted Brewster.

"One way to get cooperation," rumbled Lewis, "is to give the workers of this country enough to eat."

Young Senator Joe Ball of Minnesota leaped as if stung.

"Why that's demagoguery pure and simple," he shouted. "You are not seriously trying to tell the committee that any large number of workers in the United States don't get enough to eat, are you?"

The great eyebrows shot upward. The famous, much-photographed wide mouth fell open. Lewis directed a scornful glare at his prey, the young, inexperienced mouse daring to squeak at the battle-wise lion. It was just what he had been waiting for. The words were slow, deliberate, even-paced, but emitted in a bellow that rose to the rafters.

"When you call me a demagogue before I can reply, I hurl

130

it back in your face, sir. When you ask me are the coal miners hungry, I say yes, and when you call me a demagogue, I say you are less than a proper representative of the common people of this country."

Truman intervened. "We don't stand for any sassy remarks. I don't like that remark to a member of this committee."

Lewis made a poohing sound. "Who," he demanded with righteous indignation, "cast the first stone?"

Hour upon hour the committee quizzed John L. Lewis. Hour after hour he parried questions with quotations from Shakespeare, the Bible and the Lewisian archives.

The committee learned nothing. John L. Lewis had an enormous amount of fun, and when it was over, he stepped from the witness chair and left in a majestic recessional, the flowers in his lapel not even wilted.

As Senator Truman adjourned the session, he shook his head sadly.

In all of 1944, John L. Lewis remained fairly silent and his miners mined coal. He sat back while the rest of the labor front exploded into unrest and tried to capture the same gains that Lewis had won for his miners. The other leaders failed.

In 1945, before the war had ended, he called two more strikes, one in which he demanded a royalty of 10 cents a ton for the union funds for every ton of coal mined in the United States, and the other, a four-week strike for recognition of the foremen's union, but in both instances Lewis sent the miners back to work without getting what he really wanted.

His tactic was to demonstrate that he could, if he wished, close down the mines, no matter what the law said, and to get out into the open the demands that he would press, and win, after the war.

Everyone knew what his motives were and all could observe his methods.

When all was said and done, every impartial observer had to admit that among all U.S. labor leaders, John L. Lewis was not only the most colorful, damnable, obtuse and flamboyant, he was also the most able.

Of all industrial workers, the coal miners gained the most permanent benefits from the wartime economy.

It was all due to John L. Lewis, the last of his kind. It was

131

not until the era had passed that perspective showed him to be as important and as necessary to the Roosevelt scene as the New Deal itself. For all his adroit leadership qualities, Roosevelt needed a scowling adversary. No scowler in modern times could compete with John Llewellyn Lewis, the coal miner from Iowa.

10

The Sounds in the Air
1943

The New Year had barely begun when the nation was stunned by shocking news. It was announced that "Amos 'n' Andy" would leave the air within the month. The show was closed, over, ended. It was an unbelievable announcement. People refused to credit it as the truth.

For fifteen years and for 4,000 consecutive airings, Amos, Andy, the Kingfish, Ruby Taylor, Sapphire Stevens, Madame Queen and others of their little community had beguiled Americans with their regular nightly broadcasts, five times a week, and only once in all that time, back in 1934, had the hard-working pair taken a vacation. They were tired, but even so they would have continued had not their very program become a wartime casualty. Campbell Soup Company, its sales cut in half by the shortage of tin, could no longer afford to spend the $1.8 million each year to keep "Amos 'n' Andy" on the air, and CBS was unable to find anyone else, during the belt-tightening period, to pick up the tab. Their old sponsor, Pepsodent, faced the same problems that Campbell Soup did.

So devoted were their fans that the announcement stating that their program would end was viewed as a national tragedy. Arthur Brisbane had not lived to see the sad day. When he was alive, the great Hearst editor would sometimes become so engrossed in the evening's episode that he would call the studio to ask what was going to happen the next night.

Other fans who were frequent letter-writers included J. Edgar Hoover, Henry Ford, Vincent Astor and James Thurber, as well as millions upon millions of less-famous Americans. It was known that President Roosevelt was an ardent listener, but ethics would not permit him to say so.

Freeman F. Gosden, as the patiently suffering and put-upon Amos, had been born in Richmond, Virginia, in 1899. His first job had been as a road salesman for tobacco and tobacco prod-

133

ucts. Then, as an assistant to Thurston the Magician, he became fascinated with show business and in the early 1920s came to believe that radio had the brightest future for performers.

In Chicago he met up with a bricklayer from Peoria, Charles J. Correll, who shared his view about the future of radio. As a consequence, they teamed up and went to work on a script. To support themselves they promoted a series of "theatricals" around the Chicago area while they perfected a serial comedy talk-show called "Sam and Henry," which featured Sam as a slow, gullible Negro who was used as a foil by his big-talking, vocabulary-mutilating companion, Henry, but who always managed, somehow, through native shrewdness, if nothing else, to rescue the pair from trouble of one kind or another. It was the precise format of "Amos 'n' Andy."

Gosden and Correll persuaded the program director of station WGN in Chicago to schedule "Sam and Henry," and the show was such an instant success that the pair was signed with good (for those days) contracts. Their show ran on WGN from 1925 to 1927, when they switched to WMAQ in Chicago and started a show with a new name—"Amos 'n' Andy."

In 1929 "Amos 'n' Andy" switched to NBC and their first network show. They brought with them an announcer by the name of Bill Hay, who became almost as famous as the two stars with his unvarying introduction: "Aaannd, here they are . . . " They were to remain with NBC for ten full years and then switch, in 1939, to CBS.

And now, in February of 1943, they were ending it all. Neither one of the stars had been feeling well for some time. Gosden had lost his wife, Leta Marie, in the spring of 1942 but had not allowed his personal tragedy to interfere with his work.

"Amos 'n' Andy" had been radio's first great national program, and had fostered a massive audience that had the habit of listening to the same program at a fixed time, night after night.

So momentous and saddening was the news of their plan to terminate the show that newscaster Gabriel Heatter (WOR-Mutual Broadcasting System), who styled his show on the happier news of the day ("Ah, yes, there's good news tonight . . ."), felt obliged to withhold the announcement until the end of his program.

The war had brought many new names to prominence in

radio—those of the men who broadcast from the scenes of war-fare and those of men who analyzed the events on the fronts—but in all other respects, Americans stuck to their listening habits.

Joining the list of such well-known newscasters as Elmer Davis, H. V. Kaltenborn and Raymond Gram Swing, were network reporters who had previously worked in relative obscurity. They included Edward R. Murrow, whose nightly CBS broadcast began with the dramatic words "This—is—London—"; Bill Henry, CBS; Farnsworth Fowle, CBS; Winston M. Burdett (North Africa, CBS); Howard K. Smith (Berlin and Switzerland, CBS), Charles Collingwood (North Africa, CBS); Larry Lesueur, (British fleet, CBS); Charles Shaw (London and ETO, CBS); Richard C. Hottelet (London and ETO, CBS) and Eric Sevaried, CBS.

NBC had an equal number of correspondents on the far-flung fronts and scattered them behind the enemy lines whenever possible. Americans heard daily or nightly from such experts as Francis McCall, Wright Bryan, David Anderson, Tom Traynor (who was to be killed in action) and W. W. Chaplin, who pronounced his initials as "Doub-yuh-Doub-yuh."

For analysis there were Lowell Thomas, Quentin Reynolds, George Fielding Eliot, Roy Porter, Upton Close, Edward Tomlinson, John B. Hughes, John Gunther, John W. Vandercook and Graham McNamee.

For the rest of their radio-listening time, Americans remained loyal throughout the war's worst year to their old stand-bys—"Fibber McGee and Molly" (ranked No. 1 in popularity by Crossley), followed by Jack Benny; the "Chase and Sanborn Hour" with Edgar Bergen and Charlie McCarthy; the "Bob Hope Comedy Hour"; "The Aldrich Family," with Ezra Stone; "Lux Radio Theatre," produced by Cecil B. deMille and starring Les Tremayne and Barbara Luddy; "Kraft Music Hall" with Bing Crosby; Walter Winchell ("Good evening-Mr.-and- Mrs.-North-America-and-all-the-ships-at-sea-let's-go-to-press")   and Kate Smith, whose theme song was her best seller, "When the Moon Comes over the Mountain," in spite of the fact that she had smashed all records with her rendition of "God Bless America."

Her record was broken, of course, by Bing Crosby's "White Christmas." Despite the advent of Sinatra and other popular singers, Crosby was, in the 1940s, and remained throughout most of the next decade, radio's most popular vocalist. Crosby's "Music Hall" featured comedian Bob Burns, the "Arkansas Traveler," and John Scott Trotter's orchestra, with, always, a special guest. Announcer Ken Carpenter, whom Crosby continuously needled about his girth, and Trotter, remained with Crosby for many years.

A durable weekly feature was "Information Please" with Clifton Fadiman as moderator and regular panelists Oscar Levant, John Kieran and Franklin P. Adams, plus a distinguished guest. It was, perhaps, the most sophisticated and urbane quiz show ever on the radio airwaves.

Other radio fare that garnered big audiences in 1942 and 1943 included Andre Kostelanetz and opera star Grace Moore; "Suspense Theatre"; "Mister District Attorney"; "Duffy's Tavern," with Ed Gardner as Archie and Shirley Booth as Miss Duffy; "Ed Sullivan Entertains"; Arthur Godfrey's "Arthur Godfrey Time"; Burns and Allen; Arthur Lake and Penny Singleton in "Blondie"; Phil Spitalny and the All Girl Orchestra; Glenn Miller's band; Benny Goodman's band; Jimmy Durante and Garry Moore; Abbott and Costello; Fred Allen and Portland Hoffa; comedian Henry Morgan; and, favorite of the young folks, "Your Hit Parade," under the direction of Mark Warnow and starring Frank Sinatra, among others. "Hit Parade" also featured the second best salesman of the day (ranking only behind Arthur Godfrey), L. A. "Speed" Riggs, who entertained with the chant of a tobacco auctioneer.

The Lone Ranger, and his faithful Indian companion Tonto, galloped across the airwaves all through the forties for the children. In the wartime years there were some other excellent children's programs, such as "Let's Pretend," Irene Wicker as the "Singing Lady," "Red Lantern," "Corliss Archer," "Uncle Don," "Superman," "Tennessee Jed" and "Captain Midnight."

Millions of American housewives started their mornings listening to Don McNeil's "Breakfast Club" from Chicago. During the day they listened to "Ma Perkins," "Myrt and Marge," "Stella Dallas" and "Young Doctor Malone."

Nighttime fare included "Mr. First Nighter," from "the little theatre just off Times Square"; "Grand Central Station"; "I Love a Mystery"; "Suspense Theatre"; "The Shadow"; "The Great Gildersleeve"; "Abie's Irish Rose"; "Grand Old Opry"; "Mr. and

Mrs. North" and "Take It or Leave It," the quiz show with the $64 question, which in 1956, on TV, would become a $64,000 question.

Early in 1943, radio and the world of letters lost Alexander Woollcott, the ascerbic and petulant drama critic of the *New York Times*, who was satirized as "The Man Who Came to Dinner" by his one-time assistant in the drama department, George S. Kaufman.

Woollcott had built an enormous audience of devoted followers as radio's "Town Crier." On a blustery January night Woollcott moderated the "People's Platform" on CBS. He appeared with two authors and two college presidents. The subject before them was: "Is Germany Incurable?"

Woollcott responded to the question wryly: "It is a fallacy to think that Hitler was the cause of the world's present woes. Germany was the cause of Hitler." These were the last words he ever spoke on the air. Moments later, unknown to the radio audience, he suffered a heart attack. Alexander Woollcott died later that night at age fifty-six.

Radio had long since been networked nationwide, but by 1943 it had become worldwide, thanks to recordings and transcriptions. Favorite programs were sent to the troops on the fighting fronts, at hospitals and at all rear echelon areas. Also sent were more than 1,000 special programs, recorded by the top stars of stage, screen and radio, some of them combining talents that would have been prohibitively costly to even the wealthiest producer. Under the supervision and emceeing of Bob Hope, the special programs were designed to give the boys anything they asked for, and their requests ranged from Bing Crosby singing "When the Blue of the Night Meets the Gold of the Day" to Rita Hayworth singing in Spanish and Ann Sheridan preparing a steak dinner.

"Command Performance" the show was called, and Bob Hope ended one session with the gag that if the boys wanted lilting songstress Ginny Simms to sing another number, they had only to tear off the top of a Zero and send it in. Bit by bit the wing of a Japanese plane was sent through the mail to "Mr. Bob Hope, Hollywood, California." Assembled, it showed the Jap symbol of the rising sun. Ginny Simms hurriedly prepared another special program of favorite songs for the boys.

Incongruity, as it was so often to do in the future, characterized the musical tastes of Americans in 1943. Take for instance, the sudden emergence of country music. It sprang onto the scene almost unnoticed, and Nashville, rather than Tin Pan Alley (who scorned it as "hillbilly"), dictated the tunes that would go out to the recording studios. Country music, sometimes sheer corn, often poignant and lyrical, sprang into sudden national prominence because so many military installations were located in the South and Southwest, where such music was featured on local radio stations, and because southerners and westerners in the armed services performed missionary duties for their favorite sounds wherever they were stationed.

Yet some of the most popular music in America was being made by the man who was by far the biggest soloist around, the inventive pianist with the amazing and heavy left hand, Thomas Wright ("Fats") Waller, a 270-pound, five-foot-ten-inch food-and-gin-loving musical genius from Harlem, a marvelous entertainer who revered Bach and played a solid bass beat.

Waller played the hottest stride and barrel house piano anywhere, banging out a violent and complex bass with his left hand while making magical improvisations with his right. He played many of his own tunes: "Honeysuckle Rose," "Ain't Misbehavin'," "I Got a Feelin' I'm Fallin'," and "Keepin' Out of Mischief Now," supplementing them with pure dixieland and jazz.

Fats Waller's record sales and jukebox royalties nudged out both Crosby and Sinatra in 1943.

And one of the most popular vocalists was the new singing sensation of the posh Manhattan lounges, the Brooklyn-born chorus girl fresh from Ethel Waters' show at the Cotton Club, with a hauntingly beautiful face, a seductive body and a honeyed voice that was unique, Lena Horne.

In an interview Lena said, "I haven't got any voice. I don't know anything about music."

No one believed her.

Selling on the discs as never before at the same time were the country-style ballads of Gene Autry and Al Dexter and the more authentic sounds of the Carter Family and Roy Acuff. Dexter's "Pistol Packin' Mama" reached first place on the jukebox favorites.

Crosby and Sinatra began to sing more songs with a smoked ham flavor. Hollywood continued to turn out hundreds of singing cowboy movies, some of them below the grade of Z.

Tin Pan Alley responded with what could only be described as "country-oriented" songs, such as "Comin' in on a Wing and a Prayer," "Don't Sweetheart Me," "Do Nothin' till You Hear from Me," "Goodbye Sue," "How Many Hearts Have You Broken?" and "Take It Easy."

It was the sperm of rock music, much of it, and it was adored by the GI's and their girls, most of whom, a generation later, would deplore the matured version of the same music played and sung by their offspring.

Both Frank Sinatra and the Mills Brothers had hit records in '43 with their versions of "Paper Doll," and it could be heard day and night on almost every juke in the land. Busy with their myriad chores, few Americans knew the story behind one of the most popular tunes of the war.

"Paper Doll" was brought out in 1942, but it had been written twenty-eight years before by a dance-hall violinist, Johnny S. Black. No publisher would touch it, so Black put it away and went to work on another. He named it "Dardanella," and it was the smash hit of 1919 and has enjoyed several revivals since. Trouble was, Black had sold "Dardanella" outright for $25 and received little more, though the sale of copies made millions for its publisher.

In the early 1930s, Johnny S. Black gave up Broadway and music and went to Hamilton, Ohio, to run a roadhouse. There, in 1936, a customer knocked him down in a brawl over 25 cents; he struck his head on the pavement and died three days later.

There was another strong revival on jukeboxes and radio in 1943 with the plaintive "I'll Be Seeing You," which had been written in 1938 (words by Irving Kahal, music by Sammy Fain), though it was not until the loneliness of war began to be felt that it fit into the American mood.

Late in January the entire musical world set aside a special week to pay tribute to the undisputed king of jazz, the modest, elegant Bible-reading bandleader and pianist, Edward Kennedy ("Duke") Ellington. The Duke was celebrating his twentieth year as a bandleader, and the poll in the trade journal *Down Beat* listed his band as a first-place favorite, followed in popularity rank by Benny Goodman and Harry James.

The American Federation of Musicians officially designated a National Duke Ellington Week to mark the anniversary. In observance of the occasion, Duke Ellington gave a concert at

Carnegie Hall for Russian War Relief. He and the fifteen members of his band showed up in extra-length gray coats with a jet black carnation in each buttonhole.

With dignity they bowed to the standing-room-only, elbow-to-elbow audience, addressed their instruments and then, for two solid hours, beat out what critics said was the finest jazz ever to be heard in an American auditorium of any size anywhere. Included, of course, were such Duke Ellington favorites as "Mood Indigo," "Rockin' in Rhythm" and "Black and Tan Fantasy."

The most unexpected song hit of the year to become a best-seller in every category—records, sheet-music, jukeboxes and radio usage—was "As Time Goes By," sung by (Arthur) Dooley Wilson in the film *Casablanca*, starring Humphrey Bogart and Ingrid Bergman.

Again, Americans forgot that it was a revival. The song had been written in 1931 by Herman ("Dodo") Hupfeld for a Broadway show called *Everybody's Welcome*, where it had been introduced by Frances Williams. It had been recorded by Rudy Vallee, sold 40,000 discs and then dropped from sight and sound. Warner Brothers pulled it out of the files for their highly successful movie and with Dooley Wilson's magic, it went right to the top in popularity.

"Nobody can sing it like Sam," Ingrid Bergman said in the movie, the "Sam" being Dooley Wilson, and all of America agreed with her.

When the record ended its run in jukeboxes in restaurants and taverns, the patrons would shout, "Sing it again, Sam," just as Bogart supposedly had done in *Casablanca*. (Actually Ingrid Bergman asks Sam, "Play it once Sam. Sing it, Sam.")

Throughout 1943 the recording industry continued to have difficulties with James Caesar Petrillo, head of the American Federation of Musicians. The year before he had notified record-producers that in order to guarantee full employment for his musicians he would no longer allow them to make recordings that could be played on radio or in jukeboxes without fair compensation to either the musicians or the union.

The federal government challenged the legality of this kind of strike, but the ban was still in effect, operating loosely and somewhat ineffectively, in 1943. It was not until the following year that a royalty system of payments was worked out between the record-makers and the musicians.

Some of the record companies got around the Petrillo edict by using all-vocal ensembles, since vocalists were not union members. Dick Haymes had three hit records with an all-vocal background—"You'll Never Know," "In My Arms" and "Wait for Me, Mary." Frank Sinatra also had all-vocal hits with "Close to You" and "You'll Never Know."

Another record manufacturer transferred his entire business to Mexico and had the musicians and vocalists go there to do their recording.

More serious music enjoyed an excellent year in 1943. Two of the greatest conductors of the world were visitors in America, Sir Thomas Beecham, the arm-waving, shouting, goateed Briton, and Arturo Toscanini, the most famous Italian and a bitter anti-Fascist.

Beecham conducted the orchestra at the Metropolitan Opera. He also undertook a program to conduct symphony orchestras across the continent—in Salt Lake City, Montreal, Seattle, New Orleans, among other places. Americans came by tens of thousands to see the special performances of the ebullient conductor who waved his arms, shook his fists, kicked his feet, glowered, yelled and stamped at the musicians and managed, either by cajolery or fear, to produce beautifully controlled, flowing music from his charges.

Toscanini, who had resigned as director of Milan's famous La Scala Opera House in protest over Fascist policies, was later beaten by Mussolini-controlled police and had virtually renounced his career in defiance of the *Fascisti*, popped up unexpectedly in New York and recorded a radio program to be short-waved to Italy as well as longwaved across America. He directed the famous and flawless NBC Symphony Orchestra in a program of his own choosing. It was the first movement of Beethoven's Fifth Symphony, the overture to *William Tell* and the "Star Spangled Banner." Tears streamed down the face of the snow-haired seventy-six-year-old master as he conducted the unforgettable program, which he had titled: "Victory, Act I."

Instantly the opening phrase of Beethoven's Fifth Symphony became the victory theme of all of the Allies. Moreover, the opening notes, dit-dit-dit-dah, dit-dit-dit-daah, were the exact

Morse code of three dots and a dash (. . . -) for the letter *V*.
V for Victory. The love and admiration that the Italians had
withheld from Toscanini because of his refusal to conduct
"Giovinezza," the Fascist hymn, at La Scala, was bestowed on him
in abundance by cheering, weeping Americans, and NBC was
obliged to play his concert or excerpts from it over and over
again by tidal waves of public requests. Never before had so
many Americans become so enamored of symphony music or
a symphonic conductor.

Arturo Toscanini, at an age when most people were retired,
was fighting the *Fascisti* with one of the most powerful weapons
ever devised—music. He settled down in New York to prepare
two more acts for "Victory" to be broadcast to his countrymen
in Italy and to his adoring American friends.

Under the baton of Sir Thomas Beecham at the Metropolitan
Opera there was heard a man who was hailed by the critics as
the world's greatest operatic basso, possibly the finest singing
actor of all time and certainly the top one in his generation. His
name was Ezio Pinza. He had been a protege of Arturo Toscanini's and had been hired personally by the Maestro for the
La Scala Opera Company. It was there that he had been signed
for the Metropolitan by the impresario, Giulio Gatti-Casazza.

Now they were both producing their incomparable artistry for
the enjoyment of Americans, Toscanini, the master, and Pinza,
the basso profundo, one from Italy's pre-Mussolini *haute monde*,
the other, the seventh child of a Roman carpenter.

Copyrighted in 1943 was a song written in 1942 by three fun-
loving gentlemen, Milton Drake, Al Hoffman and Jerry Livingston. The song: "Mairzy Doats." Not until the spring of the next
year, around February, would it set new records in sheet music
sales.

It was the freak hit of the decade, ranking with "Yes, We Have
No Bananas" of the twenties and "The Music Goes 'Round and
'Round," of the thirties.

There were other good tunes to come out in 1943, one of the
most productive years for Tin Pan Alley since 1931.

Three of them were Spanish or Portuguese songs and they
gained much popularity: "Amor," "Besame Mucho" ("Kiss Me
Much") and "Tico-Tico."

The musical comedy *Oklahoma!* had opened on Broadway and

almost instantly the Rodgers and Hammerstein music swept through the airwaves and into the nation's heart with great and lasting hits: "Oh What a Beautiful Mornin'," "Oklahoma!," "People Will Say We're in Love" and "The Surrey with the Fringe on Top."

Hollywood also contributed its share of hits with songs from some of the finest musical films of all time. These included: "How Sweet You Are" and "They're Either Too Young or Too Old" from *Thank Your Lucky Stars*, "I Couldn't Sleep a Wink Last Night" from *Higher and Higher*, "If You Please" and "Sunday, Monday or Always" from *Dixie*, "In My Arms" from *See Here Private Hargrove*, "My Heart Tells Me" from *Sweet Rosie O'Grady*, "Shoo Shoo Baby" from *Three Cheers for the Boys*, "Speak Low" from *One Touch of Venus*, "Star Eyes" from *I Dood It*, "You Keep Coming Back Like a Song" from *Blue Skies* and from *Hello, Frisco, Hello*, "You'll Never Know," the Academy Award-winning song of 1943.

Movie critics in 1943, after two years of ballyhoo, finally got to see the $2 million epic produced by Howard Hughes, *The Outlaw*, starring his new discovery, bosomy Jane Russell. It had been years in the making, had involved fights with the censors, had cost more than any movie to that date and had been press-agented almost to death by the time Hughes released it. It was almost unanimously voted the flop of the year.

Mixed reviews greeted the equally long awaited Paramount production of Ernest Hemingway's *For Whom the Bell Tolls*, his prize-winning story of the Montana school teacher who participated in the civil war in Spain. Gary Cooper turned in one of the finest performances of his career. Ingrid Bergman was so good she was projected immediately to the plateau of Greta Garbo. Excellent performances were also rendered by Akim Tamiroff and Greek actress Katina Paxinou. Yet, somehow, it was a poor movie, unflowing, jerky.

My Friend Flicka, as innocent a film as had come along in years, starring Roddy McDowall and a skittish filly, plus hundreds of other horses and a Utah landscape, became one of the most popular shows in the movie houses.

Alfred Hitchcock had made his impression on cinema audiences back in 1941 with *Suspicion*, a chilling and tension-building drama in the unique Hitchcock style. He did it again in 1943 with *Shadow of a Doubt*, which was even superior as a film, and ensured stardom for two young, already-good actors—Teresa Wright and Joseph Cotton.

It was in 1943 that Orson Welles, twenty-eight, and Rita Hayworth, twenty-four, got married, each for the second time. Only a few months earlier Rita had announced that after the war she was going to marry coastguardsman Victor Mature. Welles had been using Miss Hayworth in a Hollywood magic show, where the romance blossomed. Commented Mature from shipboard: "The way to a girl's heart, apparently, is to saw her in half."

It was also in 1943 that actor Mickey Rooney, twenty-two, was divorced by actress Ava Gardner, twenty, after not quite a year and a half of marriage, two separations and two reconciliations. Tens of millions of American males showed interest in the fact that the beauteous, sultry, aloof-appearing Ava Gardner, whom some thought to be the personification of sex, was free to choose another mate.

On radio, a whole generation of listeners had formed the regular habit of listening to Ben Bernie, "The O-O-O-Old Maestro, and all the lads," who had been sponsored by Pabst Blue Ribbon Beer and previously, during Prohibition, by Pabst Blue Ribbon Malt, which he described as "The malta-with-the-mosta-of-the-besta." He was famous for his sign-off, which invariably went, "Au revoir, a fond cheerio, a bit of a tweet-tweet, God bless you, and pleas-s-sant dre-amms." He signed off for the last time on January 15, and died shortly after, at age fifty-two.

11

Red Points and Ration Books
1943

Even to the pool hall generals and armchair strategists it became apparent that 1943 marked the turning point of the war. The Allies were winning it, painfully and at great cost, but winning nonetheless. Time was on the side of the Allies, time which permitted the giant American war machine to turn out the tools of death needed by the armies and navies and to produce the supplies required to sustain men at war. America was feeding, clothing and supplying all of the free world.

In his State of the Union message, Franklin D. Roosevelt permitted himself to crow just a little:

> The Axis powers knew that they must win the war in 1942—or eventually lose everything. I do not need to tell you that our enemies did *not* win this war in 1942. We know that as each day goes by, Japanese strength in ships and planes is going down and down, and American strength in ships and planes is going up and up. The eventual outcome can be put on a mathematical basis.

And then he revealed to the world some hard facts:

> I can report to you with genuine pride on what has been accomplished in 1942. We produced 48,000 military planes—more than the airplane production of Germany, Italy and Japan put together. We produced 56,000 combat vehicles. We produced 670,000 machine guns. I think the arsenal of democracy is making good.

What he did not report was that planes, ships, tanks, guns and ammunition were virtually flowing to Britain and Russia and that there were strong supply lines to China, Burma, India, the Middle East and North Africa. Nor did he report on the food and clothing being shipped to allies in a steady stream, or the fact that American GI's, no matter where they were, were the best-fed, best-clothed military men in all history. A soldier had to be in a very remote spot if he couldn't get his favorite cigarettes, chewing gum, candy and Coke. So good were the supply lines of such things that Hershey bars, cigarettes and chewing gum were the common currency for barter among servicemen at the front. Nor did Roosevelt bother to tell the American people what they already knew, that in the midst of mankind's most costly war, and despite rationing and controls, nearly all who were left behind on the home front were eating well and living well, and many were faring better than they ever had in peacetime.

A few days after his State of Union message, Roosevelt handed Congress his second war budget, so gigantic that even the most open-handed lawmakers were taken aback. Only a few scientists and visionaries knew about the possibility of space flight at the time, but FDR's budget ran right out of the atmosphere. For the fiscal year beginning July 1, 1943, Roosevelt said, the United States would spend $108,903,047,923. It was more than the combined income of all Americans, men, women and children, in any year except 1942. It was more than the budget of any other nation in all history. Not until the mid-1960s would the budget again reach such proportions.

Conservative columnists began to calculate how long it would take a person to count out just one billion in single dollar bills (over sixty years, one estimated) and cried that even with machines to help, we couldn't count as much money as Roosevelt wanted, much less spend that much.

There was, of course, great bickering in Congress, but in due time FDR got his way, as he usually did.

Wall Street was delighted with the prospect of so much prosperity in the economy and responded with a bull market that sent prices to levels they hadn't reached since the Market Crash of 1929.

Those concerned with smaller business operations were not so cheerful. If the nation was to gear up even more to wartime production, they reasoned, it would squeeze out the little fellows. Shoe stores, for example, were running low on inventories except for basic styles. Haberdashers found it difficult to offer any great variety of styles or colors. The women's shops were equally limited in their offerings. As for "notions"—such things as clothespins, pots and pans, kitchenware and the like—they were virtually nonexistent, or became available only through the use of plastics and other substitutes.

Despite forebodings, there had been fewer business casualties in 1942 than in any year since 1933. Most miraculous had been the ingenious ways in which automobile dealers had saved their businesses when the supply of new cars was shut off. Most of them expanded their repair shops and enjoyed an increasing business in trying to keep the aging civilian cars on the roads.

Large numbers of them had converted their empty showrooms to little factories and were engaged in subcontracting work for the war plants. Skilled patternmakers became the premium blue collar workers as subcontractors bid for their services against the giants of industry. A man who knew how to design a special tool to do a special job could practically name his own price.

Starting back at Thanksgiving time in 1942, the most noticeable shortage was in meats, and it grew worse after the first of the year. Week after week housewives found that they were unable to spend their allotted red meat stamps and had "points" left over simply because there was no meat to be had. It was easier to buy sweetbreads or tripe than it was to get steak or even hamburger. Stew meat seemed to be nonexistent.

Then, in the first week of March, the Office of Price Administration announced that beginning March 29 the meat ration would be twenty-eight ounces per person per week, and that this would include a yet-to-be-determined amount of cheese.

Steak-lovers set up an outcry, blaming the British, who, they said, were getting our meat. The ration allowance in England was sixteen ounces of meat, four ounces of bacon or ham, and four ounces of cheese per week per person. They were, by golly, getting a total of twenty-four ounces to our twenty-eight ounces, said the American carnivores.

The charges didn't hold up. Lend-Lease Administrator Edward R. Stetinius revealed that Britain was given this allowance with a shipment of only 5 percent of the total U.S. supply of meat.

So the people on the home front wouldn't blame the armed forces for gobbling up all the meat, the government released a scholarly study which showed that even if all 8 million men under arms ate 20 percent more meat than they did as civilians, they would be the equivalent of only 1 percent added to the population.

Then where had the meat gone? A small percentage had gone into freezer lockers owned by hoarders. A certain amount had been frozen by the supply branches of the armed forces. Another small amount had gone to the bottom of the Atlantic or Pacific with torpedoed cargo ships. Most had gone into home-front tummies. The truth was evident everywhere—there was virtually no unemployment in America; personal income was at an all-time high; people were spending as never before; the OPA price freeze was inhibiting the supply-demand factor that would have responded to the upsurge in the demand for meat and other foodstuffs; and Congress wouldn't raise taxes to syphon off some of the excess purchasing power of the American consumer. Result: not enough meat to go around.

The reaction to tougher rationing was short-lived. Americans had meatless Tuesdays and meatless Fridays and learned to make substitutions. Eggs were plentiful. So was fish. Young wives of the mid-forties learned to stretch their meat dishes just as their mothers had done during the Depression years. Casseroles, meatless meat pies and other concoctions appeared on the tables. Dried beef gravy on toast—creamed chipped beef—known as "s.o.s." to the GI's, became a weekly dinner course in millions of homes.

Even with this, the severest meat rationing of the war, Americans were better fed, as a people, than they ever had been before, and they were far better fed than any other people anywhere else in the world. Pancakes without bacon could be tolerated, and so could broiled halibut on a Tuesday and trustworthy old s.o.s. on Wednesday, if there were a small roast for Sunday, a small steak on Thursday and franks with beans on Saturday. A cheese souffle wasn't at all bad, and who would ever have thought that an omelette *avec fines herbes* would be so popular in the American Midwest?

Butter was in constantly short supply and there were rumors rife, never denied, that the Army had a year's supply of the stuff, frozen and stored in a great mountain cave. Minnesota dairymen admitted to enormous purchases by supply officers. But even that didn't matter too much to the citizens. The margarine-makers came to the rescue with improved varieties that closely resembled butter after, at long last, getting Congress to allow them to precolor their products. Heretofore margarine had come in white cakes, looking like lard, and the housewife had to blend in the vegetable coloring matter to make it look somewhat like something resembling butter. This was in response to a law designed to protect the dairy interests, but those interests had to be sacrificed to the war. For years Congress had done everything in its power to make margarine unappealing, unappetizing, unpopular. Suddenly the farm-state lawmakers had the assignment of convincing housewives that it was not just an acceptable alternate for butter, but a viable replacement for it.

The situation gave margarine-manufacturers the foot in the door of the American market that they needed and they moved forward from that point on. Postwar figures were to reveal that if the dairy-state legislators hadn't been so anxious to load the armed services with butter at high prices, there would have been a sufficient supply to satisfy all of the markets, and if this had happened it is possible that margarine might not have gained its popularity among consumers. Since butter is colored gold and margarine is colored gold, latter-day economists, reviewing the situation, could only think of Midas, whose greed for gold also led him into trouble.

The affluence that sustained the citizenry in its darkest hours caused pressures on almost every facet of society as people, their pockets bulging with money, formed into queues to make their basic purchases or to obtain almost any service. From barbershops to barrooms, from meat markets to mortuaries, from pleasure houses to picture galleries, from theatres to theological seminaries, there were more customers than there were available services or products. Servicemen who wrote home complaining about having to stand in line for everything, from going to church to going to the bathroom, found the home folks to be responsive and understanding, for they were experiencing the same frustrations.

Suddenly there seemed to be just too many people to fit into the space afforded by the suddenly shrunken nation. The lonely stretch of land by the river, where neckers used to park, now sported a roadhouse, a small machine shop and a jerry-built motel for the wives of servicemen at the nearby post.

The empty stores on Elm Street were now all occupied, selling only heaven knew what, and it was impossible to find a parking space there anymore. The corner movie house expanded the schedules of its films with an early morning show and a late night show, but it still didn't eliminate the waiting lines. When there was a floor show at the nightclub, it was usually impossible to get a seat unless one was reserved for an hour or two before showtime. It was understandable that in wartime one might have to stand in line to get a drink at a bar, but why should it be necessary, people asked, to queue up just to get a Coke? Making an appointment with the doctor or dentist became a major assignment, since so many were in the service. The traditional house call by doctors was dropped, never to return.

In the cities, as taxicab companies patched, repaired and prayed over their gasping automobiles, the demand for their services increased tenfold, and wartime regulations decreed that cabbies must take as many passengers as their vehicles would legally seat, thereby giving rise to some unique romances, a rash of short stories on the subject in magazines and a few forgettable movies.

As the manpower shortage tightened, bosses began to pamper their employees, exerting every effort to keep them working and happy. Almost all production plants piped in music to tranquilize assembly-line workers and perk up output. Coffee breaks were instituted. Bowling leagues were organized.

Some clever industrial relations managers persuaded the prettiest girls in their plants to form clubs whose rules precluded dates with any male production workers who did not have absolutely perfect attendance records. Accountants were set to work dreaming up fringe benefits for employees, such as more life insurance, improved hospitalization with maternity leave, special bonuses for speeded-up production and cash-instead-of-vacations programs. There were also awards for those who bought the most Victory Bonds. Suggestion boxes came into existence in the industrial plants and acceptable ideas were rewarded by management sometimes with promotions. Special acknowledgement and even cash was bestowed on those who successfully organized the most effective car pools to bring workers to and from their chores.

It became a sort of manless world, with the eligible bachelors off to war and the nondraftable ones working full tilt either for the government or for the war effort. The male shortage was felt in every part of the country, except, of course, in the immediate vicinity of military posts or bases. In New Hartford, Connecticut, pretty, pert Miss Kathryn Fox, after spending two hours on the phone in a fruitless search for an escort to a party, summed up the attitude of young womanhood everywhere when she said: "For heaven's sake, I wish they'd call the whole war off."

The ladies didn't have too much time on their hands, either. Their services were needed not only in war plants but in offices throughout the land in almost every form of endeavor. Moreover, the birth rate was soaring, and large numbers of them had babies to tend to.

Women at home were reading serial stories in the current magazines by Clarence Buddington Kelland, I. A. R. Wylie and Rex Stout, and short stories by Faith Baldwin and Temple Bailey. There was a rash of fan magazines, and many girls doted on such fare as a description of the home life of movie great William Powell.

The magazines offered such familiar ads as "I'd Walk a Mile for a Camel" and "Join the Regulars with Kellogg's All-Bran." Missing from the ladies' journals were those coupon ads that had fascinated little girls for a generation, inducing them to send a dime for a tiny tube of free Pond's cold cream or a packet of Tangee Theatrical lipstick, rouge and powder for the same amount.

In their newspapers the home folks read the frontline dispatches of a modest little homespun man, Ernie Pyle. He was the most widely read war correspondent in the world, a wedge of American apple pie in the foreign fields where his countrymen were fighting, bleeding, dying.

He didn't write much about the dying, though. He wrote about the living. He lived with the troops. Ernest Taylor Pyle, an Indiana farm boy who had made it big as a columnist in New York and Washington before the war with his homey approach to writing, had made it even bigger as the Scripps-Howard columnist at war.

He wrote of things as he found them. He interviewed not generals but enlisted men and combat field officers. He told of the food they ate, of the clothes they wore, of the places they slept, of their need for baths. He found out if their socks were warm enough, and comfortable. He relayed their complaints about slow mail delivery and the occasional lack of toilet paper. He shared the raunchy humor about nurses and Red Cross ladies who were permitted to date only officers. He wrote of body lice and blisters, of exhaustion and thirst, of aching muscles and sex-starved yearnings, of fallen arches and soggy blankets, of flies and mosquitoes. But most of all he wrote about the plain, simple nobility of men, of common men who did not regard themselves as heroes, but were. He wrote of their dignity.

Ernie Pyle lived with them and marched with them into battle. His only weapon in combat was a battered portable typewriter, supported by a heart that was bounteously filled with under-standing and a pair of keenly observant and perceptive eyes.

From covering the blitz in London he went to the sands of North Africa, a companion in combat to the guys in the dirty uniforms who washed their socks in rationed water in their hel-mets and horrified the Arabs by whistling at their veiled and burnoosed womenfolk. A little man in his early forties, slight (110 pounds), with a tonsurelike bald spot widening at his crown, Ernie was no civilian liaison in the ranks; he was no chaplain who relayed gripes; he was simply and only one of the guys in the outfit—and the guys loved him. They talked with him, pro-viding him with the greatest news stories of the war.

His columns appeared in more than 400 newspapers with a combined circulation of 14 million, which gave him a total readership of something like 60 million. The home folks worried about him, called their newspapers to inquire about his health and prayed for his safety. Repeatedly Ernie Pyle had narrow squeaks with death, some of which he deigned to write about. Strangely, he stood in awe of the big by-lined war correspond-ents and felt himself incapable and unqualified to be one. He be-lieved he didn't know enough about making war professionally.

In the beginning, when he was covering the London blitz, he tried to conform to the war correspondent's style of "hard" reporting—giving the facts and telling what they meant—a deft combination of reporting and analysis. About forty newspapers carried his column then.

The change came one day in North Africa when French Admiral Darlan called a press conference in order to meet the members of the correspondents corps. Scripps-Howard cabled

Pyle to be sure and attend. He was hurrying across an air strip
to attend the interview when a force of Stukas streaked down
from the azure blue sky and covered the field with a rain of
bullets. Ernie leaped into a ditch beside a GI who had been crossing the field just ahead of him. When it was over, he put his
hand on his companion's shoulder and said, "Wow, that was
close, 'eh?" The soldier fell backward into the ditch. He was
dead.

Dazedly, Pyle sat through the interview with Darlan, then went
back to his tent and sat on an upended wooden ration box and
stared at his typewriter for hours. At length he cabled Scripps-
Howard that he could not write about Darlan. Instead he wrote
of the stranger, the young boy who had died in the ditch beside
him. From that point on, though he loathed the war and the
life he led, Ernie Pyle wrote of people, not of generals or admirals or high government officials unless they just happened to
be sharing his lot with his GI's.

An example:

> The men are walking. They are fifty feet apart, for dis-
> persal. Their walk is slow, for they are dead weary. It is
> the terrible deliberation of each step that spells out their
> tiredness. Their faces are black and unshaven. They are
> young men, but grime and whiskers and exhaustion make
> them look middle aged. In their eyes as they pass is not
> hatred, not excitement, not despair, not the tonic of their
> victory—there is just the simple expression of being here
> as though they had been here doing this forever.

From North Africa Pyle went on to the landing at Anzio,
where on four occasions he was nearly killed. He went with the
men onto the mainland, forging foot by foot into the Italian
mountains, learning with them about the German 88-millimeter
gun, which GI's said was so accurate it could light a matchhead
at a thousand yards. Again he missed death by a whisker.

From a point near Monte Cassino, where the Germans held
a superior position after having installed artillery observation
posts in an ancient abbey that the Americans felt they should
not shell, Ernie Pyle sat down one night to write of the death
of a Texan. Ernie's column is believed to have been instrumental
in causing General Eisenhower to reverse his decision and order

the bombing and shelling of the 1,400-year-old Cassino abbey. Ernie wrote:

> In this war I have known a lot of officers who were loved and respected by the soldiers under them. But never have I crossed the trail of any man as beloved as captain Henry T. Waskow of Belton, Texas.
>
> Captain Waskow was a company commander in the 36th Division. He had been in this company since long before he left the States. He was very young, only in his middle twenties, but he carried in him a sincerity and gentleness that made people want to be guided by him.
>
> I was at the foot of the mule trail the night they brought Captain Waskow down. Dead men had been coming down the mountain all evening, lashed on the backs of mules. Then a soldier said there were some more bodies outside. We went out into the road. Four mules stood there in the moonlight. The soldiers who led them stood there waiting.
>
> "This one is Captain Waskow," one of them said quickly.
>
> Two men unlashed his body from the mule and lifted it off and laid it in the shadow beside the stone wall. The uncertain mules moved off to their olive groves. The men in the road seemed reluctant to leave. They stood around, and gradually I could sense them moving, one by one, close to Captain Waskow's body. Not so much to look as to say something in finality to him and to themselves. I stood close by and I could hear.
>
> One soldier came and looked down, and he said out loud: "God damn it!"
>
> That's all he said, and then he walked away.
>
> Another came and he said, "God damn it to hell, anyway!" He looked down for a few last moments and then turned and left.
>
> Another man came. I think he was an officer. It was hard to tell in the dim light, for everybody was grimy and dirty. The man looked down into the dead Captain's face and then spoke directly to him, as though he were alive: "I'm sorry, old man."
>
> Then a soldier came and stood beside the officer and bent over, and he too spoke to the dead Captain, not in

a whisper but awfully tenderly, and he said: "I sure am sorry, sir."

Then the first man squatted down, and he reached and took the Captain's hand, and he sat there for a full five minutes holding the dead hand in his own and looking intently into the dead face. And he never uttered a sound all the time he sat there.

Finally he put the hand down. He reached up and gently straightened the points of the Captain's shirt collar, and then he sort of rearranged the tattered edges of his uniform around the wound, and then he got up and walked away down the road in the moonlight.

That column also inspired a movie, released in 1945, whose script Ernie Pyle supervised. It was called *The Story of G.I. Joe*, and it starred Burgess Meredith as Ernie Pyle and Robert Mitchum as Captain Waskow (called Captain Walker in the film.) General Eisenhower called it "the greatest war picture I've ever seen." It showed the war that Ernie Pyle knew and lived. It revealed warfare as a craft at which the ordinary, gallant, grimy, noble young men of the day were experts. It made it clear that there was no glory in fighting and no glamor in dying.

Ernie Pyle went on from Italy. He landed with the invasion troops at Normandy, then, in September of 1944, left France to go to the United States to be lionized for a couple of months and look over the script of the *G.I. Joe* picture. Then he left for the Pacific.

On March 31, from Okinawa, he wrote to his wife: "I've promised myself and I promise you that if I come through this one I will never go on to another one." To fellow correspondents he confided: "I have begun to feel I have about used up my chances."

On April 18, 1945, on the tiny Pacific islet of Ie Jima, off the coast of Iwo Jima, Ernie Pyle was killed by a Japanese machine-gunner. Ernie Pyle's war was over. So was his coverage of it, which had been cherished by so many millions of Americans.

Besides their newspapers, Americans found much other reading matter in 1943. When Wendell Willkie's *One World* came out on the spring booklist it immediately smashed all records and astounded book-sellers. Within eight days half a million copies had been sold, outstripping Margaret Mitchell's *Gone with the Wind*, Dale Carnegie's *How to Win Friends and Influence People* and J. K. Lasser's *Your Income Tax*. Only the Holy Bible came close to matching its popularity.

Much of the reading public roared with glee, some of it sulked and some of it was downright peeved when Philip Wylie's *Generation of Vipers*, a set of moralizing sermonettes, hit the bookstalls. The angry young sportsfisherman from Miami poked pins into such sacred American institutions as mom and "momism," the Boy Scouts, the PTA, baseball and even the "Star-Spangled Banner." Though Wylie was in dead earnest, his book was read by most as a refreshing intellectual exercise at a time when people found it hard to indulge in the needed purgative of laughing at themselves. The sacrifice of mom as a "noisy neuter by natural default or a scientific gelding sustained by science, all tongue and teat and razzmatazz," in exchange for a few laughs at oneself, seemed a small price. "She is a middle aged puffin," raged Wylie, "with an eye like a hawk that has just seen a rabbit twitch far below. In a thousand of her there is not enough sex appeal to budge a hermit ten paces off a rock ledge."

Rushing right to the top of the best-seller list was a hard, factual war story by a talented Boston newspaperman, skinny, six-foot-seven-inch, twenty-six-year-old Richard Tregaskis. *Guadalcanal Diary* was quite simply the story of the Marine invasion of that island in the Solomons, told in stark, brutal but absolutely factual prose that flowed with a clackety-clack as relentless as an unfeeling teletype machine. Shortly after Dick Tregaskis' manuscript arrived in the States it had been picked up by the Book-of-the-Month Club and sold to Hollywood, and no sooner was it in print than the book soared to the top of the best-seller list.

In 1943 the talented short-story writer and essayist William Saroyan brought out his first novel, *The Human Comedy*. It, too, became a movie a year later, but it was first received as an excellent and pleasing book, the story of a happy family in a small town in wartime, whose members found goodness around themselves and a purpose in living, and even in dying.

Two other novels were destined to leap to the top of the list and remain there for weeks. *A Tree Grows in Brooklyn* by Betty Smith, the story of a poor, muddling but happy Brooklyn family during World War I, and *Taps for Private Tussie*, Jesse Stuart's deep-felt story of a poor southern hill family's reaction to the death of a soldier son and the receipt of his $10,000 National Service Life Insurance payment.

In retrospect critics might agree that the two most significant works of fiction that year were *The Apostle* by Sholem Asch and *The Fountainhead* by Ayn Rand.

Books brought out in 1943 that won the Pulitzer Awards in 1944 included *The American Leonardo: The Life of Samuel F. B. Morse* by Carlton Mabee, *The Growth of American Thought* by Merle Curti, *Western Star* by Stephen Vincent Benet (poetry), and *Journey in the Dark* by Martin Flavin (fiction).

The Pulitzer Prize for music in 1943 went to William Schuman for his Secular Cantata No. 2 (*A Free Song*). It was the first Pulitzer in that field.

Twice in 1943 radio station WRGB, Schenectady, owned and operated by the General Electric Company, televised full-length operatic performances, quietly launching a new era. The first was Offenbach's *The Marriage by the Lantern* (an operetta) broadcast in May, and the second, Humperdinck's *Hansel und Gretel*, aired in December. The performances were given with full scenes and settings and were sung in English by performers from the Hartt Opera Workshops of the Julius Hartt Musical Foundation of Hartford.

A few doctors on the home front and a few working in war theatres began to experiment again, in 1943, with the drug called penicillin, which had been discovered back in 1929 by Sir Alexander Fleming. Because of the then laborious process of creating laboratory mold, only small quantities were available. Those who used it said it produced excellent infection-killing results. The standby for wounds remained the more easily produced sulfa drugs.

The news story that intrigued millions of home front Americans and, indeed, many millions throughout the free world, was the mysterious murder of the fabulously wealthy Sir Harry Oakes on the night of July 7 in his tropical palace in Nassau, the Bahamas.

It was a story set in a palm and hibiscus fairyland, involving enormously rich people, a bit of spice and titled foreigners from the Continent. There was even the classical "poor little rich girl" who defied her daddy. To top it off, the Duke of Windsor, now governor of the Bahamas and a close friend of the murdered man, had called in detectives by plane from Miami with orders to find the murderer whoever he might be. There was the unstated implication that it might be someone rich and famous.

The victim was a storybook figure himself. Born in Sangerville Maine, in 1874, he graduated from Bowdoin College in Brunswick and then rushed off to the Yukon to prospect for gold.

For thirteen years Oakes searched fruitlessly for gold in Alaska, the Philippines, Australia, New Zealand, Africa, Mexico, California and Nevada. By 1911 he was back in Canada, hopefully exploring likely looking spots and still finding no gold. One day, flat broke, without resources of any kind, he was kicked off a train at a place called Swastika, in northern Ontario.

Forlorn, dejected, Oakes squatted down beside an equally impoverished and beat-down Chinese near the railroad tracks. By way of making conversation he explained that he was a gold prospector.

Gold? asked the Chinese. Gold? If that's all he wanted, there was plenty of it all around Swastika. Oakes searched around and found that the Chinese was telling the truth. He staked out Lake Shore Mine and soon learned that he owned the second richest mine in the world.

When he was prospecting in Australia, Oakes had met a girl named Eunice McIntyre, and in 1932, fabulously rich, he married her. They built a showcase home on the Canadian side of Niagara Falls, bought great mansions at Bar Harbor and Palm Beach, bought a town house in London and a shooting box in Sussex.

In 1937, provoked by the rising Canadian taxes, Oakes decided to move to Nassau, where he would be taxed only 5 percent on his declarable annual income. He bought the largest hotel in the Bahamas, built a private airport for the hotel and himself, rebuilt the Bahamas Country Club and created a luxurious and huge home at water's edge, as well as getting himself elected to the Bahamas House of Assembly, where he became friendly with Britain's former king. For his charitable contributions Oakes was made a baronet.

The year before, in 1942, the eighteen-year-old daughter of Sir Harry and Lady Eunice, Nancy, eloped with a smooth-talking Continental weekend houseguest, the titled and thrice-married Count Marie Alfred de Fouguereaux de Marigny, called Freddy de Marigny. Sir Harry did not approve. He had greeted the news of the marriage with anger, then stony silence.

After their elopement Nancy and Freddy went to Mexico City to live and Nancy came down with typhoid fever and trench mouth and was declared dangerously ill. Her parents flew to her bedside and Sir Harry, in silence, watched Freddy come each day to visit his bride and twice to give her blood transfusions.

Then, a short time later, when she was recovering in Miami, Nancy confided to her mother that she was pregnant. Lady Eunice told the doctors and they were startled. Nancy, they said, was too weak to allow the baby to go to term. On their advice, the pregnancy was ended. That was enough for Sir Harry; he forbade Count Freddy to enter his house. Back in Nassau, Sir Harry and Lady Oakes changed their wills, reducing the amount Nancy would receive in the event of their deaths, if she were still married to Freddy de Marigny.

When Sir Harry Oakes was bludgeoned to death and burned in his bed on the night of July 7, the sixty-nine-year-old tycoon was worth about $400 million. Lady Eunice and Nancy were summering in Bar Harbor (Nancy was planning to go to Bennington College in September) and Sir Harry had intended to join them on July 6, but had changed his schedule.

But Sir Harry was not alone in Nassau. With him was his son-in-law Alfred de Marigny, who inexplicably had been welcomed back into the household in Nancy's absence.

It was Freddy de Marigny who was arrested by the detectives hired by the Duke of Windsor, and charged with the murder of Sir Harry Oakes, one of the world's richest men.

Soon, to an avid reading world, there began to unfold one of the most suspenseful courtroom dramas ever recorded by real-life people. Freddy lolled in the courtroom, tweaking his slim Vandyke beard, waving to friends occasionally, seeming to be bored most of the time. Over the horizon in every direction, war raged and earth and men were torn and shattered, but on the green jewel of an island set in a peaceful bright blue sea, soft palm-filtered sunlight dappled the walls of the quiet courtroom while Sir Oscar Bedford Daly, the chief justice of the Bahamian Supreme Court, bewigged and black-robed, presided over proceedings that would determine life or death for a romantic storybook Frenchman who had the unwavering support of his beautiful, chic, rich young wife. It was tailormade for the sob sisters of the world, and from all over the world, where the war permitted, they came, and they wrote.

159

Someone had crushed Sir Harry's skull with four blows from a blunt instrument and had set fire to his bed. The fire had blistered his face and body but had burned itself out.

The prosecution presented evidence. Freddy de Marigny had burnt hairs on the backs of both of his hands. His soot-smudged fingerprint was found on the windowsill of Sir Harry's bedroom. A witness testified to the fact that a light had burned late in Freddy's room.

Harold Christie, unmarried friend and real estate associate of Sir Harry Oakes, was also a houseguest. He and Sir Harry had enjoyed dinner the night before the murder with two guests, Dulcibel Effie Heneage and Charles Hubbard, but both had retired, Christie said, shortly after the guests departed. Police Captain Edward Sears testified, however, that he had seen Christie downtown, driving, after the time he said he and Sir Harry had retired.

Enter Grisou, a gray Maltese cat, to alibi for the light in Freddy's room.

Freddy and a friend, also a houseguest, the Marquis Georges de Visdelou-Guimbeau, had been having a night out on the town. After the party Freddy drove the wives of two RAF pilots home, then drove home and went to bed just after 1 A.M. Guimbeau testified that at 3 A.M. he drove his friend Betty Roberts to her home and then returned to the Oakes mansion to find Freddy's light on. He investigated and learned that Freddy was having trouble with Guimbeau's cat, Grisou, who, wanting to go out, wouldn't let Freddy sleep.

Other evidence showed that Freddy's fingerprint got on the windowsill two days after the murder. Someone else said they saw him burn the hairs on the back of his hand with an accidentally flaring matchbook.

The trial dragged on week after week and the headlines jousted with those concerning the war for space on page one. Sunday supplements were filled with mouthwatering descriptions of the proceedings and juicy sidebar stories about the members of the Oakes household and the rich "international set" Bahamians who crowded the courtroom, paying a pound a day to natives to hold their seats for them.

At length it came to its inevitable end about a week before the American Thanksgiving holiday. Freddy de Marigny was found not guilty of the charge against him. However, the jury

160

recommended that Freddy and his friend, the Marquis de Visdelou-Guimbeau, owner of Grisou, the alibi cat, be deported immediately. Two days later the Colonial Executive Council voted to honor the jury's recommendation and ordered the count and his friend the marquis to leave the country. There was nowhere to go for Frenchmen but North Africa. The pair chose instead to try Latin America. They disappeared from the scene and from the newspapers.

In 1949 Nancy Oakes' marriage to Count de Marigny was annulled. And the murder remains unsolved.

Since the beginning of the war effort, the personnel managers of Detroit's manpower-needy industrial plants had scoured the South looking for willing hands to perform the necessary tasks. Most accessible, most eager to leave were those who had the least to leave behind, the Negroes from the shantytowns, the dried-out farms and the unproductive piney woods.

The war plant representatives loaded whole families onto buses and trailer trucks, lashed their meager belongings on top, and whisked them off to Detroit where they tried, as best they could, to fit them into the already jammed and strained community. By mid-1943 Detroit was the new home of countless tens of thousands of black people, forced by circumstances to live in neighborhoods that had previously been ethnically unmixed, all Polish, all French-Canadian, all Irish, all Italian, all German, all Swedish. Trouble was brewing.

It exploded on Sunday, June 21, started by a fist fight between a white man and a black man on the Belle Isle Bridge. For twenty-four hours of nightmare, Detroit was looted, burned, pillaged. Cars were destroyed on the streets. Fires sprang up simultaneously in dozens of places. Pawnshops were smashed and their guns stolen, sporting goods stores were split open and the arms seized. Shots filled the air. Citizens, black and white, fell to the pavement, many mortally wounded.

Only a personal proclamation by Franklin D. Roosevelt ended it. Federal troops marched in with fixed bayonets to insist on order. The tally: 23 dead; over 700 injured; over 600 jailed. A year earlier *Life* magazine had warned that the Ku Klux Klan was stirring up trouble in Detroit. Subsequent investigation—after the riot—showed that *Life* had been right. It was simply that nobody had heeded the warning.

The angry blacks of Detroit now had money. They could

travel. Some went to New York and in Harlem told of the indignities and the plots in Detroit.

On August 1, a white policeman in Harlem tried to arrest a black woman on a charge of disorderly conduct, a mild misdemeanor under New York's laws. A black soldier, celebrating leave, tried to intervene. Hot words ensued. Blows were struck. The policeman wound up in the hospital with a battered head, and the Negro soldier joined him there with a bullet wound in the shoulder.

Quickly the news spread throughout Harlem that the policeman had shot down the black woman and the black soldier in cold blood.

For twenty-four hours Harlem rioted. The damage was well over $1 million. The toll was 6 dead, 543 rioters and police injured, a chasm between Harlem and the rest of Manhattan that would take years to close.

The Pentagon, the world's largest office building, covering thirty-four acres just outside Washington and costing $64 million, was opened to the brass of the armed services, relieving the strain on scores of downtown buildings in the sardine-packed "Capital of the World."

In Chicago, the world's largest hotel, the Stevens, which had been taken over by the Army, was finally sold at a near loss, after an embarrassing display of military financial naivete, to the Kirkaby hotel interests. Chicagoans were more interested in trying out their first subway, which, being newer, was cleaner than New York's, and, said the folks of the Windy City, much quieter.

In the late spring of 1943, all of the Nazi Afrika Korps had been cleared out of North Africa. General Rommel had gone back to Berlin to see Hitler and find out why he wasn't getting the support he needed.

In July, British and American troops, commanded by General Eisenhower, invaded Sicily, and two months later were on the Italian mainland en route to Rome. In the Pacific, after the fall of the vital Solomons, the U.S. Marines wrested the key island of Tarawa from the Japanese in one of the war's bloodiest battles.

Early in the year President Roosevelt and Prime Minister Churchill conferred at Casablanca, Morocco, on the "unconditional surrender of Germany, Italy and Japan." In late November and early December, President Roosevelt, Prime

Minister Churchill and Premier Stalin met at Teheran, Iran, to agree on final plans for victory and the surrender of the enemies.

On July 25, Premier Benito Mussolini, the Duce of a defeated, hungry and angry people, was forced to turn the government back to King Victor Emmanuel III, who placed him under arrest. On September 8 Italy terminated hostilities with the United States and sued for peace. On October 13, Italy declared war on its former ally, Germany. Mussolini, who had been whisked into hiding by the Nazis, was living under German military "protection" somewhere with his mistress, the arrogant, blonde Clara Petacci. Some reports said they were in Germany, others that they were in northern Italy.

For a while impoverished Italy was to receive some military help—meaning food and supplies—from the occupying American forces.

But in November the United Nations Relief and Rehabilitation Administration (UNRRA) was organized by forty-four nations to supply food, clothing, medicine and other necessities to liberated peoples of the world.

The Italians were regarded as having been "liberated" from the Nazis and were among the original beneficiaries of the novel organization—forerunner of the United Nations.

(*Photos by Frederic Le*

(*Top left*) Horsedrawn wagons returned to the streets of New York, replacing gasoline powered trucks. (*Middle left*) Gas stations counted cars that they could supply. The last car on line was lucky. (*Bottom left*) A War Bond Rally on the steps of the Sub Treasury building at Broad and Wall Streets, New York City. (*Top right*) Victory Gardens took over every corner lot and unused plot of land in the country. (*Bottom right*) Assembly line workers posing in front of a suggestion box. Note the tin hat on the soldier in the poster.

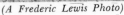

(*A Frederic Lewis Photo*)

(*Top left*) Durable Eddie Cantor. (*Middle left*) Fred Allen and his wife, Portland Hoffa. (*Bottom left*) Al Schacht, "The Clown Prince of Baseball," entertained fans of the Great American Pastime throughout the war years. (*Top right*) Radio's favorite comedy team, Amos 'n' Andy. (*Bottom right*) Kay Kyser, conductor of "The Kollege of Musical Knowledge."

(*Top left*) H. V. Kaltenborn, NBC newscaster, and the dean of war commentators. (*Center left*) Jack Benny, left, and Fred Allen, March 1937. (*Bottom left*) Fibber McGee and Molly (Jim and Marian Jordan). (*Top right*) Arturo Toscanini, conductor of the NBC Symphony Orchestra. (*Bottom right*) Comedy team George Burns and Gracie Allen, October, 1941.

(A Frederic Lewis Photo)

(*Top left*) W. C. Fields, Dorothy Lamour, Charlie McCarthy and Edgar Bergen. (*Middle left*) Red Skelton, October, 1942. (*Bottom left*) Sgt. Joe Louis. Joe learned he was drafted into the Army the night he knocked out Buddy Baer in 2 min. 56 sec. His purse for that fight went to charity. (*Top right*) Bob Hope. (*Bottom right*) Bing Crosby, July, 1940.

This inflated model of a landing craft (*above*) was part of a ghost army made by Uniroyal, Inc. as decoy targets. They collapsed easily for storage, and were quickly inflated at a new location.

The medium tank (*below*) looked real from the air.

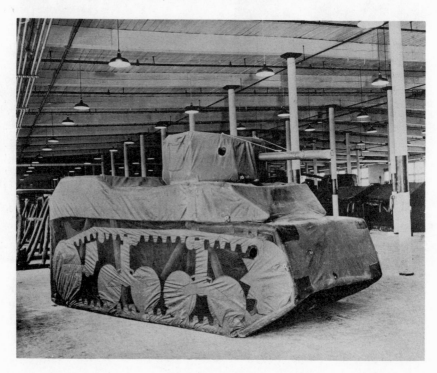

The keel of this Liberty Ship (*above*), the Robert E. Peary, was laid on November 8, 1942, at 12:01 a.m. The finished ship was launched at 3:30 p.m. on November 12. A typical launching of a Kaiser ship (*below*), on July 4, 1942. Henry J. Kaiser brought mass production techniques to shipbuilding, saving months, and building a fleet of ships practically overnight.

LAUNCHING, 7-4-42

The 1941 Ford (*above*) and Chevrolet (*below*) were fated to be driven with minimum maintenance for the next five years. Not until 1946 did American carmakers resume auto production for the civilian trade. Meanwhile, cars like these logged upwards of 200,000 miles.

(*Top left*) From 1940 to 1945, General Motors ceased production of peacetime products, as did most other industrial operators, and plunged into all-out war effort. By war's end GM, the nation's largest war materials producer, had turned out military equipment with a dollar value of more than $12.5 billion. (*Top right*) War plants received Army-Navy "E" for Efficiency Awards honoring their service in keeping the goods flowing to the war front. The Bay City, Michigan Chevy plant had 282 workers in the armed forces. (*Below*) B-29 bombers rolled out of Willow Run as though they were two-door Fords. They were produced so fast they were stacked in lines before being fueled and flown off to war. Here Henry Ford II inscribes one for luck.

(Photos by Frederic Lewis)

(*Top left*) Window banners proliferated during the war, telling passers-by that the household had a man in the service, reminding people to buy bonds, or, as in this case, asking for a little peace and quiet—everybody's prayer. (*Top right*) Unofficial V-E Day, May 7, 1945, Times Square, New York. You are looking south towards 43rd Street. (*Below*) The Commander-in-Chief takes time out for a family get together. Young David B. Roosevelt, the President's grandson, is on his lap. David's mother, Mrs. Elliott Roosevelt, his brother, Elliott, Jr., 6, sister Chandler, 8, and grandmother, Mrs. Eleanor Roosevelt, complete the family scene.

Built for Main Street . . .
But they made good on the Burma Road

A typical example of B. F. Goodrich leadership in truck tires

THE Burma Road is an incredible highway. It's a 700-mile corkscrew twisting perilously through jagged mountain ranges. It's narrow, unpaved, "scratched out of the mountains with their fingernails," as an American engineer described it. Yet this road with its treacherous curves and steep grades, often blocked by landslides and pockmarked by bombs, soon earned the name of "China's lifeline."

Here a fleet of American-built trucks, many equipped with B. F. Goodrich truck tires, several years ago began to deliver the goods over a road called impassable.

These tires are the same "First in Value" tires that are the choice of truck owners on Main Street, U. S. A. In fact, they were built for the everyday job of hauling food and steel and motor freight.

The fact that these B. F. Goodrich Speedliner Silvertowns made good on the Burma Road is an indication of the extra quality built into Silvertowns.

If you are permitted to buy tires for your trucks, get these tires which last you longer, serve you better and conserve rubber for defense. All Silvertown Tires are now fortified with Duramin, an amazing B. F. Goodrich chemical discovery which adds thousands of miles to tire life. See the B. F. Goodrich man *first*, for B. F. Goodrich is First in Rubber.

In war or peace

B.F. **Goodrich**

FIRST IN RUBBER

Advertisement for B. F. GOODRICH,
Saturday Evening Post,
April 4, 1942

"If My Mess Sergeant Could Only See Me Now!"

WHEN MESS CALL sounds in Uncle Sam's Army we know we're going to get the best 'eats' a soldier ever had. But after all, nothing can really take the place of mom's cooking...and the pickin's foraged 'between times' from her G-E!"

Folks at home may take their General Electric Refrigerator for granted, but not your young man in the service! He knows what it's like to be *without* one for raiding day or night—and does he miss it!

Today the importance of a dependable, economical refrigerator is recognized more than ever! Five of the six essential foods required daily for proper diet need constant refrigeration to retain their valuable vitamins! So if you have a refrigerator that maintains temperatures below 40 degrees, keep it in good working order.

There will not be many new refrigerators available this year, but if you buy a G-E you can be certain it will be of the same high quality that has made the General Electric "tops in preference, tops in performance." Actually, the new 1942 G-E Refrigerator provides *even lower temperatures and better food preservation with even less current than the 1941 model*—and, of course, the General Electric 5-year Protection Plan applies as always.

JUST OFF THE PRESS—Timely new 24-page booklet "How To Get The Most Out Of The Food You Buy." Write General Electric Co., Dept. XG-274, Bridgeport, Conn. Enclose 3c stamp to cover postage and cost of mailing.

GENERAL ⊕ ELECTRIC

Advertisement for GENERAL ELECTRIC,
Saturday Evening Post,
April 4, 1942

Advertisement for PLYMOUTH,
Saturday Evening Post,
October 9, 1943

EVEN THESE BIG ONES STAY HOOKED
ON AN *ASHAWAY LINE!*

ONE hundred and nineteen years ago in the little New England town of Ashaway, R. I., a retired sea captain settled down to make fishing lines.

Ever since that day in 1824 Cap'n Lester Crandall's ASHAWAY LINE & TWINE MFG. CO. has grown more and more famous for the excellence of its lines and for its pioneering tradition.

The first fish line made entirely of *nylon* yarn, for example, was produced a few years ago by ASHAWAY.

But then came the war . . . and with it, ASHAWAY's determination to have a hand in winning it.

And so, armed with more than a century of line-making skill and with early experience in handling nylon yarn, ASHAWAY has been cooperating closely with the Plymouth Cordage Company, world's largest makers of fine ropes and twines, in the successful development of a super nylon rope for towing U.S. Army gliders.

But this is only one of ASHAWAY's wartime contributions. Today our plant is turning out *not* fishline, but parachute shrouds for our fliers . . . non-stop pick-up lines for the air mail . . . signal flare cord . . . surgical sutures for our medical corps . . . and other vital control cords for our fighting forces.

Not until it's over 'over there' will we again be ready to wade hip-deep in tumbling mountain streams . . . to pit our strength against a sounding swordfish . . . to fill our lungs once more with the clean, sweet air of a free world—happy and proud that we have had a hand in helping to *earn* that freedom.

For FREE catalog write Box 103, address below:

FAMOUS ASHAWAY RECORDS

Here is the All-Tackle World's Record Bluefin Tuna catch . . . 927 pounds! Taken on an ASHAWAY 54-thread line by Dr. J. Vernaglia in 1940 from Ipswich Bay, Mass.

ASHAWAY LINE & TWINE MANUFACTURING CO., ASHAWAY, R. I

Advertisement for ASHAWAY,
Field & Stream,
March, 1943

IF you've been inclined to look upon outboard motors only as vacation equipment, take another look. Outboard motors have come of age. Years of development have made them mechanical marvels—and today they are doing man's work in the armed services everywhere.

With their amazing maneuverability they have uncovered a new mode of movement in a war where movement is supreme. A few pounds of metal, fashioned into a modern Sea-Horse, provide power to handle tons of equipment and supplies and men. With dispatch. And with DEPENDability.

Johnson has made the outboard motor an instrument to be reckoned with—in industry as well as in war—and an instrument of infinite pleasure for days of peace. Development goes on. Someday, after the war is won, you'll see even finer models—lively, rugged offspring of the grand Sea-Horses that are in the war today.

JOHNSON MOTORS, WAUKEGAN, ILLINOIS

DO YOUR DUTY—BUY WAR BONDS

PUSHIN' THE BRUTES AROUND

THERE IS
NO SUBSTITUTE
FOR
EXPERIENCE

JOHNSON SEA·HORSES
for Dependability

Advertisement for JOHNSON Sea Horses,
Field & Stream,
August, 1943

A Lift from the Front at Guadalcanal

FOR all its grimness, modern war is merciful to our wounded. The life-giving miracle of blood plasma* ... the swift, efficient treatment behind the lines ... plus speedy transport to finely-equipped base hospitals ... result in an incredibly high portion of recoveries among even desperately stricken men.

Speedy Transport! It may be by giant transport plane, by ambulance or nimble-footed Jeep ... or at jungle fronts in the South Pacific, by outboard-driven small craft threading narrow rivers, saving priceless hours between front lines and the base.

Evinrudes are busy at innumerable tasks for the Army and Navy, Marine Corps and Coast Guard ... driving swift assault boats ... propelling pontons, lighters, ferries . . . powering huge rubber rafts, wherries, small craft of every type. After Victory there will again be Evinrudes for all who love the water ... peacetime Evinrudes worthy of the traditions of their fighting forebears!

EVINRUDE MOTORS, Milwaukee, Wisconsin
Evinrude Motors of Canada, Peterboro, Canada

EVINRUDE
OUTBOARD MOTORS

*A pint of your blood can save the life of a wounded soldier or sailor. The need is constant, pressing. Call your local Red Cross Chapter for an appointment.

Advertisement for EVINRUDE,
Sports Afield,
October, 1943

THE GIRL WHO LANDED A PILOT

Her complexion was always so charmingly
fresh...so wonderfully *real* looking!
Not *artificially* pretty! Is your
man proud of *your* looks?
Help keep your skin looking clear,
clean, smooth as a baby's, with
Tussy Emulsified Cleansing Cream
and Tussy Rich Cream.

To hasten the return of your
serviceman, our plant is making ammunition fuzes. So if
your favorite store is tempo-
rarily out of any Tussy preparation, please be patient.

Tussy
EMULSIFIED
CLEANSING CREAM
Softens and cleanses at the same time! Tussy
Emulsified Cleansing Cream whisks off stubborn
dirt, stale make-up, clogging grime. Leaves
your face looking ever so much cleaner...and
years softer, too! 4-oz. jar, $1*

Tussy
RICH CREAM
Smooth on Tussy *Rich Cream* at night. This
fragrant, richly lubricating cream helps ease
away roughness, tiny wintry-dry lines. By morning your skin feels much smoother...less rough,
velvety instead of *papery*. 2-oz. jar, $1*

*All prices, tax additional

TUSSY COSMETIQUES
683 FIFTH AVENUE
NEW YORK 22, N. Y.

Tussy *for that young, young look*

Copyright, 1944, by Lehn & Fink Products Corp., Bloomfield, N. J.

Reproduced by permission of Tussy Cosmetics, Inc.

Advertisement for TUSSY,
HARPER'S BAZAAR,
February, 1944

"Don't mail them, John — *bring* the Camels — and <u>hurry</u>!"

"HOME ON FURLOUGH!"— what heart-warming words those are when you have a man in the service!

First in the Service... CAMELS

YES, Camels are the number one cigarette with men in the service—here at home and abroad. They are following our men on every ocean, to every continent.

And it's Camel's job to see that our soldiers, sailors, and marines *everywhere* get their cigarettes *fresh*—cool smoking and slow burning, the way they like 'em.

That's why Camels are packed to go round the world—packed to seal in that famous Camel flavor and extra mildness—anywhere, for months at a time.

The Camel pack keeps *your* Camels fresh and full-flavored, too—preserving for *you* the extra goodness of Camel's matchless blend of costlier tobaccos.

R. J. Reynolds Tobacco Company, Winston-Salem, North Carolina

BUY WAR BONDS STAMPS

CHOICE QUALITY

CAMEL

TURKISH & DOMESTIC BLEND CIGARETTES

WHEREVER HE IS...

The favorite cigarette with men in the Army, Navy, Marines, and Coast Guard is Camel. (Based on actual sales records.)

Advertisement for CAMELS,
HARPER'S BAZAAR,
March, 1944

YOUR BLOOD CAN SAVE HIM

BLOOD DONOR CENTER

BE A CADET NURSE

"Serve your country while you prepare for a professional career with a secure and important future. If you are 17 or 18, a graduate with good scholastic standing from an accredited high school and are accepted by the U. S. Cadet Nurse Corps, you will receive complete nurse education under an all-expense scholarship.

"Never before have you been offered such an opportunity. Address inquiries to U. S. Cadet Nurse Corps, U. S. Public Health Service, Box 88, New York, N. Y. . . . or apply at your nearest hospital."

THOMAS PARRAN, Surgeon General
U. S. Public Health Service

Wamsutta hopes to have enough Supercale* sheets for all Uncle Sam's nieces when they come home again. And enough, too, for all you war brides who have never had your full share of Wamsutta Supercale . . . the famous, fine, long-wearing "Trousseau Sheet of America."
WAMSUTTA MILLS, NEW BEDFORD, MASS.

Wamsutta SUPERCALE SHEETS

Springfield Blankets . . . Wamsutta-Somerset Towels

Advertisement for WAMSUTTA,
HARPER'S BAZAAR,
April, 1944

Advertisement for WAMSUTTA,
HARPER'S BAZAAR,
June, 1944

Test Pilot

— SIZE 10

NINE THOUSAND feet above the flying field, a Hellcat fighter plane screams down in the dark blur of a power dive. Holding the stick of this four-hundred-mile-an-hour ship is a small, firm hand. It belongs to Barbara Jayne, whose job it is to "first-flight" planes just off the production line of Grumman Aircraft...to put them through their preliminary paces before their final delivery to the Navy.

Mrs. Jayne is one of the women helping shorten this war by replacing a man in vital civilian work...and she thinks her job's the most exciting in the world! She's learned to streamline her busy life...mapped an efficient schedule for her brief leisure time. That's why, when it comes to caring for her looks, she's devoted to DuBarry Beauty Preparations.

While taking the famous Success School course, she learned

Du BARRY

BEAUTY PREPARATIONS
by RICHARD HUDNUT

that these preparations are more effective because they're correlated. Not only is each one scientifically formulated for a specific purpose, but they're blended to work together...each helping the other for better results.

More than 130,000 Success School pupils have been taught the greater effectiveness of co-related DuBarry Beauty Preparations, how well they fit into busy lives today. Take, for instance, DuBarry Face Powder, which Mrs. Jayne finds so flattering in the exciting new summer shade, *Tropical.*

Balanced blending! DuBarry is a medium-textured powder for any type skin. It's heavy enough to cling longer; light enough so you'll never look over-powdered.

Light, but clinging! DuBarry Face Powder wears even longer if you'll pat DuBarry Skin Freshener on after to "set" your make-up.

Get-acquainted size! DuBarry Face Powder is now available in a new $1 size. In all fashion shades.

Featured in the Richard Hudnut Salon and DuBarry Success School, 693 Fifth Ave., New York 22, N. Y....and at better cosmetic counters everywhere

Advertisement for DUBARRY,
HARPER'S BAZAAR,
June, 1944

12

Business *Not* as Usual
1943

There are many Americans who still look back on July 1, 1943, as one of the most disastrous days in the nation's history. It was the day that the withholding tax went into effect. Thirty years later there remain some taxpayers who still claim that the government had no right to force employers to do its tax collecting for it, and yet others who continue to complain that the government should not be allowed use of money withheld from employees without paying interest on it.

In mid-war, the government's problem was cash flow. Its costs of borrowing were rising and the customary procedure of raising cash to operate the government by issuing treasury notes or bills that were, in effect, "tax anticipation notes," seemed wasteful.

As a result, Roosevelt, with the help of Treasury Secretary Henry Morgenthau, Jr. (whom the President affectionately called "Hank the Morgue" because of his sober, banker's mien) developed the withholding tax program as the best possible way to create a good cash flow, reduce borrowing costs and automatically eliminate cheaters. Everyone who worked paid his tax weekly, or whenever he got his paycheck.

Overnight several million Americans became taxpayers who had never before filed a return. Anticipating the bookkeeping problem that this would cause, the Internal Revenue Service (then called the Internal Revenue Department) required that those from whom taxes were to be withheld file affidavits listing the dependents on whom they were claiming deductions, *and* stating their Social Security numbers.

Cries of Big Brotherism rent the air, of course, at this linking together of the old age insurance program with the tax-collecting agency. Many feared that through their Social Security records the government would find out that they hadn't been filing proper returns prior to withholding. The revenuers might have done that, had they chosen, and scouted out many delinquents, but they were too busy with the new program, and there was a tacit agreement that all would be forgotten and forgiven, now that everyone was on a current-paying basis.

The withholding schedule went into effect at exactly the same time that an income tax boost became effective, so that in their first paychecks after July 1, many millions of Americans took a substantial pay cut. The shudders could be felt throughout the economy, and for a month or so—until Labor Day, actually—consumer spending took a decided plunge.

At the same time a number of states increased their taxes for workmen's compensation. Industrial accidents were mounting rapidly, and so was the cost of compensating injured workers. Thus was an additional bite taken out of the weekly pay envelope.

The summer of '43 was belt-tightening time for most Americans on the home front. They took it philosophically—the war had to be won and it had to be paid for. In all, the transition to regular tax withholding went smoothly and without too much complaint. By Thanksgiving time even irate letters to the editor about the withholding tax had all but disappeared from the nation's newspapers.

In 1943 death took from the financial world one of its leaders, spokesmen and figureheads, and from the industrial world, one of its most competent mass-producers and efficiency experts. On March 13, seventy-five-year-old John Pierpont Morgan, Jr., died of a heart attack in Florida. In May, Edsel Ford, forty-nine-year-old president of Ford Motor Company, one of the busiest war-producers in the nation, died of cancer, leaving his tough, seventy-nine-year-old father, Henry Ford, to run the empire. Edsel Ford's son, Henry Ford II, at twenty-six, was completing his second year as a naval lieutenant.

With the passing of J. P. Morgan, an era ended. The bank founded by his father, John Pierpont Morgan, Sr., a Hartford lad steeped in the investment techniques of the insurance industry, who went to New York to integrate American industry through the sheer power of finance—mergers, integrations, acquisitions—was one of the most influential private banks in the world. It was respected and feared. Its headquarters at 23 Wall Street, directly across the street from the New York Stock Exchange, was known as either the "Corner" or the "Powerhouse" in every bourse of the world. The House of Morgan had personified the "personal banking" of the time, just as the House of Rothschild had personified it in an earlier period. A nod from the Morgan House could mean millions to a man. A thumbs-down word from Morgan House could condemn him to a life of failure.

J. P. Morgan, Jr., was not the ruthless man his father had been. He was not so acquisitive. He had been born to enormous wealth and schooled for tycoonery. He was modest, publicity-shy, but shrewd, sharp and a driving worker. He knew the power of money and used it.

Morgan money had been mixed with Du Pont money in several ventures, not the least of which was the reorganization of General Motors, which set that company on the road that would lead it to the position it held when Morgan died—the largest, wealthiest and most efficient industrial corporation in the world.

In the wave of remorse that had surged across the nation in the aftermath of World War I, John Pierpont Morgan, Jr., became the personal scapegoat of one of the great lies of the century, and it had bothered him until his death. It was only with his interment that the great lie was laid to rest.

The great lie was a fairy tale created by the Marxists to aid their cause and to foster the isolationism that was taking root and spreading throughout the country. It held that it was the international bankers, of which J. P. Morgan and Company was the leader, that duped the nation into World War I, a conflict that had supposedly left the tycoons richer than ever. In scores of radio harangues, Morgan was described as a "merchant of death." J. P. Morgan and Company's role, if it can be described as such, was to lend money to the United States and to England, and, of course, if the "merchant of death" had not made the loans, the taxpayers of those nations would have been obliged to make up the difference.

Morgan himself, in fact, led a valiant postwar fight to restore the economies of the European countries so that their war debts to the United States might be repaid. Such efforts did not make news headlines, so his personal efforts, backed by not only his bank's wealth but his own, were never made public, and were known only to a few on Wall Street and in Washington.

Yet to come were the epithets of the New Deal—"prince of privilege" and "economic royalist"—which were to be hurled at

Morgan in the early days of the Depression, following the Market Crash of 1929. In 1933 it is probably true that John Pierpont Morgan, Jr., was the most discredited and maligned man in America, next to Herbert Hoover.

On the day the market crashed, October 24, 1929, Morgan headed a group of four other prominent bankers to create a pool of $240 million, which was poured into the market in an effort to stem the avalanche of sales, and though the true facts were never known, it was always said by insiders that the major part of that money came from Morgan himself. Morgan was absent that day, but he authorized the use of the money by his partner and second-in-command, Thomas W. Lamont. The other bankers involved in the heroic effort to avert the market crash were Charles E. Mitchell, chairman of the board of National City Bank (now First National City Bank); Albert H. Wiggin, chairman of the board of Chase National Bank (the Rockefeller bank, now called Chase-Manhattan Bank); William C. Potter, president of Guaranty Trust Company (now Morgan Guaranty Trust); and Seward Prosser, chairman of the board of Bankers Trust Company.

With the New Deal came the investigation of the market crash, and the spectacle of showmanship was conducted under the aegis of Ferdinand Pecora. After someone compared the clowning to a Roman circus, a press agent got a great idea and placed a circus midget on the lap of the ultra-dignified and portly Morgan while photographic flashlights flared.

It made photographic history. To the surprise of all concerned, however, the indignity backfired. The picture of Morgan and the midget, printed in virtually every periodical in the country from the *Hobo News* to the *New York Times*, showed Morgan to be amused and apparently chuckling and, of all things, kindly.

From that day on it was hard to think of J. P. Morgan as an ogre or an economic royalist or a prince of privilege or a merchant of death. The public's image of him was more of a portly grandfather, capable of love, indulgence and humor.

The Pecora banking investigation provided the foundation for the special committee headed by Joseph P. Kennedy, at that time a New Dealer himself and unfriendly to big banks, which created the Banking Act of 1933, bringing an end to private banking and splitting commercial banking, which handles deposits and checking accounts and lending operations, from investment banking, which finances the bonds of governments and businesses and the securities of corporations.

After that the House of Morgan was ended as a private bank. J. P. Morgan and Company, Inc., became a commercial bank —only the eighteenth largest in the country. The investment business went to Morgan, Stanley and Company under the leadership of J. P.'s son, Harry.

All of his life through, J. P. Morgan, Jr., contended that a private bank could gain power only in one way, and that was through its reputation for integrity. No one ever successfully or seriously questioned the integrity of J. P. Morgan or of his bank.

Because of the nature of his disease, Edsel Ford had known that he was to die some weeks before. He had been sent home from Ford Hospital, internationally famous for its advanced laboratories and its skilled surgeons, and told that nothing more could be done for him. He awaited the grim reaper in his beloved stone mansion on the shore of Lake St. Clair.

His death was considered by many to be the most grievous blow in the life of his father, Henry Ford, who had never expected to outlive his only son. He and Edsel had worked shoulder to shoulder throughout the young man's life, erecting a relationship that transcended even the closeness of father-and-son. It was Edsel who modernized the Ford Motor Company and its products. It was Edsel who fulfilled the promises that his father made. It was Edsel who restored order in the wake of his father's temper and abrasive ways.

But even in his late forties, Edsel was still the pupil, while his father was the teacher, instructing him on the intricacies of managing an empire.

Edsel Ford was only two years old in May, 1896, when, in a little seat made especially for him, he rode on the first journey his father made in his first horseless carriage, down rutty Bagley Avenue in Detroit. Like his father, he fell in love with the contraption.

In the years to come he was never far from his father's side while the progeny of that first contraption coughed and churned dust throughout the land. He took time out for grammar school and high school but decided he could not waste time on college when he was needed in the plant.

So at age nineteen, donning greasy coveralls, he went to work in the plant of Ford Motor Company, never, really, to emerge again. It wasn't long, however, before he was to learn just what it meant, just what was involved, when you were the only son of ultra-high-principled Henry Ford.

Edsel Ford was twenty-three years old when World War I broke out, and as a non-college man, highly eligible for the draft. He intimated that he might like to enlist.

Henry Ford was deeply opposed to the war, strongly, uncompromisingly opposed to it, and to any war. He could not possibly see himself allowing his son to don the uniform. Instead, he announced that Edsel was a key man at the factory, much needed for wartime work, and got him deferred.

Instantly, in a nationwide press that was frenetically patriotic, Edsel was branded yellow. Quietly the boy lived it down, did his "key man" work and turned out the goods of war that his country needed.

Only two years later, in 1919, Henry Ford got into a verbal donnybrook with his stockholders, which led to a bitter parting when Henry bought them out for $75 million, of which $70 million was raised from Ford's pet hate, bankers in Wall Street, Morgan among them, and quickly installed Edsel as president.

It was probably no real favor to be made president of Ford Motor Company (wholly owned by Dad) at age twenty-five. Henry Ford had learned, however, that Edsel Ford had great value smoothing the waters that he, Henry, had churned up.

As Edsel had grown into the job, the job itself had grown. Ford was the biggest auto producer in the 1920s. Edsel learned that though his father was an unquestioned genius, it would be his job to keep Ford Motors up to date. Edsel, after much persuasion, got Henry to junk the Model T and bring out the Model A with a gearshift transmission. Edsel pushed constantly for brighter colors and more pleasing design, sparking the "design revolution" in the entire industry. And Edsel insisted on introducing a full line of low-priced cars, again setting a pattern for the industry.

When war clouds darkened again in the late 1930s, it became Edsel's chore to overcome his father's rigid pacifism, and to convince the old man that it wasn't *his* decision to make—that the country needed Ford Motor Company's production facilities to produce the goods of defense.

Carried away, perhaps, by his son's rhetoric, Henry Ford promised the nation he could produce 1,000 planes a day. It

189

became Edsel's task to try to live up to it. At Willow Run, at the time of his death, Ford was producing better than 500 planes a month in the most amazing mass-production effort ever made, a flow of planes that alone might have stopped the Axis in a matter of time.

When Edsel died, Henry Ford reappointed himself president, and started negotiations with the government to get his grandson, Henry Ford II, out of uniform and into the factory "where he belonged." The government agreed that young Henry belonged at Willow Run. So did the Navy.

The government had good reason to accede to Henry Ford's request for the release of his grandson. The giant Ford complex (Willow Run was the biggest industrial plant in the world) was working day and night, seven days a week, on $4 billion worth of vital war contracts. If Henry Ford said he needed Henry Ford II, he could have him.

Thus, in the early autumn of 1943, Henry Ford II put away his Navy uniform and reported for work, not in the front office as might befit the grandson and heir apparent, but on the production line. In a short time Henry Ford II might well have wished that he were back in the Navy and in combat.

Under the regimen his grandfather prepared for him, young Henry put in a twelve-hour day, six days a week, arising each morning except Sunday at 6 A.M., and spending long hours, first with Harry Bennett, Ford's top administrative man, and then with Charles E. Sorenson, Ford's production head. His assignment: Get production know-how as soon as possible. That was what built Ford, and Henry Ford the elder intended that it was what would keep it going. It wasn't long before Henry Ford II knew production from top to bottom, from one end of the line to the other. His only complaint: he was producing airplanes, not Fords.

Also producing airplanes, and at a fantastic rate, was a relatively new industrial tycoon, Donald Douglas, aviation's greatest innovator, a lanky engineer who hated to fly and found no romance in the wild blue yonder except in the precise design of his metal birds.

A Navy dropout—Douglas had gone to Annapolis but after three years quit to attend Massachusetts Institute of Technology, where he worked on the first aircraft wind tunnel in the country—Douglas in 1942 had made one-sixth (by weight) of all planes produced in the United States and in 1943 would produce nearly 25 percent of them, by weight.

The DC-1's grandchild, the DC-3, which in the 1940s was the workhorse plane of every commercial carrier, was being made by Douglas as a transport for the Army and called—the C-47. "The way you can tell 'em apart," an old Air Corps sergeant explained, "is the DC-3 is silver and the C-47 is painted olive drab so that it's easier to spot 'em in a bright sky and shoot 'em down."

In addition to the C-47's, Douglas in 1943 was making the Douglas A-20 light bomber; the Navy's single-engine SBD dive-bomber, which accounted for more enemy tonnage in the Pacific than any other U.S. weapon; four-engined Flying Fortresses under contract from Boeing; four-engined Liberator bombers under contract from Consolidated Vultee; four-engined C-54 transport and cargo planes; and parts and equipment for all of them.

Donald Wills Douglas, who had started with capital of $600 and an order for one plane in an office over a barbershop in Los Angeles, by 1943 operated six mammoth plants in the United States worth nearly $200 million and employed 153,000 workers. In addition Douglas had small plants in corners of the world from Ireland to Africa to China. His giant factories in the United States were in Santa Monica, Long Beach, El Segundo, Tulsa, Oklahoma City and Chicago.

Mid-war business problems hit show business, too. Perky, dimpled Sonja Henie, cute darling of Darryl Zanuck movies for Twentieth-Century-Fox and highest-paid Hollywood star (over $210,000 a year), applied to Lloyds of London for $250,000 insurance on her last five pairs of ice skates because no more were being produced due to the war. After some bouncy flights to entertain troops at various camps, Jimmy Durante let it be known that he was insuring his precious nose—"the nose that knows"—for $50,000. Fox also cut out all big banquet scenes from movies in production.

Big league baseball also suffered severely. The big cause, of course, was lack of patronage. Only subway and trolley-car riders could get to ball parks. Others couldn't drive. Moreover, because of the overcrowded condition of the rails, spring training camps had to be abandoned. But perhaps the biggest reason was that the best baseball players were with the biggest big league teams—in the armed forces.

Private Joe DiMaggio was swatting homers at Camp Santa Ana, California. At the Great Lakes Naval Training Station, Seaman Johnny Mize was the station nine's first baseman.

The Cardinals' pitching hero of the previous season, Johnny Beazley, was now Lieutenant Beazley of the Air Force and a pitcher for the team at Berry Field in Nashville.

In Norfolk, Virginia, the Navy had corraled some of baseball's finest. Playing for the Norfolk Naval Training Station were Dom DiMaggio, Phil Rizzuto and Don Padgett. At the Norfolk Naval Air Station were two beloved Dodgers, Peewee Reese and Hugh Casey.

Elsewhere the business world plodded on, but not quite as usual. The War Production Board faced up to a grave emergency. On July 1, 1942, it had ordered a halt in the production of civilian alarm clocks because the parts were needed for more important items. By the spring of 1943, war plant managers were complaining because so many of their workers were coming in late. The reason: no alarms to wake them. After high-level sessions, the WPB officials got clockmakers to agree to a "victory model" clock that would be economical on metal but not on noise. WPB ordered about 1.75 million of them on a hurry-up basis.

McCall's in March and *Collier's* in November showed one eye of Veronica Lake peeking slyly (seductively?) from behind her long hair to advertise Ivory soap. Soap was in short supply but it wasn't rationed, except on a voluntary basis by some local stores.

In the home, housewives were finding cooking chocolate hard to get and there were very few candy bars available to use as substitutes. They had joined many other items in the battle areas.

The ladies were doing their own recycling, and making their brown-paper grocery bags serve for as many as five trips to the store. They discovered that the girl who came into a grocery with her own bags under her arm usually got better attention from the clerks than one who didn't.

The paper shortage caused a sentimental problem. There were very few Christmas cards available in the stores in 1943. Hand-written notes of greeting had to fill the bill. Even the telephone wasn't a good substitute for sending greetings, for people were asked to limit long-distance calls to five minutes so that the lines would be available for servicemen calling home. Even so, a soldier calling from Florida to New York might have to wait three or four hours to get a free circuit.

The most surprising businessman to hit the headlines in 1943 was a cigar-maker by the name of Julius Klorfein, president of Garcia Grande Cigars, Inc., producers of some of the finest nickel and two-for-a-nickel stogies on the American market.

He was discovered in Gimbel's bargain basement in New York among a group of 1,000 who had gathered to bid, with war bond pledges, for numerous historical items, included among them, a letter written by George Washington and the personal Bible of Thomas Jefferson.

When Danny Kaye, the master of ceremonies and auctioneer, held up Jack Benny's violin, a $75 instrument that sought in vain to be an imitation Amati, but much beloved by the comedian and his constant prop for twenty years, an attendant pushed his way through the crowd and handed him a letter.

Kaye opened the letter, glanced at it and blanched.

"I—I have a bid for this violin for $1 million!" he said. The room broke into thunderous applause, and everyone looked around for the successful bidder, the generous American who had pledged to buy a million dollars' worth of war bonds.

At length, after a series of impatient nudges from the lady sitting beside him, who was obviously his wife, a short, solid, aging gentleman arose and bowed shyly.

The cityside reporters who were covering the affair asked him his name. "Julius Klorfein," he said.

They scampered back to their newspapers' files to dig out background information on this quiet man. There was none.

Tracked down later that night, Mr. Klorfein was asked about his anonymity.

"I've been too busy," he explained.

At the turn of the century he had come to the United States from Russia and began making his own cigars in a tiny shop in Brooklyn. Now, at fifty-eight, he had bought Jack Benny's violin and a million dollars' worth of bonds, and was receiving the publicity he had always avoided.

Doing a booming business—if the word can possibly be used in that context—were the churches of America of all denominations. Easter fell on its latest possible date, April 25, and there was beautiful spring weather in most parts of the country. Churches were jammed by people anxious to hear again the story of the Resurrection. By that time more than 18,000 American boys had been killed in action and, including that number, there were more than 94,000 casualties. People turned to faith.

The Bible, ever the world's best seller, increased in sales by more than 25 percent according to *Harper's*. A book of prayers and meditations, *Daily Strength for Daily Needs* by Mary Tileston, doubled its peacetime sales and went to over half a million copies.

The best-seller list in 1943 included two religious books, *Song of Bernadette*, the story of Our Lady of Lourdes, written by Franz Werfel, a Jewish refugee, which had sold over 500,000 copies, and *The Robe*, a story of Christ's Passion, written by Lloyd C. Douglas, a Protestant minister, which had sold more than 250,000 copies.

A big song hit was "Praise the Lord and Pass the Ammunition," based on an actual incident in the Pacific where a chaplain had joined his comrades on the firing line. Folks of all religious persuasions were quoting the words of the Rev. William T. Cummings, a Maryknoll priest and army chaplain who survived Bataan and the dreadful "Death March."

His now-famous saying: "There are no atheists in the foxholes."

There weren't many atheists on the home front in 1943, either.

13

Sense and Nonsense
1944

The zoot suit, the wartime adornment of young urban civilian males, customarily came in wide stripes and loud colors. The coat had overpadded, almost peaked shoulders, wide, sharp-pointed lapels and a single button. Usually it was worn unbuttoned, the coat ajar, to display the long watch chain that dangled in a loop down the right pantleg. The pants were baggy, like knickers that had fallen down, and they pegged in to tight little cuffs at the bottom that just crested the tops of the shoes.

The true aficionado allowed his hair to grow long in the back, a forerunner of the "ducktail" that would come in the 1950s.

It was the most extreme fashion that men had worn in the twentieth century and students of mass movements and fads said it was a sort of "last-fling syndrome," a desire to wear gaudy, attention-arresting plumage before donning the dull uniforms of the enlisted personnel of the armed services.

Those over thirty resisted, of course, for a while, but the sparse selection on the ready-made racks in the men's clothing stores gradually began to offer suits that were modified zoots, with stuffed shoulders, longer, pointier lapels and pants that were slightly pegged at the bottom. Unless one could afford a tailormade suit, he had to go slightly zooty.

Women's fashions, too, acquired the "new look," and since the ladies (whose hemlines were one inch above the knee by OPA decree) were going all-out for tailored suits, the jackets adapted handily to the heavily padded shoulders, sharp lapels and single center button. The Andrews Sisters, for instance, rarely appeared in a movie scene without their tailored suits with huge shoulders preventing them from getting too close together.

For awhile the civilian population of America, male and female, looked like a gargantuan football team composed mostly of fullbacks and linemen. The men wore bow ties, but so did some of the women.

The year 1944 was a very serious year both politically and economically on the home front, and a vital, decisive year on the war front, and it may have been because of the very gravity of the situation that items of small consequence were highlighted and a feverish nonsense prevailed.

Feverish was the word to describe the reception Frank Sinatra got from 30,000 young fans when he opened a three-week engagement at Manhattan's huge Paramount Theatre, mecca to all performers. It took 421 policemen, 30 policewomen, two dozen patrol cars and a pair of trucks to control the Sinatra enthusiasts, a preponderance of them girls, who did manage, somehow, to tear off most of the singer's clothes.

Not so well publicized was the fact that Sinatra's twenty-four-year-old wife, Nancy, gave birth to their second child, Francis Wayne Sinatra, in the swoonster's home town of Jersey City. Tens of thousands of young girls didn't want to think of their idol singing a lullaby to his own infant. The image didn't go with that of the biggest male sex symbol of the time.

The strange part of it was that Sinatra seemed to do it all with his voice; he appeared to be anything but what a sex symbol should be. He was narrow-shouldered, un-zoot-suited, skinny, even scrawny, with what, to the very observant, seemed to be a receding hairline. Moreover, although jitterbugging was the dance of the day, most of Sinatra's big selections were unsuited to that frantic rhythm. The jitterbug was an ultra-athletic dance, requiring not only vigor but endurance, consisting, as it did, of much hopping and leaping along with some genuine calisthenics. If, as some psychologists of the time said, it was a mating dance that emulated sexual foreplay, it was adapted only for the very healthy young and must have come from a simian strain of great muscular achievement, far superior to that possessed by the adult members of the softening and decadent human race of the mid-twentieth century. The truth was, few people over thirty-five could jitterbug well. Yet the nonjitterbugging Sinatra's strength and popularity was with the youthful jitterbugging set.

There was no question about Sinatra's husky voice, though, or his fabulous phrasing. His record sales soared, and so did his box-office receipts.

Another entry in the celebrity sweepstakes was made by a soft-voiced violet-eyed twelve-year-old girl in *National Velvet*—Miss Elizabeth Taylor. Both film and girl were a success.

The *Motion Picture Herald* reported that the year's biggest box-office draw, male or female, was the lovely limbed, firmly packed Betty Grable, the top female star of Darryl F. Zanuck's talent pool at 20th Century-Fox, now that Alice Faye, having helped Don Ameche and Tyrone Power through innumerable Zanuck productions, was showing signs of preferring the role of house-wife to that of star. Not since Shirley Temple, another Zanuck star, had an actress been tops at the box office for an entire year. Shirley's reign had been for four consecutive years, 1935-38. Betty Grable, who imitated no one and was basically just her own self on screen, was *the* blonde that Hollywood had been lacking since the death of Jean Harlow.

In Hollywood, Humphrey Bogart and his wife, actress Mayo Methot, whom he called "Sluggy," separated after years of squabbling, and the tattle-tale columnists of the town whispered it was because Sluggy was for Dewey and Bogy was for Roosevelt. In a Hollywood hospital, W. C. Fields explained a badly bruised nose—it had prevented him from falling flat on his face when a cane slipped on a polished floor in his bedroom. He said he was obliged, therefore, to resort to the frequent potation of medicinal mixtures.

Bob Hope, No. 2 at the box office in 1944, was off on a continuous tour of military posts at home and abroad. Fred Astaire was a headliner in a number of overseas USO tours. Clark Gable was serving in the Air Force, and had already seen some of the he-man action that he once did for cameras. Major James Stewart, having been the pilot-commander of a dozen missions over Germany, was awarded the Distinguished Flying Cross for his participation in a successful raid on aircraft factories in Brunswick in which twenty U.S. planes had been shot down.

They, and numerous others, including Darryl Zanuck himself, who was in North Africa, were not around as Hollywood celebrated the fiftieth anniversary of motion pictures with a couple of galas and some illicit whiskey, and the U.S. Post Office Department brought out a special purple-colored commemorative stamp in honor of the occasion.

A couple of other heroes, both from Boston, captured fleeting headlines at home. Navy Lieutenant John Fitzgerald Kennedy, second son of Joseph P. Kennedy, former ambassador to Britain, was given the Navy and Marine Corps Medal for "extreme heroic conduct." He had rescued two sailors when a Jap destroyer sliced his PT-boat in half, and he had brought his crew safely to an island in the part of the hull that remained afloat. Lieutenant Colonel Henry Cabot Lodge, Jr., who had resigned from the Senate to join up, captured a four-man Nazi patrol single-handed. The grandson of the isolationist who, after World War I, led the Senate to vote against entry into the League of Nations, spotted the Huns, drove his jeep up to them, pulled his service .45 and ordered them to come along. They did.

One Air Force captain who got himself a furlough hurried out to Beverly Hills to marry himself an actress of considerable note, Paulette Goddard, thirty-three, who was the "Cheesecake Girl" of 1944. The captain: Burgess "Buzz" Meredith, thirty-six, the stage and movie star with the pixie grin. It was Meredith's third trip to the altar, as it was Miss Goddard's.

There began to filter into the domestic press occasional cartoons from *Yank* and *Stars and Stripes* and soon Americans were writing to their editors demanding more of "Willie and Joe," by a youngster named Bill Mauldin.

Mauldin seemed to reflect most dramatically, and with uncanny humor, life at the front. There was good reason for this; he was drawing his cartoons at the front, and had picked up a Purple Heart for wounds in Italy to show for it. He, along with George Baker who drew "Sad Sack" in *Stars and Stripes*, was already an enormous favorite with the GI's by the time his cartoons were "discovered" on the home front.

Somehow Mauldin captured the very spirit of the war; a cartoon without caption, for instance, showing a cavalry officer mournfully pointing his .45-caliber pistol at the radiator of his hopelessly disabled Jeep. But his unshaven, grimy, baggy-suited, flat-footed heores, Willie and Joe, with their serious eyes and half-smoked butts dangling from their lips, won him acclaim from continent to continent, throughout the world.

MP's had been an early target of Mauldin's penetrating wit, and then hyper-discipline-demanding young second lieutenants. The causticity that was directed at these two stern structures of military life softened in time as Mauldin realized that MP's and shavetails died in action just as readily and as horribly as his beloved EM's—enlisted men.

By the time the home folks were reading Mauldin, his cartoons reflected a broader humor, such as the one showing Willie and Joe standing in a freshly captured Italian wine cellar with its huge wine casks lining the wall, each one leaking out its last drops of the precious stuff from myriad holes caused by a spray of machine gun bullets, and as Willie tries to capture the last few drops in his steel helmet, Joe mutters: ". . . Them lousy——— ———Krauts; Them atrocity-committin' Huns!"

Bill Mauldin was only twenty-three when, still foot-slogging his way through Italy's bloody battles, his talent projected him into the big time as a front-rank caricaturist and cartoonist. He had been a swollen-footed infantryman for five years by that time. But that was nothing, really—he had started *drawing* when he was three. Thus his talent was that of an expert, both as an artist and as a dogface infantryman.

The year had started with an influenza epidemic in the East that ultimately raged nationwide. It seemed that everyone had either had it, or was just recovering from it. Starting with the troops stationed at domestic posts, camps, bases and other facilities, the military inoculated all of its personnel with the new influenza vaccine, which was made from the specially treated membranes of hen eggs.

For a good part of the year—until fall, with the football games—sports fizzled, never sizzled. The all-star game, highlight of the baseball season, was played in Pittsburgh and was said by spectators to be the dullest affair in the history of the game, caused primarily by the absence of so many top players in military uniform. The National League won 7-1 in a contest that didn't even feature one homer.

The most exciting night in baseball occurred *before* a game when, in midsummer heat nearing 100 degrees, at a time when the subways and buses were immobilized by strike, nearly 30,000 home-fronters packed into Philadelphia's Shibe Park to pay homage to Cornelius McGillicuddy, who was observing his fiftieth anniversary in baseball management.

Connie Mack, then eighty-one, sprinted out to home plate, vigorous, lean and youthful-appearing in suit and sport shoes after Bud Abbott and Lou Costello had gone through some mirthful antics and Master of Ceremonies Ted Husing, the "Voice of Baseball," had read a telegram of congratulations from President Roosevelt. Connie summoned to the infield his personally selected all-time all-star baseball team. One by one they jogged from the dugout as he called their names.

The lineup: George Sisler at first base; Eddie Collins at second; Frank Baker, third base; Honus Wagner, shortstop; Bill Dickey, catcher (who got special leave from the Navy); Tris Speaker, center field; George Herman "Babe" Ruth, right field. Missing from the all-star team were Lieutenant Commander Mickey Cochrane, catcher, who couldn't get leave from the Navy, and Ty Cobb, left field, who was at his California retirement home with a case of poison ivy.

Shortly after the baseball season ended, the mulish, hard-as-a-rock, scowling, profane commissioner of baseball, Judge Kenesaw Mountain Landis, seventy-eight years old, was admitted to a Chicago hospital with multiple problems associated with old age. Judge Landis had ruled supreme with absolute dictatorial powers over baseball since 1920, but not many had begrudged him his power or had thought it was improper, for baseball, under his iron rule, had matured and prospered.

A joint commission of the American and National Leagues rushed to his bedside in Chicago and informed him it was recommending him for yet another seven-year term in office. For this kindly gesture, Judge Landis smiled, one of the few times he was known to have done so during his reign as organized baseball's supreme czar. A few days later he succumbed to a heart ailment.

Never before had football commanded so much attention as in 1944. Baseball teams might be suffering from recruitment problems, competing, as they were, with the armed services, but the colleges and academies were not. They were getting the cream of the crop of young men and training them in officer-candidate courses. The influx of brawn and brains showed itself on the gridiron.

Almost as if responding to orders from Army recruiters, West Point enjoyed one of its most spectacular football seasons in history, creating three giant stars who would become all-time greats, and turning in its first unbeaten, untied season since 1916, proving somehow that military belligerence does, indeed, stimulate West Point to super deeds, which was a comforting thought.

Throughout the world, GI's in Army uniform, many of whom didn't even know where West Point was located, were joined by their loyal home folks in cheering on the dream team of Army coach Lieutenant Colonel Earl Blaik, the perfector of the "T" formation of attack. Military bands relearned the notes of "You've Got to Be a Football Hero."

On that best West Point team in twenty-eight years were all-America halfback Glenn Davis, ferocious fullback Felix ("Doc") Blanchard, another all-America, and agile quarterback Doug Kenna.

The Army started out the season by giving Notre Dame the worst trouncing in its history and beating the Irish 59-0. It ended the season on the "new" Thanksgiving Day by slashing the Navy to ribbons 23-7. (By Presidential decree, Thanksgiving fell on the third Thursday of November, rather than the fourth, to allow more time between Thanksgiving and Christmas.)

Another footballer garnered fleeting headlines. Tommy (Thomas Dudley) Harmon, two times all-America Michigan halfback, got leave from the Army Air Force to go to Ann Arbor and marry Hollywood starlet Elyse Knox. Twice Tommy Harmon had been reported lost in combat; twice he had returned. His bride wore a silk gown made from his bullet-lacerated parachute.

Since October, 1942, American distillers had been forbidden to produce drinking liquor. The alcohol was needed for explosives. In early 1944 several experimental types of potables were permitted, the most important of which was a concoction whose base was alcohol made from surplus and waste potatoes and their skins. It tasted like a popular-priced blend, and sold for $3.32 a fifth in Manhattan. There was only one thing wrong with it: there wasn't enough to go around. There was a certain amount of domestic gin to be found, but to the connoisseurs it seemed oily and to the uninitiated it seemed altogether too potent and fiery. Beer and wine had to fill the bill.

Then, in June, the War Production Board announced that come August it would allow distillers to resume production of neutral spirits for blending.

The news was greeted with more enthusiasm than had heralded the end of Prohibition twelve years earlier. The ingredients of the blending process—rye and bourbon—had been aging for a long time, awaiting the neutral spirits, and by mid-August familiar brands were beginning to reappear on the shelves of liquor stores. Some of the blenders experimented with a domestic-type "scotch," which, while embodying something of a smoke taste, never made it as a substitute. It would not be until mid-1946 that a sufficient quantity of scotch whiskey—the genuine stuff—was to reach the American market.

The shortage that *really* pinched, nipped at the cramped toes of Americans. There was shoe rationing and under it the average civilian was allowed two pairs of shoes per year, just about half of the normal consumption. Until 1944 Americans had lived off the large inventory of shoes that had been building up prior to rationing. In the third full year of war, the shortage made itself felt. Those who owned sneakers cherished them highly, for there was no such thing as rubber-soled shoes, because there was no rubber. Seriously affected were those who needed specially built shoes. The leather was simply not available.

While the local shoestore was suffering a wartime slump the neighborhood grocer enjoyed an unexpected boom. Hit hard by the evolvement of the big chain supermarkets in the late 1930s, the corner grocer came back into his own. For one reason, people didn't care if his prices were somewhat higher than those in the supermarket. For another, they found it more prudent to preserve their precious gas-rationing stamps and to shop at the higher-priced neighborhood stores. Never before had women shopped so carefully, preserving their ration stamps. They bought pickles and relishes instead of catsup because the latter was rationed. They bought Jello instead of deserts and rationed canned fruits. They bought only the best grades of everything, because the ration "cost" in stamps was the same, regardless of quality.

Americans learned of some scientific developments that were considered portentous but perhaps not as portentous as they turned out to be.

At Harvard, newsmen were invited to see what the university's press agent described as "the world's greatest mathematical calculating machine." It was an awesome thing, functioning behind a fifty-foot panel of electrical hardware, which plugged into 500 miles of wire and over 3 million electrical connections.

Home from the Navy to see his "gadget" introduced was Commander Howard H. Aiken, a Harvard professor, who, with engineers of International Business Machines Corporation, had designed and built the monster. With IBM executives he was presenting it to Harvard for use in research projects.

The machine could solve any mathematical calculation suggested by any man on earth, and was able to add or subtract in a third of a second. Moreover, said Commander Aiken, it could solve problems in celestial mathematics, making it possible to pinpoint star movements, problems that, at the time, were not tackled because the computation was too involved and tedious.

Then there was a momentous announcement by the U.S. Surgeon General's Office of a war-discovered insecticide that was wiping out malaria on the fighting fronts, had ended a typhus epidemic in Naples and promised, when the war was over, to eliminate on the home front such common pests as flies, mosquitoes, lice, fleas, moths, Japanese beetles, corn borers, fruit worms and aphids.

So important was the discovery that the WPB joined with Agriculture Department officials in supplementing the surgeon general's announcement.

The name of the stuff—dichloro-diphenyl-tri-chloroethane —or, for short: DDT.

"DDT," said the Surgeon General's Office, "will be to preventive medicine what Lister's discovery of antiseptic was to surgery."

Sprayed on a wall, DDT would kill any fly that alighted there as long as three months later. Clothing on which it was dusted would be lice-free for a month, even after eight washings.

The developers of DDT, the J. R. Geigy Company, a textile dye firm based in Basel, Switzerland, revealed that DDT was first synthesized in 1874 by a German chemist named Othmar Zeidler. Then, in 1939, when a plague of potato beetles hit Switzerland, a Geigy chemist, Paul Müller, rediscovered the formula and found that it stopped the plague.

In 1942 the U.S. Department of Agriculture began to experiment with the stuff, whose chief ingredients were chlorine, alcohol and sulfuric acid, and had such remarkable results that other agencies became interested, notably the military.

The WPB announced that no less than seven American laboratories and hundreds of biochemists were concentrating on refining and improving DDT and that the production of about 350,000 pounds per month was all going to the Army.

One of the more significant events of 1944 was a wedding. It united in matrimony Sergeant Skeezix Allison Wallet, twenty-three, the cowlick-haired son of Walt Wallet, with his boyhood sweetheart, Nina Clock, age twenty-two. The ceremony took place in Gasoline Alley. Skeezix was home on furlough.

More than three generations of comic-strip doting Americans had been great friends with Frank O. King's character Walt Wallet, had groaned through his innumerable antics, had chuckled at his humor, had watched him find Skeezix on his doorstep and had, in amazement, watched Skeezix grow up and Walt grow older. In time they would watch Walt become a grandfather.

Skeezix's and Nina's marriage was a wartime wedding, one of tens of thousands taking place with furloughed servicemen and their girls in 1944.

14

The Fourth Term
1944

Throughout the first half of 1944 the big political question—in fact, the biggest political question in the history of the republic—was whether or not Franklin Delano Roosevelt would run for what was invariably described as "an unprecedented fourth term." That the third term had been unprecedented, too, the phrasemakers overlooked.

Early in February, the kindly, people-loving vice president, Henry A. Wallace, on a mild and modest mission to California, revealed at a press conference in San Francisco that there was no doubt in *his* mind that the President would run for Term 4. That made it all pretty official. It could be made truly official by only one higher source, and as usual that source was keeping quiet and pretending to ignore the whole thing.

Transcending all other considerations in the minds of home-front Americans was the state of the President's health. For twelve long years, since 1932, he had been the nation's first citizen. At first not many had known that he was a cripple, confined to a wheelchair. Press and newsreel cameramen had carefully avoided photographing his useless legs or his wheel chair. It was known that he had once suffered an attack of poliomyelitis, or, as most referred to it, infantile paralysis, and that he was not the most robust of men, but the full extent of his disability was not common knowledge.

It was only after the unbelievably taxing years of the war, however, that the general public began to worry about him. And now it appeared that he wanted another four grueling years in the White House. Could he—could *anyone*—stand it?

Roosevelt had created the Infantile Paralysis Foundation to do research toward finding a cure for the dread disease that killed and crippled so many of the young, and only recently he had let it be known that he frequently enjoyed the therapy of the swimming pool at Warm Springs, Georgia.

It served only to focus attention on his disability.

In more specific political areas, Roosevelt was in trouble with Congress. He had lost control, for the first time since taking office. After the 1942 elections, Republicans had a majority in the House of Representatives and there was no reason to expect them to be less than positive in the use of the power that had been denied them since Herbert Hoover's exit from the White House with the election, not only of Roosevelt, but of overwhelming Democratic majorities in both houses.

At the very beginning of the year, Roosevelt confided to a press corps friend that he wished reporters would stop using the term "New Deal" to describe his administration. It was getting embarrassing, since a New Deal wasn't needed at the time. Yet, aside from his stewardship of the nation during its biggest and bloodiest war, the New Deal was Franklin Roosevelt's major contribution to American political history.

He had started it all on his initial campaign tour in 1932 when, in Chicago, he said: "I pledge you—I pledge myself—to a new deal for the American people." Now the New Deal was no more, even in Roosevelt's mind.

Clearly, if Roosevelt were to run, it would have to be on his wartime record as commander in chief. The armed forces were doing very well. The tide of war seemed to be turning. Ahead were some of the major battles of the conflict, decisive battles. Both in Europe and the Pacific the war news was of Allied victories, Allied gains, Allied progress.

There was the fact, though, that some of the people were getting tired of Roosevelt and wanted a change. The President laughed heartily at the dinner marking the eleventh anniversary of his first inauguration on March 4, 1933, when comedian Bob Hope quipped a much-quoted line:

"I've always voted for Roosevelt as President. My *father* always voted for Roosevelt as President."

Some who read of the joke in the papers, next day, thought there was more sarcastic truth than humor in the gag; they, too, felt that they had been voting for Roosevelt for too long.

But the fourth-term politics hadn't even begun to heat up. Before electiontime, it would prove to be one of the hottest of the Roosevelt campaigns.

There remained the issue of FDR's health. In April, the President wound up in the Naval Hospital at Bethesda, Maryland, suffering, the doctors said, from a mild case of bronchitis that had persisted for three weeks. It would be better, they said, if he'd quit smoking. The chief shook his great, shaggy head, stuffed a Camel into his ubiquitous cigarette holder and continued to puff away.

Reporters covering the White House noticed that he was nervous, edgy, drummed his fingers on the arms of his chair. He looked tired.

A few days later there was a birthday party on the South Lawn of the White House for Fala, the President's black scottie dog. Fala received reporters and photographers, sniffed uninterestedly at a birthday cake with four candles and accepted with grace his birthday present of an extra bone.

No one paid much attention at the time to the fact that the President was not there.

Within a few days his absence was noted, however, and inquiries at the White House elicited no information. Rumors began to spread. Some had it that he was at the Mayo Clinic, as was, indeed, "Assistant President" Harry Hopkins. Others said he had gone to London to confer with Winston Churchill. There was one happy little rumor that he had gone fishing off Key West. The world away from the newsrooms was subjected to even harsher rumors. One had it that the President had died suddenly and had been buried at sea and that the military chiefs were keeping it a secret so that the enemy wouldn't be heartened by his passing.

Then, in mid-May, the secret came out. For a solid month, Franklin Roosevelt had been resting and relaxing—on doctor's orders. It was the longest rest he had had in his eleven years in the White House. He had been the guest at Hobcaw Barony, Bernard Baruch's twenty-one-room home on his 23,000-acre, 226-year-old plantation, in South Carolina.

Tanned and relaxed, the President revealed that he had done a lot of "just sitting on the front porch" at Hobcaw, but pressed for more details he recited a long list of piscatorial activities. He had fished the Black and Waccamaw rivers, had cast for bass on the plantation ponds, had gone crabbing from the pier that protrudes into Winyah Bay, and under a sheltering umbrella of blimps and patrol planes he had trolled for bluefish and bonito out in the Atlantic, and once was almost caught at sea in a squall that had been kicked up by a tornado that had wreaked havoc on the mainland.

This was one of his largest press conferences. Just about every accredited White House reporter and photographer attended. All were curious about the President's health and they took a careful look at the face that was more familiar to more Americans than any other in history. Though the lines were gone, the face was thinner. The tan shone through the top of the head. Yes, he had undeniably grown bald. Suddenly, for the first time, many of the reporters realized that, though he was only sixty-two, Franklin Delano Roosevelt had become an old man. The vitality of his middle age had been sacrificed to the war.

Taking a toll of the man's nerves and equanimity was his increasing trouble with Congress, much of it stemming from within the ranks of his own party.

Trouble had started at the beginning of the year when Roosevelt, in a testy message, accused the Senate of attempting to perpetrate a "fraud on the soldiers and sailors and marines," and "on the American people," for voting down the administration-backed bill to give the vote automatically to all eligible servicemen and women, 'and substituting a measure which threw the question back to each state. The 11 million men and women in the armed forces would be deprived of the vote in 1944, Roosevelt said.

Angered and flushed, the generally mild Robert Taft leaped to his feet and termed the President's message a "direct insult" to Congress and charged that he was attempting to line up the military vote for his fourth term.

Whatever Roosevelt's reason, clearly his message was not designed to persuade Congress to change its mind, but to make it out the culprit, and everyone in Congress knew that when it came to devious and lofty politicking, Franklin D. Roosevelt was the master.

When the measure got to the House, opposition was led by New Deal-hating, Roosevelt-baiting John Rankin, the Mississippi Democrat, who scored a new low in bigotry in his speech.

"Now who is behind this bill? Who is the chief sponsor of it? The chief publicist is *PM*, the uptown edition of the Communist *Daily Worker* that is being financed by the tax-escaping fortune of Marshall Field III, and the chief broadcaster for it is Walter Winchell—alias no telling what . . ."

"Who is he?" asked Clare Hoffman, Michigan Republican.

"He's the little kike I was telling you about the other day, who called this body the 'House of Reprehensibles.'"

Perhaps someone would have stopped Rankin's ravings, but members of the House were so enraged at Roosevelt's gibes that all sat silent.

Republican Leader Joseph W. Martin, Jr., took a quick check, saw that he had the votes to defeat the administration's bill and quickly ordered a roll call vote. The bill was knocked down 224-168. Then Congress passed the Eastland-Rankin bill, calling for state balloting for GI's, 328-69.

Even before he went away for his rest in South Carolina, Roosevelt had embroiled the Congress in another bitter battle and had outraged and angered his longtime friend and faithful courier, Senate Majority Leader Alben Barkley.

It had started when the President announced at his Monday morning conference of Democratic leaders that he was going to veto the new tax bill. At the meeting were Barkley, Vice President Wallace, Speaker of the House Sam Rayburn and House Majority Leader John McCormack.

Roosevelt read excerpts from his message. After they had listened in silence, Barkley, Rayburn and McCormack tried to persuade the President to change his mind. Why not, they suggested, let the bill become law without his signature? To veto it would throw away $2 billion in new revenues. The bill, after all, was the work and the will of Congress.

Barkley got to the nub of it. If the President persisted in his veto, Barkley would have to stand up on the floor of the Senate and defend his position, which was not good for a majority leader to have to do. Roosevelt said that this was understandable. The meeting broke up with a show of cool good humor.

Next day Roosevelt sent the veto to the Capitol. It was the first time in history that a President had ever vetoed a general revenue bill.

Alben Barkley read his copy of the veto, at first incredulously, then with anger. The bland words that FDR had read aloud the preceding day were still there, but prickering and barbing throughout the message were other, thorny words: "inept," "indefensible special privileges to favored groups," "fail the American taxpayers" and then—"It is not a tax bill but a tax relief bill providing relief not for the needy but for the greedy."

Barkley was stunned. A quick check of fellow senators revealed that all were angrier at the President than they had ever been. Barkley went to his office and sat and thought about it throughout the afternoon and during the entire evening until midnight when, his mind made up, he called his secretary and asked her to show up for work extra early next morning, then went off to catch a few hours sleep.

When the Senate convened next forenoon, Barkley was there, a half-completed manuscript in his hand, with typists back at his office racing through the rest of the speech he had dictated and dispatching finished sheaves of the manuscript to the rostrum in relays.

Barkley cleared his throat, swept his eyes around the jampacked gallery and let them rest for a long moment on Vice President Wallace. Then, step by step, he proceeded to lacerate the President's veto message and rip it to shreds. The Presidential gibe about the bill providing relief for the greedy, Barkley said, was a "calculated and deliberate assault upon the legislative integrity of every member of the United States Congress."

"As for me," he said, "I do not intend to take this unjustifiable assault lying down."

In emotional tones, Alben Barkley recalled his thirty-one years in Congress as a representative from Kentucky:

> For twelve years I have carried to the best of my ability the flag of Franklin D. Roosevelt. I dare say that for the last seven years of tenure as majority leader, I have carried that flag over rougher territory than was ever traversed by any previous majority leader . . . I have called a conference of the Democratic majority for 10:30 o'clock tomorrow morning at which time my resignation will be tendered . . . If the Congress of the United States has any self-respect yet left, it will override the veto of the President and enact this tax into law, his objections to the contrary notwithstanding.

There was a moment of silence. A staccato of handclaps broke out on the floor. Suddenly there was a great roar from the galleries, shouting, cheering, applauding, just plain yelling.

Beseeching the galleries to stop their wild cheering, Alben Barkley said: "Now I am content. My cup runneth over. I have never felt calmer in my life."

The ball was back in Roosevelt's court. The great professional, the master politician of the day, reacted swiftly so that Barkley would not garner *all* of the political headlines in the afternoon newspapers.

He dispatched a wire to "Dear Alben," and saw to it there were sufficient copies for the press. The "Dear Alben" letter became famous, not only for its political adroitness, but because it was in response to the most serious political attack ever launched against Roosevelt from within his own party.

He had never intended to attack the integrity of "yourself and other members of Congress," Roosevelt said, and explained that at the Monday conference "I did not realize how very strongly you felt about the basic decision." Then he urged Barkley not to resign. If he persisted, FDR said, he hoped his colleagues would not accept the resignation; but if they did, he sincerely hoped "they will immediately and unanimously re-elect you."

That, of course, is precisely what the Democratic conference leaders had planned to do, but the general public did not know that, so, in effect, Roosevelt regained some prestige the next day when the conference accepted Barkley's resignation, then immediately and unanimously re-elected him majority leader of the Senate. Barkley balked at first, saying he wanted a few days to think it over. He didn't want the public to think he was giving in to the President and his "Dear Alben" letter. He needn't have worried. Everyone with the least political savvy knew that Alben Barkley was no longer Franklin Roosevelt's drummer boy and standard bearer.

Term 4 was off to a very rough start. The President's cough worsened. His fingers drummed more nervously on the green leather arms of his chair.

That very afternoon the House overrode the President's veto with 299 votes to 95. Next day the Senate clobbered the veto by overriding it 72-14.

Republicans, delighting in the President's discomfort, began to sharpen their pencils for the impending campaign. Who

211

would run against Roosevelt? Would it be General Douglas MacArthur? It looked that way, though there were some in the GOP who wanted to run Wendell Willkie again, now a world-famous "ambassador-at-large" for the United States government. Still others said that California's Governor Earl Warren showed great potential as a candidate.

In February Senator Arthur Vandenberg of Michigan had written a piece for *Collier's* magazine titled, "Why I Am for MacArthur," which was widely reprinted and quoted. He wrote: "MacArthur . . . is granite in the face of duty, a composite of all our necessities. Mr. Roosevelt intends to run primarily as our commander-in-chief. Should we not offer the people a better commander-in-chief?"

Even as Roosevelt was warring with Congress, however, it was Wendell Willkie who was generating the most steam for the Republicans. Although he was out of favor with some of the party leaders, not only because of his liberal views, but because he had so willingly represented and helped Franklin Roosevelt, Willkie determined to go on a vote-garnering tour himself to test the temper of the people rather than the chieftains.

At first it seemed that the people were enthusiastic about the big, burly former utilities executive. They came in large numbers to hear him talk as he whistle-stopped across the land in an ancient Pullman so old that some railroads would not allow it to be coupled into their high-speed crack trains. People talked eagerly of his book, *One World*, which had become a best-seller.

In April, when the first primaries were held (Wisconsin), Wendell Willkie learned that the support for him was disastrously poor. The choice was for uncommitted delegates, not for those pledged to Willkie, the only candidate running. In Omaha, Wendell Willkie read the writing on the wall and bowed out. "It is obvious now that I cannot be nominated," he said. "I therefore am asking my friends to desist from any activity toward that end and not to present my name to the convention."

In October, less than a month before the election, Wendell Willkie died at fifty-two, the big, oak-strong Indianian felled first by a coronary thrombosis, then by a strep infection of the throat. He was not to see whether or not there was a Term 4, though in opposing Roosevelt for Term 3 he had made political history with his booming crusade and the Willkie train, the caravan that presented America with a spectacle not seen in the hustings for a century. His big voice had roared over and again: "Only the strong can be free, and only the productive can be strong," while amazingly large crowds chanted, "We Want Willkie! We Want Willkie!"

Suddenly, in death, Wendell Willkie seemed to Republicans everywhere to be exactly the man they had needed to guide the nation in the days ahead. But it was too late.

At almost the same time the Democrats lost a stalwart—the Happy Warrior—New York's famed and fabled Al Smith, the first Catholic to run for the Presidency, and the man who set the machinery in motion for repeal of the onerous and crime-creating Volstead Act, the law that brought Prohibition to a tormented land. Victim of a vicious whispering campaign (Drys and redneck anti-Catholics in the Bible Belt spread the rumor that he already was in possession of plans to build a tunnel from the White House to the Vatican), Smith had been defeated by Herbert Hoover in 1928. Although he had supported his old friend Franklin D. Roosevelt in 1932, by the time Term 2 rolled around in 1936, Smith was dead-set against the proliferation of government that Roosevelt was fostering. He coined the phrase "alphabet soup" to describe the agencies Roosevelt was creating. After a few brief statements *against* Roosevelt and *for* Alf Landon in 1936, New York's former governor, the Happy Warrior, retired from politics to become president of the Empire State Building and director of a number of corporations. Smith's wife had died in the spring, and afterwards he grew old quickly. For a generation, no New Yorker would hear "The Sidewalks of New York" without thinking of Alfred Emanuel Smith, the East Side Irish kid who made it big.

After Willkie's death some Republicans turned with renewed interest to the idealistic but politically disinterested Douglas MacArthur, who already had a twenty-four-hour-a-day job with the war in the Pacific.

Suddenly, a Republican freshman congressman from Nebraska, Albert L. Miller, recalled that he had files containing some interesting correspondence with General MacArthur, in which he had urged him to run for the Presidency and MacArthur had *seemed* to be amenable to the idea. He released the letters to the press. In one, the congressman had written:

There is a tremendous groundswell in the country against the New Deal. You should permit the people of the country to draft you for President . . . I am certain that unless the New Deal can be stopped this time our American way of life is forever doomed. You owe it to civilization and the children yet unborn to accept the nomination . . . You will be our next President.

Replied MacArthur:

I do not anticipate in any way your flattering predictions, but I do unreservedly agree with the complete wisdom and statesmanship of your comments.

To this, Miller might have replied, "Huh?"
Instead he wrote back:

If this system of left-wingers and New Dealism is continued for another four years, I am certain that this monarchy which is being established in America will destroy the rights of the common people.

Most graciously and quite eloquently, General MacArthur replied to the congressman—in effect, one of his "bosses":

Your description of conditions in the United States is a sobering one indeed and is calculated to arouse the thoughtful consideration of every true patriot.
We must not inadvertently slip into the same condition internally as the one which we fight externally. Like Abraham Lincoln, I am a firm believer in the people, and, if given the truth, they can be depended upon to meet any national crises. The great point is to bring before them the real facts.
Out here we are doing what we can with what we have. I will be glad, however, when more substantial forces are placed at my disposition.

Here was a typical response from a lifelong soldier, an indoctrinated member of the military establishment, with a traditional

214

and understandable suspicion of political innovation. MacArthur was, presumably, merely writing to a politician who shared his worries about the home front.

The letters were blown all out of proportion, and before he was aware of it, on the other side of the globe, MacArthur was a front-rank candidate for the Republican nomination for the Presidency.

Learning of it, MacArthur wrote: "I have not sought the office, nor do I seek it."

When that didn't dampen his enthusiastic supporters, he made it clear and final:

> I have had brought to my attention a widespread public opinion that it is detrimental to our war effort to have an officer in high position on active service at the front considered for nomination for the office of President. I have on several occasions announced I was not a candidate for the position. To make my position unequivocal, I do not covet it, nor would I accept it.

Thus ended the MacArthur candidacy.

Within a month, the Republican leadership belonged to Thomas Edmund Dewey, the New York governor with the impressive public record. It was he who would sweep into the convention and come away with the Republican nomination, considered to have the best chance of defeating Roosevelt of any Republican since 1932. To run with him as vice presidential candidate, the GOP chose Senator John W. Bricker of Ohio.

Tom Dewey, a Michigan boy, had swept into New York's State House in Albany in 1942 with what amounted to a landslide after having rolled up one of the most glittering records in history as district attorney of New York County. As a special prosecutor prior to his election as DA, he had won seventy-two convictions out of seventy-three cases brought to trial. He had also sent racketeer Lucky Luciano to jail with a sentence of thirty to fifty years, dispatched Prohibition hoodlum "Legs" Diamond to Atlanta to serve a four-year term, dive-bombed "Dutch" Schultz, the policy-racket king of Harlem and smashed what was undoubtedly the nation's largest loan-shark operation.

By training and instinct, Dewey was a prosecutor, seemingly

215

cold, always methodical and deliberate, impeccably groomed, an orator with a practiced, modulated voice. Someone said he looked like the bridegroom on the wedding cake, and the image lingered.

A week later, it was "Dear Alben" Barkley, still smouldering a bit, who nominated Franklin Roosevelt for his fourth term at the Democratic convention in Chicago. An ostentatiously pre-planned "spontaneous demonstration" broke out, led by the forces of Chicago's mayor, Big Ed Kelly.

Roosevelt made his acceptance speech by radio from his private railroad car on the West Coast. Delegates sat in the convention seats, staring at an empty speakers' rostrum, brilliantly illuminated by spotlights, and listened to his voice come from four giant amplifiers overhead. Said the President, immediately launching the campaign:

> I shall not campaign in the usual sense. In these days of tragic sorrow, I do not consider it fitting. And besides, in these days of global warfare, I shall, however, feel free to correct any misrepresentations.
>
> The people of the United States will decide this Fall whether they wish to turn over this 1944 job, this world-wide job, to inexperienced or immature hands, to those who opposed lend-lease and international cooperation, or whether they wish to leave it to those who saw the danger from abroad, and met it head-on.

Selected to run with him, after much backroom bloodletting, was Franklin Roosevelt's personal choice for vice presidential nominee, Senator Harry S. Truman of Missouri.

Said John Bricker: "Who? Truman? I can't seem to remember that name."

Dewey set out to convince America of his worth. He did it coolly, calculatingly, with the utmost precision. His train always arrived on time, never late, never early. He alighted, smiling, holding his gray homburg in his left hand. If it was a big town, a twenty-five-car motorcade escorted him to the hotel. There he granted a half-hour press conference, then closeted himself with important political leaders for exactly one-half hour.

In those towns where he was to deliver a speech, the rostrum was preset for him at an exact height, and a place was made for him in the wings, offstage, where he could await his introduction, and with the mention of his name, march forward right to the podium of precise height.

The wily veteran campaigner in Washington kept his promise. He didn't stump the country. Instead he granted press interviews in the Oval Room or elsewhere in the White House, and he spoke at the biggest dinner meetings, such as the Teamsters', or allowed trusted colleagues of the press or radio ask him pointed questions.

The question of Roosevelt's health kept popping up, and Republican newspapers seemed invariably to point out that Dewey was a young, healthy forty-two. Roosevelt was sixty-two.

Vice Admiral Ross T. McIntyre, White House physician, made a public statement about the President's health: "Nothing wrong organically with him at all. He's perfectly O.K. He does a terrific day's work. But he stands up under it amazingly. The stories that he is in bad health are understandable enough around election time, but they are not true."

On November 4, 1944, Franklin and Eleanor Roosevelt were back at Hyde Park, New York, to cast their votes. Voter No. 251 of Hyde Park Village, wheeled into the voting booth jiggled a handle. The voice, familiar to many millions, said: "The goddamned thing won't work." An embarrassed election official whispered some advice. The gears clinked and the curtain parted. FDR had voted.

Two days later, in pouring rain, Roosevelt was helped off his special railroad car at Washington's Union Station and went to his long, black limousine with the bulletproof windows, there to look out, with surprise, at a crowd of over 30,000 persons standing in the downpour.

As the limousine moved off he could see that tens of thousands more were lining the streets under an endless canopy of umbrellas. He ordered the automobile-top put down so they could see him sitting there beside Harry Truman and Henry Wallace.

At the press conference that followed immediately in the Executive Mansion, Roosevelt, after a little urging, agreed to

217

reveal what had been his private guess about the division of electoral votes. From a desk drawer he withdrew an envelope he had sealed before Election Day.

On a slip of paper inside, he had given himself 335 votes and Dewey 196.

The actual final vote was: Roosevelt 432, Dewey 99.

15

The Black Man's War

The whole end of education . . . is found in burning into the heart and brain of the youth entrusted to it an instinctive and comprehended sense of race.

Adolf Hitler in *Mein Kampf*

All who are not of good race in this world are chaff.

Ibid.

At the close of World War Two, national liberation movements in the colonized world picked up new momentum and audacity, seeking to cash in on the democratic promises made by the Allies during the war. The Atlantic Charter, signed by President Roosevelt and Prime Minister Churchill in 1941, affirming—"the right of all people to choose the form of government under which they may live," established the principle, although it took years of postwar struggle to give this piece of rhetoric even the appearance of reality.

From *Soul on Ice*
by Eldridge Cleaver
Copyright 1968 by Eldridge Cleaver
Used with permission of
McGraw-Hill Book Company

Eldridge Cleaver was only six years old when the Atlantic Charter was signed and only ten years old when the war ended. He knew, though, as did most other Negroes in America, that it was a black man's war, as were all American wars, right from the Revolution, and that this was, for the black, a special war.

This attitude required no great spurt of patriotism on the part of the black man in America. The reasoning was very fundamental. Hitler was a racist, eliminating Jews to the horror of the outside world. Japan was a racist country, intolerant even of other

Orientals. America was fighting racism, committed to stamp it out. Surely, reasoned the American black man, America would no longer tolerate racism on the home front. Eagerly, then, tens of thousands of American Negro boys sought and volunteered for active combat, just as did tens of thousands of American Jewish boys, and for exactly the same reason—to fire as many bullets into racism as possible, in the hope that with the defeat of Hitler and Tojo and the arrogant, strutting Duce, its ugliness would be ended throughout the world.

While it was for Eldridge Cleaver's generation to discover that the struggle had only started in World War II, the truth is, despite the bitter race riots in Detroit and in Harlem (see pp. 161-162) and the zoot-suit riots of Mexican-Americans in Los Angeles in 1945, that considerable progress was made by both the blacks, in moving closer toward equality, and by the American whites, in learning acceptance of integration, in principle, at least, and in broadening their understanding of the Negro problem.

When the war started, Negroes who volunteered or were drafted, were segregated. They were welcome only in the Army and not at all in the Marine Corps. In the Navy they could serve only as messboys and stewards. At first they were not allowed at all in the Army Air Corps.

There was, at first, rank discrimination against Negroes, not only in the military, but also on the home front. When Wright Aviation in Ohio hired two unskilled Negro workers in 1941, its thousands of white workers went out on strike. This, along with several other incidents similar in nature, and the plans of A. Philip Randolph (with sanction of the NAACP) to have 100,000 Negroes march on Washington to end discrimination in defense plants, caused President Roosevelt to issue Executive Order 8802, forbidding employment discrimination in government and defense industries. This directive was followed by the Fair Employment Practices Act and the Fair Employment Practices Commission. The legislation was fine, but employers were under the gun to get out production, else suffer financial penalties, and all of the unions were lily white and, in most areas of the country, intended to stay that way. As it was from the time of Emancipation, white men seemed afraid of losing their jobs to Negroes.

Back in 1936, the Republicans, remembering that they were

"the party of Lincoln," had written a plank in the party platform which said:

> We favor equal opportunity for our colored citizens. We pledge our protection of their economic status and personal safety. We will do our best to further their employment in the gainful occupied life of America, particularly in private industry, agriculture, emergency agencies and the civil service. We condemn the present New Deal policies which would regiment and ultimately eliminate the colored citizen from the country's productive life, and make him solely a ward of the Federal government.

The platform of the Democrat party in 1936 made no mention of the Negro. Indeed, during the Democratic convention, Senator "Cotton Ed" Smith of South Carolina and Charleston's Mayor Burnet Maybank walked out when a Negro minister opened a session with prayer. Smith walked out again when Negro Congressman Mitchell of Illinois delivered a speech. Ultimately the entire South Carolina delegation officially protested the presence of Negroes and Cotton Ed Smith warned that he "would not support any political organization that looks upon the Negro and caters to him as a political and social equal."

Yet the Republicans didn't receive much Negro support for their public stand. Instead it went to the Democrats, though the party embraced such as Cotton Ed Smith, Mississippi's Theodore "The Man" Bilbo, Georgia's Governor Eugene Talmadge and Louisiana's Huey Long, segregationists all. The reason for this was that the Negroes liked Roosevelt, if not the Democrats. It must also be remembered that there was some influence at this time from the Communists, who had made inroads in the Negro population, and that the Communists liked Roosevelt, especially for his undisguised views about Hitler. *Crisis*, the official paper of the NAACP, rejected the Republican platform with its pledge of protection for the Negro economic status with: "That is precisely what the Negroes do not want. His present economic status is the chief cause of his discontent."

The figures supported the NAACP viewpoint.

In 1936 the average southern rural Negro's income *per family* was $556; for whites it was $1,535. For southern urban Negroes it was $635, for whites $2,019; for northern urban Negroes it was $1,227; for whites, $2,616. Of the urban Negro work force, 36 percent of the males and 26 percent of the females were unemployed. For urban white males, unemployment was 21 percent and for females, 19 percent.*

In the 1940 election year, Republicans made their platform tougher:

> We pledge that our American citizens of Negro descent shall be given a square deal in the economic and political life of this nation. Discrimination must cease. To enjoy the full benefits of life, liberty and the pursuit of happiness, universal suffrage must be made effective for the Negro citizen.

Democrats in 1940, for the first time in the twentieth century, mentioned the Negro in their party platform. It cited what the administration had done for the Negro in economic and social advances, and went on:

> We shall continue to strive for complete legislative safeguards against discrimination in Government service and benefits, and in national defense forces. We pledge to uphold due process and the equal protection of laws for every person, regardless of race, creed or color.

As the year waned and the draft was stepped up and defense production was intensified, Roosevelt made an announcement about the Negroes that was calculated to offset the mildness of the Democratic platform position.

He announced that Negro strength in the Army would be in proportion to the Negro percentage in the total population. (There were 12,866,000 Negroes in the United States—roughly 9 percent of the total population of 140,000,000.) He said that Negro groups would be organized in every major branch of the service, combatant as well as noncombatant. Negroes would have the opportunity to become officers—there would be Officer Training Schools for them. Negroes, pledged Roosevelt, would

*According to Peter M. Bergman in *The Chronological History of the Negro in America*, Bergman Publishers, New York, 1968.

be trained as pilots, aviation mechanics and technical specialists. But Negroes and whites would not be mingled in the same units, he said, because that "would produce situations destructive to morale and detrimental to the preparation for national defense."

Then the Navy announced that it would permit Negroes in the enlisted ranks other than as messboys and stewards.

Northern, midwestern and western Negroes, when they were recruited or drafted, were shipped off to military centers in the South and many of them learned for the first time what Jim Crowism was all about. Traveling from the Northeast down to the South they were obliged to get off their trains in Washington's Union Station, the Capitol dome visible in the background, and climb into "Jim Crow cars" for the remainder of their journey. On passes in the southern towns and cities they found they had to use separate toilets, eat at separate restaurants, trade in different parts of the stores and sit in segregated sections of the movie theatres. The only bars they could patronize were in "niggertowns," operated by avaricious local blacks who charged outrageous prices.

The uniform of the United States, they learned, could not protect them in the South.

Incident after incident began to creep into the press. Charges of treason were filed against Negro soldier Harry Carpenter in Philadelphia when he told a Negro sergeant: "This is a white man's war and it's no damn good."

In Alexandria, Louisiana, twenty-eight Negro soldiers were shot down by white civilians and officers during a race riot. Other race riots broke out at Fort Bragg, Camp Davis and the Mobile Navy Yard.

After Pearl Harbor the military hierarchy began to think a little differently about the caliber of the Negro fighting man and gradual, almost unnoticeable integration began to take place in combat ground units and in some of the specialized services such as Engineers and the Quartermaster Corps.

One of the heroes of Pearl Harbor was a Negro, Navy messman Dorie Miller. When the white gunner at Miller's battle station on the U.S.S. *Arizona* was killed, Miller seized the gunner's controls on the antiaircraft gun and shot down six Japanese planes. He was awarded the Navy Cross for outstanding bravery. Still serving as a messman, Dorie Miller was killed in action in the Pacific in 1943.

In January, 1942, the more than 200,000 Negroes living in Harlem got their first representative on the New York City Council, Adam Clayton Powell, Jr., the handsome, tall, young pastor of the Abyssinian Baptist Church, whose 14,000 members comprised the largest Protestant congregation in the world.

Hugely popular in Harlem (except for a few ladies in his parish who frowned on his marriage to nightclub singer Isabel Washington), Powell's election proved him to be popular in the white sectors of the city as well. He ran third among the six councilmen elected to the City Council. In Harlem, where he had mailed out 200,000 sample ballots to voters instructing them how to mark the complicated proportional representation ballot, there were fewer spoiled ballots than anywhere else in the city. It became clear to political strategists that when the impending redistricting of congressional districts was completed, Harlem would have its first U.S. congressman in Adam Clayton Powell, Jr. It did, in 1945.

An incident in 1942 that angered the nation and served to emphasize the white supremacy policy in the South took place in July, in Rome, Georgia. It involved Roland Hayes, fifty-five, who earned as much as $100,000 a year when he was the world's greatest Negro tenor, a man whose recordings were still eagerly sought by music lovers.

He lived quietly in retirement on a 600-acre farm sixty miles northeast of Rome. It was the farm where his parents had once worked and lived as slaves. He was known and respected among the neighborhood whites, who were grateful when he gave one charity concert each year in nearby Calhoun.

In Rome, Hayes was less well known, though it was the place where he and Mrs. Hayes did most of their shopping. On an extremely hot day when the Hayes family was doing its marketing, Mrs. Hayes took their nine-year-old daughter Africa (pronounced Afree-ka) into a shoe store and sat down in the second row of six rows of seats, directly under a ceiling fan. Though Mrs. Hayes had traded in the store for several years and wanted to purchase shoes for Africa, there was a new clerk on duty and he asked Mrs. Hayes to sit in a seat at the rear reserved for Negroes. Mrs. Hayes said that because it was so hot, she preferred to stay under the fan. The clerk insisted. An argument started. Mrs. Hayes, shouted: "This is no time to talk about racial prejudice and segregation! Hitler ought to have you!"

Someone called the police and reported "nigger trouble." Roland Hayes, learning of the incident, hurried to the store to see if he could make amends.

The modest artist told what happened next. Here is what he said, as reported by *Time* magazine:

> I went to the store to rectify any trouble that might have been caused, and as I left, a policeman caught me in the belt and dragged me back. I protested I had done nothing and I denied my wife had cursed. I told them my wife didn't curse. When I said that, a man *not* in officers' garb gave me all he had on the jaw. Then I was dragged to the patrol car, handcuffed between two officers. I was struck again by this man not in uniform, who leaned through a window to hit me. My wife and I were put in a cell and our little girl left on the outside.

It wasn't long before Police Chief Charles I. Harris learned the name of his prisoner. It rang a bell. He called Governor Gene Talmadge, who told the chief to handle the situation as best he could.

Mr. and Mrs. Hayes were released on $50 bail. Next day the bail was sent back to them. When the case was called in court, no one appeared to prosecute.

Rome tried to hush up the incident but the *Rome News-Tribune* carried the story and it was picked up by the wire services and spread to the rest of the world. America, warring against racism on two continents and six oceans, was not doing much about it on the home front.

Back on his quiet farm, the internationally honored tenor, who had never been active in the struggle for Negro rights, said: "I'm not bitter toward anyone and the humiliation is on the other side. I am only ashamed that this should happen in my native state. I love Georgia."

But another Negro singer moved the black cause a tiny step forward that year, rubbing America's nose in its prejudice. She was Marian Anderson, the famed contralto, who in 1939 had been denied use of Constitution Hall by its owners, the Daughters of the American Revolution, and had given her Easter concert instead, thanks to Interior Secretary Harold Ickes, on the steps of Lincoln Memorial.

Miss Anderson's manager, Sol Hurok, again asked for use of Constitution Hall in 1942 and the ladies of the DAR, perhaps having learned that two Negroes, Peter Salem and Salem Poor, were heroes at the Battle of Bunker Hill (or Breed's Hill, as the ladies refer to it) and that the chief navigator on Columbus's ship, the *Niña*, was probably a Negro, went Mr. Hurok one better: they formally invited Miss Anderson to be star soloist at one of their war-relief concerts. It was a standing-room-only sellout.

A heart-rending case in 1942 stirred the national conscience even deeper and caused thoughtful people throughout the land, white and nonwhite alike, to ponder the plight of those at the lowest end of the economic scale.

The story was that of twenty-five-year-old Odell Waller, a Negro sharecropper who worked a poor wheat and tobacco farm in Pittsylvania County in southern Virginia that was owned by a white tenant farmer, Oscar Davis, who, it turned out, was just about as poor as his sharecropper.

When the government curtailed Davis' tobacco allotment under one of the myriad wartime controls, Davis, deeply in debt and threatened with foreclosure, cut Odell Waller's acreage and denied Waller his due, which was a one-quarter share of the threshed wheat.

Waller pleaded with his landlord for his share of the wheat, fifty sacks, but Davis was adamant—he wasn't going to give it up. Waller explained that without it he and his family would starve. Davis was unmoved.

Waller talked it over with his wife, decided that since the wheat was his under the law (his contract with Davis) he would get it by force, if necessary. Accordingly he put a pistol in his pocket and confronted Davis again, demanding the release of the fifty sacks.

Davis said that never would Waller be allowed to take the wheat out of there, and reached into his pocket. He usually carried a gun. Waller said: "I opened my pistol and commenced to shoot at him." He insisted he thought it was in self-defense. Davis, shot four times, slumped to the ground, dead. He carried no weapon.

An all-white jury consisting of one businessman, one carpenter and ten farmers, listened to the case for two days and after deliberating fifty-two minutes, found Waller guilty of murder.

When Waller was sentenced to die in Virginia's electric chair at the state penitentiary at Richmond, liberals rushed to his defense, among them John F. Finerty, a well-known corporation lawyer, who pointed out the obvious—that Waller had not been tried by a jury of his peers. He argued that second-class citizens such as Waller were barred from serving on Virginia juries because they could not afford to pay Virginia's $1.50 annual poll tax.

Court after court denied Finerty's appeals for a new trial. Twice the U.S. Supreme Court refused to hear the case. But Governor Colgate W. Darden, disturbed over what appeared to be an inhumane miscarriage of justice, repeatedly granted stay after stay. The *Richmond Times-Dispatch* called for either Waller's pardon or the granting of a new trial.

Chief Justice Stone, turning Finerty down, said: "The petition presents no question cognizable in a habeas-corpus proceeding in a Federal court." And there it ended.

A short time after the nation celebrated the Fourth of July and the birth of freedom for men of all stations, Odell Waller, husband, father and sharecropper, sat in the death cell at Richmond and on notepaper wrote in an awkward schoolboy's script:

> Have you thought about [how] some people are allowed a chance over and over again, then there are others allowed little [;] some no chance at all. I accident[ally] fell and some good people tried to help me. Others did everything they could against me so the governor and the coats [courts] dont no [know] the true facts. In my case I worked hard from sunup until sundown trying to make a living for my family and it ended in death for me.

A few minutes later he was strapped into the chair, someone pulled the switch and Odell Waller died. He had never denied that he had committed a murder. The question was whether he had ever received a fair trial, and if not, whether the death penalty should have been invoked.

In the war years 1940-45 a total of twenty-six Negroes were lynched, the largest number, seven, in 1945. It was an improvement of sorts: in the war years 1917-18 there were ninety-six Negroes lynched, thirty-eight in 1917 and fifty-eight in 1918. There were also 1,100 Negro floggings in 1917.

Although it was not until 1947 that the armed forces were unified and desegregated, the American Negro, in World War II, compiled an impressive record, as he had in every American war. (A Negro, Private Henry Johnson of the 369th "Hell Fighters" Infantry Regiment, who had killed or captured twenty-five German troops, was the first American soldier to receive the French Croix de Guerre.)

During World War II 3 million Negro men registered for service. Over 4,000 Negro women served in the WAVES and WACS. Of the Negro men, 701,678 served in the Army, 165,000 in the Navy, 17,000 in the Marines and 5,000 in the Coast Guard. A half-million Negroes served overseas, mostly in Europe and North Africa.

The all-Negro 332nd Fighter Group, under the command of Negro Colonel Benjamin O. Davis, Jr., was one of the most decorated aircraft fighter units in the war. The Group flew 1,579 missions, destroyed 260 enemy planes, damaged 148 others and sank a German destroyer. Ninety-five of the 332nd's pilots were awarded the Distinguished Flying Cross. It received innumerable unit and squadron citations.

The commanding officer (now a lieutenant general and the head of the Department of Transportation's antiskyjacking program) was the first Negro West Point graduate in the twentieth century (1936) and became, in 1954, the first Negro Air Force general. He is the son of Brigadier General Benjamin O. Davis, Sr., who in 1940 was made the first Negro general in the history of the U.S. Army. He had risen through the ranks to become Inspector General of the Army, a spit and polish soldier, who retired in 1948 at the age of seventy-one after a lifetime in the service.

The first Negro unit to be sent into combat in Europe, the 92nd Division, was accompanied by prodigious publicity and fanfare. Less than two months after landing in Italy, Captain Charles F. Gandy of the 92nd, a native of Washington, D.C., was killed in heroic action on Mt. Cavala and was awarded the Silver Star posthumously. The 92nd lost 3,000 lives in Italy. It was awarded 65 Silver Stars, 162 Bronze Stars, and 1,300 Purple Hearts.

The 99th Fighter Squadron, the first Negro flying unit in the Air Force, had, by early 1944, completed its five-hundreth combat mission, ranking it with the veterans. The squadron, under the command of twenty-five-year-old Major George Spencer Roberts, received an official commendation from Air Corps Commanding General H. H. (Hap) Arnold, occasioned by the fact that the squadron had shot down eight German aircraft in one day, and four in another. The total score for three days' missions had totaled twelve kills, two probables and four damaged. In June, 1944, the 99th Fighter Squadron became part of Colonel Davis' 332nd Fighter Group. In March, 1945, the unit was given the Distinguished Unit Citation, the highest unit decoration, for a 1,600-mile round-trip air attack on Berlin. By then the 332nd had flown 1,578 combat missions. Officers and men had received 95 Distinguished Flying Crosses, 1 Silver Star, 1 Legion of Merit, 14 Bronze Stars, 744 Air Medals and Clusters, and 8 Purple Hearts.

At Anzio Beach in Italy, the 387th Separate Engineer Battalion, composed of 500 Negroes, lost four officers and eleven men and had sixty-one men wounded, even though it was not a combat unit. Three members of the 387th received Silver Stars for gallantry.

Landing at Omaha Beach, Normandy, on D-Day was the 761st Tank Battalion, the first Negro armored unit in combat in the war. General George S. Patton, commander of the Third Army, sent the men into battle with this advice: "Men, you're the first Negro tankers ever to fight in the American Army. I would never have asked for you if you weren't good. I don't care what color you are so long as you go up there and kill those Kraut sons-a-bitches."

The 761st spent 183 days in action and, according to Major General M. S. Eddy, showed "such conspicuous courage and success as to warrant special commendation." Ten tanks of the 761st were chosen to be in the honor guard at the German surrender.

The 969th Field Artillery Battalion, all Negro, fought at the Battle of the Bulge with such valor that General Maxwell Taylor wrote to the commanding officer:

> The officers and men of the 101st Airborne Division wish to express to your command their appreciation of the gallant support rendered by the 969th Field Artillery Battalion in the recent defense of Bastogne . . . This division is proud

229

to have shared the battlefield with your command. A recommendation for a unit citation of the 969th Field Artillery Battalion is being forwarded by this Headquarters.

Negro authors worked busily during the war years and some presented the reading public with serious and major contributions. These included *Native Son*, a novel by Richard Wright, 1940; *Blood on the Forge*, a novel by William Attaway, 1941; *Negro Caravan*, an anthology of Negro writing compiled by Sterling A. Brown, 1941; *No Day of Triumph*, a documentary by Jay S. Redding, 1942; *Face and Other Stories*, a collection of short stories by Roger Mais, 1942; *He Who Would Die*, a collection of poems by H. Binga Dismond, 1943; "Health Card," a short story by Frank Yerby, 1944, winner of the O. Henry award; *Rendezvous with America*, a collection of poems by Melvin B. Tolson, 1944; *30 Poems*, a collection by Frank A. Collymore, 1944; *If He Hollers Let Him Go*, a first novel by Chester Himes, 1945; *A Street in Bronzeville*, a book of poems by Gwendolyn Brooks, 1945; and *Sandyland and Other Poems*, a collection by H. A. Vaughan, 1945.

Bop, a very special kind of music, an outgrowth of swing and jitterbug, was introduced to the world in 1940 by a group of seven Negro musicians at Minton's Play House on West 118th Street, New York City. The septet, composed of players who were either well known at the time or destined to become so soon, were: Teddy Hill, Charlie Christian, Dizzy Gillespie, Dusty Young, Kenny Clarke, Thelonius Monk and Charlie Parker.

In 1943 two all-Negro movies were released. *Cabin in the Sky*, a memorable musical, starred Lena Horne, John Bubbles, Eddie Anderson (of Jack Benny fame), Ethel Waters ("Happiness is Just a Thing Called Joe"), Duke Ellington, Louis Armstrong and a host of other popular artists.

The other musical with an all-Negro cast was 20th Century-Fox's *Stormy Weather*, starring Lena Horne, Bill Robinson, Cab Calloway, Dooley Wilson and numerous other stars.

In 1943 Paul Robeson broke a record for Shakespeare on Broadway with his two hundred and ninety-sixth performance of *Othello*.

In 1944 the Negro actor Canada Lee narrated the first radio series on the race struggle. It was called "New World A-Comin'."

16

Where Were You on D-Day?
1944

On June 6, 1944, Americans, Canadians and even Britons went about their affairs as usual, except that more of them went to church than was customary on a Tuesday.

Things were not "as usual" on the European continent and never were to be the same again. The ultimate end of the Nazi Wehrmacht, Hitler's giant war machine, began that day.

The long-awaited invasion of France, the "second front," started at 6 o'clock from a bright, relatively calm sea that would reach high tide at 10:33 A.M. By 8:25 A.M., landings had been effected all along a ninety-mile stretch of the Normandy coast, placing the Allies in position to seize two major ports, Cherbourg and Le Havre. A virtual army of paratroopers had also been dropped behind the Germans' coastal defense emplacements.

The fighting on the beaches was thunderous, murderous. Vast stretches had been mined. Steel rails, barbed wire, booby-trapped obstacles impeded the invaders. From shell-impervious pillboxes German machine-gunners swept the open stretches with a deadly rain of steel. German mortars and howitzers pounded high explosives into the beach and emplaced guns hurled larger shells at the invading fleet. Overhead the Luft-waffe made pass after pass over men and ships streaming tracers into them and dropping antipersonnel bombs.

It was one of the bloodiest days in mankind's history.

But Allied troops, tens of thousands, it was disclosed later, had been parachuted behind the German defense line during the darkness that preceded the dawn landings and soon they began to link up with the bloodied units from the beaches, which began to scramble away from the dunes and into the hedgerow country to predetermined rendezvous points.

The decision to launch the invasion had been reached thirty hours earlier by General Dwight David Eisenhower, the Allied supreme commander. The moon, the tide, the carefully prepared weather forecasts were all favorable, though at the time the decision was made it was pouring rain on both sides of the English Channel.

By the time Americans and Canadians awoke to the dawn of June 6, five hours later, the story of the invasion was in many of their morning newspapers and on the morning news broadcasts. At the suggestion of President Roosevelt, many went to church and prayed for victory and the safety of Allied soldiers, sailors and airmen, before going to work.

The President himself devoted the day, closeted in his bedroom, to preparing a prayer to be read by him that night over continentwide radio.

At first many home-fronters asked if it was the real thing this time. They had been fooled two days earlier by the false broadcast of an invasion caused when a young British girl learning to operate a teletype machine experimented with the message: ALLIED FORCES INVADE FRANCE. Inadvertently her machine was plugged into a main circuit and the message was printed on teletypes throughout Britain and the Allied Command, including the news printers. Instantly the message had been flashed to North America and around the world, only to be retracted a few hours later. The young lady, mortified, broke down and had to be hospitalized.

But on June 4 in Italy, Rome had fallen after nine months of siege, and on June 5 the Fifth Army had roared across the Tiber, skirting Vatican City, with hardly a look at Rome, the beleaguered seat of Western civilization. The Fifth was en route to the mountains to engage the remnants of the German Army, which, after retreating, had dug in and was waiting. Mussolini, safe for a while in the mountains, urged the Italians to continue to resist the Allies, but his countrymen laughed and called him things even Sicilian Mafia leaders had refrained from calling him, and of all Italians, *they* claimed to hate him the most.

When the White House confirmed the invasion and announced that the President would speak that night on nationwide and Canadian radio, North Americans joined Britons in anxiously awaiting word. Sharing the anxiety was the man left behind in a farmhouse in Britain, General Eisenhower, who paced back and forth with temper wearing thin, stopping occasionally to write a memo to himself. One, which echoed the sentiments of the entire Western world, said: "Now I'd like to hear some reports."

Soon they came pouring in, first to Ike, then to the waiting world.

Father's Day fell on June 18 in 1944 and on Tuesday, June 6, to relieve their tension, many people went shopping to see what they might get for the old boy. There were certain things they could *not* get: shoes, tires, cars, lawnmowers, Camel cigarettes (they were the GI favorite), leather belts, leather wallets, golf balls, swimming trunks, radios, alarm clocks, brushes of any kind using hair or bristle, fountain pens, camping equipment and boxed candy.

Among items they could purchase for dad were good Havana cigars, some Chesterfields, Phillip Morris, Luckies and Old Gold cigarettes, British-made smoking pipes (but no British tobacco), a few cameras, several kinds of wrist watches, sweaters, jackets, hats (felt, straw and Panama), neckties, dress shirts, a limited selection of sports shirts, fishing equipment, a narrow choice of golf woods, rainwear, lawn and porch chairs, slippers made of felt, hosiery (anything but pure woolen or argyle) and flashlights.

When Americans went grocery shopping that day they found they could buy: chicken at 35 cents a pound, hamburger at 27 cents a pound, plate corned beef at 17 cents a pound, sliced veal loaf at 29 cents a pound, and sliced luncheon meat at 24 cents a pound. There was no bacon to be found in most of the stores, and few pork items.

They could buy four pounds of potatoes for 25 cents or eight pounds for 48 cents. Two heads of lettuce sold for 25 cents. Florida oranges were selling for 49 cents a dozen. A sixteen-ounce tin of hash went for 23 cents.

Butter, which a year earlier had been in extremely short supply, was now back on refrigerator shelves and selling for 39 cents a pound, a price that was considered by many housewives to be simply outrageous and there had been outcries against war profiteering. A one-pound can of coffee sold for 23 cents. A large loaf of bread cost 7 cents. Grade "A" eggs were 42 cents a dozen. Two large boxes of Rinso went for 43 cents.

Egg prices had been falling for some time. In that first week of June, including D-Day, the War Food Administration was struggling with the egg problem. The "problem" was a good one: There were too many eggs.

When Uncle Sam had called for more agricultural production, apparently every one of the 389,469,000 superpatriotic hens in America decided to give her all. In May, the month just ended, these cackling winners of the "E-for-Efficiency" award had set a new production record of 6,704,000,000 eggs. On D-Day, there were 1,400 freight cars on midwestern sidings containing 25 million dozen eggs, and there were many more in nearby Canada. Egg processors were hastily summoned who took most of them off the hands of the embarrassed War Food Administration. In a few weeks the seasonal egg slump would begin, and officials were hoping that the hens would observe it and not cling to a wartime production schedule. A period of "moult" was decreed for July and August, though it turned out that many of the feathered barnyard girls would ignore it. Eggs continued plentiful throughout the remainder of the year.

On D-Day the bigger circuses were touring the country doing one-and two-night stands—Barnum and Bailey, Hunt Shows, Cole Brothers, World of Mirth, Carnival Caravan. One month later, on July 6, the Ringling Brothers, Barnum and Bailey Circus was to be in Hartford with its new, fireproofed, nineteen-ton Big Top when fire broke out, causing the worst disaster in circus history—169 dead, 412 seriously injured. The Hartford fire marshal had not inspected the tent before the show. Five circus officials and employees were arrested on technical charges of manslaughter.

On that fateful day of June 6, the Census Bureau reported, women outnumbered men in the United States for the first time in an official count, and would outnumber them in the next election by some 600,000. There were 44,622,886 women and 44,103,669 men. The disparity was highly noticeable in retail establishments as well as in a great many manufacturing plants.

Morning newspapers carried a copyright story from the *Atlanta Journal* disclosing that the Ku Klux Klan had decided to disband and that members would not reveal the reason behind the decision.

Those same editions carried a report from the Navy that U.S. subs had sunk sixteen more Japanese merchant vessels recently, bringing the total to 589 such merchantmen that had gone to the bottom.

On June 6 the Swedish liner *Gripsholm* arrived in New York with 131 wounded U.S. and Canadian soldiers who a week earlier, at an undisclosed port, had been exchanged by the Germans for a similar number of wounded Nazi PW's.

The Fifth War Loan Drive was launched on D-Day, quite by coincidence, and before day's end was off to a very good start, treasury officials said. The offering of bonds was for $16 billion in several series, the most publicized of which was Series "E," for public participation.

Eleanor Roosevelt's column, "My Day," on June 6 dealt with her visit to the Agricultural Experimental Station at Beltsville, Maryland, where she reported having seen some phenomenal things done to plants and vegetables by scientific fertilization and hybridization and said that when she had a chance, she was going to try them at Hyde Park, though she confessed to lacking a green thumb.

In his hard-hitting column, which was generally critical of Roosevelt, the administration and the war effort, Westbrook Pegler wanted to know where New York restaurants got their superb steaks, rare wines and expensive liquors to entertain the *haute monde*.

In New York's Harlem, a nine-year-old girl poked her head out of the window to watch a street battle between two rival gangs of Harlem High School youths and someone fired a pistol. The bullet went through her neck, killing her.

A New York store, show-offy with inventory, advertised ladies' Enna Jettick shoes at $6.50 a pair. McKettrick Classic dresses sold for $8.95. A shipment of table lamps was offered at $8.95.

Two days before D-Day, at the invitation of Prime Minister Winston Churchill and General Eisenhower, General Charles André Joseph Marie de Gaulle, six-foot-four-inch head of the Free French and designated by his fellow exiles as the president of the Committee of National Liberation, based in Algiers, had flown from North Africa to London.

On his arrival he had been informed that the invasion was scheduled for that day, Sunday, but that it had been postponed for two days. He spent Sunday night reading and revising the speech that Eisenhower was to broadcast to Frenchmen at the time of the invasion, but on Monday, when he presented himself to the supreme commander, he was told that the Eisenhower speech had already been recorded and gone off to broadcasting stations.

Monday night, as loading activity went on all around him,

General de Gaulle prepared his own speech and, at Churchill's request, took it to the BBC to be recorded and broadcast to the French on D-Day. On June 6, de Gaulle, like Eisenhower and Churchill, paced the floors, awaiting reports, knowing that his words, along with Eisenhower's, were being repeated over and again on broadcasts to the people of his homeland across the channel.

In two weeks, General de Gaulle was to return to *la patrie*, debarking at Bayeux, the first French town to be liberated by the Allied forces on D-Day.

In Washington FDR stayed closeted in his bedroom, avoiding people. He received all of the reports, however, as they came in. He also considered another essential—the cost of the war. So far it had cost the United States $170 billion. The outlay was nearly $315 million per day.

Cordell Hull and members of his staff conferred about the possibility of calling delegates from the Allied powers together to formulate an international organization that would henceforth help to maintain world peace. The initial meetings, at Dumbarton Oaks in Washington's Georgetown, were to take place two months later. It would be called the World Security Conference, and the resulting organization would become the United Nations.

Also in Washington that day, a nineteen-year-old girl, a real beauty with auburn hair and blue eyes, having learned that as Miss District of Columbia she would go on to the finals, made plans for her participation in the Miss America Contest in September. She would win. Her name was Venus Ramey and her measurements were 37-1/2-25-36-1/2. She was the, uh, biggest girl in bust measurements in the history of the Miss America contests, which dated from 1921. Even by 1971, her generous proportions had not been surpassed.

Some American military men spent D-Day on Russian soil, somewhere in the Ukraine at secret air bases. Flying Fortresses had made bombing history by flying from Italy, bombing Rumanian targets and going on to the specially prepared bases in Russia.

In Berlin, Adolf Hitler, age fifty-five, huddled with his High Command, instead of with Propaganda Minister Joseph Goebbels as was his preference. He did not think the Allied invasion was too serious. There were seventy-two movie theatres in Berlin

236

still operating despite bomb devastation around the city. The High Command ordered the word "catastrophe" eliminated from all military reports and, indeed, from the vocabulary itself in ordinary usage.

In New York, where there was some open celebrating about the invasion, though people were generally restrained because of the sure knowledge that casualties would be high, there were several first-rate plays running on "browned out" Broadway.

These included *Jacobowski and the Colonel, Chicken Every Sunday, The Searching Wind, Kiss and Tell, The Two Mrs. Carrolls, Tomorrow the World, The Voice of the Turtle, One Touch of Venus* and *Carmen Jones*.

On June 6, 1944, the national debt of the United States stood at $260 billion.

Just before noon that day, while he was driving on U.S. Route 6 from Willimantic toward Hartford, the last spare tire blew out on the 1939 Dodge of Morton Bannion of New Hartford, Connecticut, and he knew that his days as a salesman were ended unless he could find a tire carcass that could be retreaded. He hitchhiked home.

All the big dailies in New York ran extra editions throughout the day and scheduled more for the morning of June 7. Most were sold out.

In Normandy the Anglo-American-Canadian troops sang "Lilli Marlene" when they were dug in, a song that had been borrowed from the German prisoners of war, and "Don't Sit Under the Apple Tree"—("with anyone else but me"). Some raw recruits had brought a new song, "Don't Fence Me In."

At home, the young and romantically inclined sang "You'll Never Know"—("just how much I love you")—the Academy Award-winning song from the movie *Hello, Frisco, Hello*, which had come out late in 1943 and had soared to nationwide popularity.

Jive was the stuff in the jukeboxes and a tempo called "eight to the bar."

At most stateside military bases that day servicemen still in training were put through extra drills and assigned to special duty to keep them off the streets. There was the suspicion that they might be needed sooner than expected, as replacements.

Going My Way, the new Bing Crosby picture with high spiritual overtones that was to win him the Academy Award, was available to some movie-goers that night. So was *Dragonseed*, with Katharine Hepburn and Walter Houston, and the much-talked-about *Lifeboat* with Tallulah Bankhead and the indomitable William Bendix. Playing in neighborhood theatres was *Lady in the Dark* with Ginger Rogers and Ray Milland, *The Lodger* with Laird Cregar and *Between Two Worlds* with Edmund Gwenn and George Tobias.

Books also were good for quelling home-front anxieties on D-Day. Americans were still reading some 1943 best-sellers like *A Tree Grows in Brooklyn* by Betty Smith, *The Fountainhead* by Ayn Rand and *The Human Comedy* by William Saroyan. Added to them were a few new ones in 1944—the eyebrow-raising *Forever Amber* by Kathleen Winsor, the moving *A Bell for Adano* by war correspondent John Hersey and Ben Ames Williams' *Leave Her to Heaven*.

It was a day that on the home fronts, Americans, Canadians and Britons did just about the same things they had been doing for months. They kept themselves busy and listened for bulletins on radio. They read their newspapers. They listened to music to get their minds off their anxieties. Some went to plays that night, others to movies, others to taverns and roadhouses. Some stayed home and read. Some made love. Some got drunk on not-quite-satisfactory spirits.

Marriages were performed that day. Births were achieved. Deaths were recorded.

It was a day like any other wartime day—with one exception.

It was a day that would never be forgotten by those who lived through it, either in Normandy or elsewhere in the world.

17

The Restless Natives
1944

As the year began, Americans rode and shipped goods on railroads that were owned by President Roosevelt. He had seized them in the name of the government two days after Christmas, warning the 1,450,000 railroad workers in the twenty unions serving the $28 billion railroad empire, that he would not tolerate wage demands that exceeded the "Little Steel" formula.

Throughout the nation labor leaders glowered at the President and reminded him that it was an election year and he would need labor's support. The railroad seizure was calculated by FDR to be a stark warning to union men that there would not again be concessions like those granted to John L. Lewis and his coal miners in 1943.

The warning worked. Phillip Murray called back 170,000 striking steel workers, and another 500,000 who had been planning to walk out were ordered to stay on the jobs. It was reasoned—incorrectly so, it turned out—that it would always be easier to deal with the private owners than with the high-handed Roosevelt government.

For twenty-two days Secretary of War Stimson held complete power over the entire 233,670 miles of trackage in America, from the one-mile-long coal-hauling Valley Railroad in McKean County, Pennsylvania, to the Pennsylvania Railroad itself, with its 24,928 miles of track.

Seven railroad presidents were sworn into the Army and made instant colonels, instructed to buy proper uniforms and report back to their desks. Other rail officials were commissioned with varying lesser ranks. Elsewhere, the Army pulled out its 201-files and found all stateside soldiers who had previous experience working on railroads and assigned them to temporary duty at their peacetime jobs. Trains rolled as usual with no change in schedules. Rail companies collected and kept their fares and shipping charges, as usual.

The President had solved the crisis, but he had not dispelled the anger of the union members. The operating brotherhoods of the railroad industry were the "gentlemen" of the labor movement, the conservatives who carefully observed negotiating protocol. Their demands for wage boosts had been shunted around in Washington's new buck-passing arenas for more than a year. A day before they were to present their case to the National Mediation Board, Roosevelt had seized the roads.

In the end the workers got more than they had asked. Example: the nonoperating unions wanted an 8 cent an hour raise, and received 9-11 cents.

In the men's rooms of all of the railroad stations on every line in the country there was, by early 1944, a universal message, sometimes repeated many times over: *"Kilroy Was Here."* Sometimes it was accompanied by a drawing:

Who was Kilroy? No one seemed to know. He had swept through America and visited just about every public men's room in the nation. He had gone to Canada and had been equally busy with crayon and pen while serving the needs of an apparently faulty bladder. He had peed his way through England and the British Isles and had scribbled away at walls throughout Italy. Soon he would decorate the walls of most of the *pissoires* in France.

In mid-1944, Kilroy's diuretic affliction apparently was cured and he moved his artwork outside of the men's room walls to more public exposure. Soon Kilroy's legend appeared on billboards, on construction-site fencing, on the sides of public buildings and warehouses and in phone booths. It was then that people knew who Kilroy really was. He was the spirit of the GI at war, omnipresent, like the spirit of Christmas, perhaps—or, more accurately, the symbol of the universality of young manhood and valor. People could be grateful that "Kilroy Was Here."

The long arm of Roosevelt's government-at-war reached out again in the spring and slapped at an old man sitting alone in his tycoon's office, providing the world with the comic-opera dramatics of the head-on collision of two extremely strong wills, Roosevelt's and that of Sewell Avery, chairman and undisputed boss of the mighty mail-order house of Montgomery Ward and Co.

It had started when the War Labor Board issued an order to Montgomery Ward to extend an expired labor contract with a CIO union until there could be an election to determine whether, indeed, the CIO union controlled a majority of the workers as the union claimed. Avery had refused.

Next, the WLB warned that the President might seize Montgomery Ward, just as he had seized the railroads. Avery had scoffed. He dispatched a wire to the White House challenging the President to take over Montgomery Ward. He didn't have to wait long for results.

Next morning the U.S. government arrived at Montgomery Ward's executive offices in Chicago, headquarters of the $295 million Avery-built empire.

The "government" was the well-tailored, rich, sophisticated, Yale-graduated, North Shore Chicagoan, Under Secretary of Commerce Wayne Chatfield Taylor, a very un-New Dealish emissary. He presented himself at Sewell Avery's spacious office. Avery rose, greeted him with a thin smile and asked him to come in and sit down. The door closed behind them.

Taylor presented Avery with the President's order directing the secretary of commerce to take over operation of Montgomery Ward and Co. "for the successful prosecution of the war." After an hour, Taylor emerged and told waiting reporters what they had expected to hear: Sewell Avery had refused to turn over his company. The government, he said, had no right to seize it.

Taylor returned to his office to telephone Commerce Secretary Jesse Jones in Washington for instructions. A short time later he was back at Montgomery Ward's with a United States marshal and eight deputies, all armed. Sewell Avery looked over the marshal and his armed squad and quietly informed them he would not surrender. The marshal and deputies left.

Then, shortly after 6 P.M., three Army trucks from nearby Camp Skokie Valley rolled to a stop at Montgomery Ward's front entrance and at once there debarked a forty-four-man unit of helmeted military police under the command of Lieutenant Ludwig Pincura. The battle squad was ordered to fix bayonets.

Followed by four of his men, Lieutenant Pincura went to Sewell Avery's eighth-floor office. Avery, sitting in his executive's chair behind his desk greeted them with a smile. Lieutenant Pincura said: "Under authority vested in me by the President of the United States I am taking over this plant."

"Does that mean I have to leave?" asked Avery. Then he answered his own question. "No," he said.

"Yes," said Lt. Pincura.

Avery looked at his watch. "Well," he said, "it's time to go home, anyway."

He left by a rear door, hopped into his limousine and drove to his Lake Shore Drive apartment.

Next morning when Sewell Avery showed up for work not only was Wayne Taylor waiting for him but also U.S. Attorney General Francis Biddle of the Philadelphia Biddles.

The Attorney General asked Avery if he would cooperate and turn over Montgomery Ward's books to the government bookkeepers. Avery refused. Biddle then asked him to call a staff meeting and explain what the government's purpose was in seizing the company. Avery said he wouldn't cooperate in any way. Thereupon Biddle informed Avery he would have to leave. Avery flatly refused.

Taylor then turned to the major heading the Army unit of occupation, and asked him to escort Avery out of the plant.

Avery sat there and refused to be budged.

The major then ordered a sergeant and a private to seize Sewell Avery and carry him out of his office and out of the building. They complied. With each soldier holding an arm and a leg and Sewell Avery sitting with his hands folded across his stomach, and his coat neatly buttoned, the head of Montgomery Ward was evicted.

Hotly angered, the blood flooding his face, he thought of the absolutely worst invective he might hurl at the Main Line Biddle who sat in his office:

"You—you *New Dealer*!" he shouted.

Sergeant Jacob L. Lepak and Private Cecil A. Dies carried him to the elevator. Avery refused to enter. They carried him aboard. At the ground floor he refused to move. They carried him outside and stood him on the curb, locked out of the plant where he was the $100,000-a-year chief executive officer. He was not to return until the labor election had been held and its results certified.

Everywhere in the world, in 1944, the Allied forces pressed their advantage—the tide of war had turned at last. For five years the Germans had had their way on the Continent. They had overrun Poland, Denmark, Norway, France, Belgium, the Netherlands, Luxembourg, the Balkans and a good chunk of Russia, not to mention most of North Africa. Now they were being beaten back, on the defensive on every front. The Japanese had spoiled for a sea fight, had been accommodated at the Battle of Midway and had been defeated. Now, in 1944, U.S. marines and soldiers were island-hopping from one Japanese-held atoll to another, across the length of the Pacific.

In France, first Le Havre was captured, then Cherbourg, after bitter fighting, and finally General Omar Bradley gave orders to break out of Normandy and the Anglo-American-Canadian forces raced on to Paris and then headed for the German frontier. There were more Allied landings in southern France in August, and by November 25, the Allies had breached the supposedly impregnable Siegfried Line, the German defense west of the Rhine. Within two days the double-tiered Siegfried Line was broken in five places at Aachen. Western Germany had been invaded for the first time since Napoleon.

Then, just before Christmas, the Germans, badly beaten on all fronts, and having fought the bloodiest battle of any war in defense of the Roer River valley between Aachen and Cologne, finally turned and struck back. On a sixty-mile front, from the blood-spattered Hurtgen Forest to the eastern bulge of Luxembourg, Field Marshal von Rundstedt hurled a desperate German force.

"You bear the holy duty to achieve the superhuman for our Fatherland and our Fuehrer," he told his troops. Behind massive artillery barrages, Germany's finest infantry and armored units drove against the Allies. The Luftwaffe was concentrated on the small area. Buzz bombs were directed against the suddenly stopped Allied advance, as well as a mysterious new V-bomb, which was also being fired at random targets in London.

In the Ardennes, east óf Malmédy, the Germans overran U.S. forward positions and smashed five miles into Belgium, cutting off American units in St. Vith and Bastogne.

Throughout the American Army, reaction was instantaneous. Cooks, truck drivers, mail clerks, finance office personnel, mechanics, quartermaster specialists, even latrine orderlies, were ordered to clean their weapons and get into the line. Back in the States all leaves were canceled. Units in the Infantry Replacement Training Centers that were anywhere near the end of their training cycle were ordered into combat alert for shipment to France.

At year's end the Battle of the Bulge was still flaming hot and bitter, but even von Rundstedt knew that the overwhelming superiority of the Allied forces throughout the rest of France and the Low Countries spelled ultimate doom for the Germans in Luxembourg. The Battle of the Bulge was the last desperate strike of a rattlesnake that had already been fatally wounded and must, in time, die.

In the winter of 1943-44, the American Fifth Army had been stopped in Italy. Under Field Marshal Albert Kesselring, more than twenty Nazi divisions held off the Americans and prevented them from reaching Rome.

General Mark Clark decided to outflank them and effected a landing at Anzio beachhead in late January, 1944. For a while it seemed that the tactic was successful, until the Germans, superbly equipped and supplied, launched a vicious counterattack. The Allies then were forced to resume their advance against Rome through the ragged mountains south of the Eternal City. It was there that they were stopped again on the mountain called Cassino, with its 1,400-year-old monastery being used by Germans as an observation post for their uncannily accurate artillery. American tanks and convoys, crowded on Highway 6, were stopped dead in their tracks by the German artillery directed from the revered Monte Cassino Abbey. Rome lay seventy miles to the north, over the mountains.

The Germans were aware that plans were afoot to invade the Continent, though they didn't know where. Kesselring's troops were known as *Kriegsverlangerer*—war prolongers. Their mission was to use up Allied strength, equipment and supplies in Italy to keep it from fighting on the second front, wherever that might be. But General Mark Clark and General Sir Harold R. L. G. Alexander also knew that the more of Kesselring's men, supplies and ammunition that were consumed in Italy, the less support could be given to defending that second front, wherever it might be.

At long last, after tremendous American losses in the vicinity of Cassino, General Eisenhower gave permission to bomb the observation post in Cassino Abbey. Three waves of B-17 bombers followed by a squadron of twenty Marauders took care of the ancient Benedictine abbey in short order.

The German radio cried "Outrage." The Vatican remained silent. Said Kesselring: "I have only the deepest contempt for the cynical and sanctimonious mendacity with which the Anglo-Saxon Commands now attempt to make me responsible for their acts." He, of course, denied that the abbey had been used as an artillery observation post.

If there had been no Nazis up there before, there were shortly after the bombing took place. They swarmed over the rubble and soon from behind the jagged stones hundreds of gun barrels pointed down to the Americans in the Liri Valley. But GI's could advance against small weapons, even machine guns. There was no more heavy artillery fire.

In the spring the Allies launched a strong offensive against the Gustav Line before Rome, and breached it on Trinity Sunday, two days before D-Day in France. The Germans fell back to their defense positions and retreated into the northern mountains, with the Fifth Army in hot pursuit.

There, in the steep, snow-crested peaks, awaited the Gothic Line, the strongest natural defense position in all of Italy, and it was there that the two opposing forces settled down for a static, stalled, bitter battle that lasted for the remainder of the year and throughout the winter.

The course of war was certainly turning in Russia in 1944. Allied bombings had devastated the German industrial machine back in the fatherland. Russian supplies, thanks to almost constant and seemingly endless shipments from the United States, were building up. In six-wheeled Studebaker trucks and in four-wheel-drive Willys Jeeps, Russians could outmaneuver the Germans in snow or mud.

Kiev had been recaptured in the winter. Next was Leningrad,

ending an 880-day siege. Lying in the snow before the shell-devastated city were the corpses of 25,000 German soldiers, and eighty-five huge siege guns.

In September the Red Army captured Praga, just across the Vistula River from Warsaw, the capital which had been under the Nazi boot longer than any other. Soon Russian forces were advancing against East Prussia. There, in the last week of October, three years and four months after Germany invaded Russia, the Russians invaded Germany, and marched on, into one of the bloodiest battles of the Eastern Front.

In the Pacific, the U.S. captured Kwajalein, then leap-frogged 400 miles to take Eniwetok. From there the task force jumped 1,200 miles into the Marianas to recapture Guam and seize the Japanese fortress of Saipan, only 1,500 miles from the southern tip of Japan.

To stop the American advance Japan hurled her entire fleet against the U.S. naval forces, and launched the biggest air attack of the war with literally hundreds of planes. The Japs lost that encounter, pulled back and planned another.

In October the light cruiser *Nashville* hove to in Leyte Gulf amid the battleships of Admiral William F. Halsey's Third Fleet and the giants of Vice Admiral Marc Mitscher's fast carrier task groups—the greatest fleet of ships ever assembled in the Southwest Pacific.

A wave of Army infantrymen stormed over the shell-scarred beaches and scouted for Japanese in the underbrush. There were only a few. A lone enemy plane ventured out. It dropped one bomb harmlessly into the ocean. Not a Japanese surface craft was in sight.

From the deck of the *Nashville* a ladder was lowered to a barge. Down the ladder scrambled General Douglas MacArthur, followed by his immediate staff. He sat erect in the barge's stern, khakis neatly pressed, cap at military angle, shoes flawlessly shined. The barge ground onto the beach and lowered a ramp. MacArthur went to the ramp's end, and stepped off into waist-deep water. Unperturbed, he waded ashore.

To the Filipinos who scrambled down to greet him, he declared:

"People of the Philippines, I have returned. By the grace of Almighty God, our forces stand again on Philippine soil. . . . Let every arm be steeled. The guidance of Divine God points the way. Follow in His name to the Holy Grail of righteous victory."

Turning to his chief of staff, Lieutenant General Richard K. Sutherland, he said, minus the rhetoric: "Believe it or not, we're here."

Thus, in October, 1944, ended General MacArthur's personal odyssey, which had begun in mid-March, 1942, when, on orders from the President, he had abandoned Corregidor, and from a haven in Australia had promised the Filipinos: "I shall return."

It was clear that with the fall of the Philippines, Japan would have to attack, else lose its defense line. The Nipponese admirals devised a careful strategy—to have three separate task forces converge from different directions.

When reconnaissance disclosed the three separate forces steaming toward the Philippine Sea, Admiral "Bull" Halsey had to make a decision. He did: attack.

When the first of the Japanese attack fleet came into Leyte Gulf it headed straight for Suriagao Strait, where an ambush of PT boats awaited them with their stinging torpedoes. They were followed by U.S. destroyers with more torpedoes. As the big battlewagons plowed on it became obvious to Rear Admiral Jesse Oldendorf that the Japs were crazy enough to go through the narrow twelve-mile-wide pass between Desolation Point and Hingatungan. He let them get deep into the pass and then blasted them all from the sea with a circular wall of fire.

It was more than fitting that among the attacking American ships were five battlewagons that had been salvaged from wreckage at Pearl Harbor—the *California, Tennessee, West Virginia, Pennsylvania* and *Maryland*.

In the North, Mitscher's force tracked down the unsuspecting remainder of the Jap fleet and brought havoc to it.

When it was over, the back of the Japanese Navy had been broken. Twenty-four Jap warships were on the bottom, including three battleships, four carriers, ten cruisers, three flotilla leaders and six destroyers. Possibly sunk also were a battleship, five cruisers and seven destroyers.

When they struggled out of the Philippine Sea, six other Jap battleships, five cruisers and ten destroyers were so severely damaged they were unusable in war.

Of sixty Japanese warships that had steamed into action, only two escaped without extensive damage.

247

The battle for Leyte raged on in the jungles, not far from MacArthur's new headquarters, and would continue to do so for the balance of the year.

Paris had barely been liberated and Germans were still fighting in France when the ladies of the free world were informed that the Parisian couturiers were ready to show their 1944 creations. Though there was strict rationing of cloth everywhere in the world, and though there was no way to transport fashion editors to the showings, ladies could hardly wait to see what Paris decreed for the new fashions, perhaps to be called "postwar fashions," though that term was a bit premature.

Instead of fashion photographers, cameramen of the Signal Corps drew the extremely pleasant job of snapping the pretty, smiling mannequins. Instead of the well-known fashion editors and designers from the United States, Canada, Australia and Britain, there were envious, uniform-clad WAC's, a few uniformed nurses, and rows of bug-eyed U.S. officers watching the presentations.

Hardened correspondents who had been foot-slogging with the ground troops all the way from Normandy were ordered by their city desks to report on the details. Supply planes, returning empty to depots in England, brought back the pictures and the stories and quickly they were presented to the breathlessly waiting world.

The grand old names of *haute couture* were all there: Lanvin, Schiaparelli, Lelong, Molyneux. There were marvelous new hats, some turbanlike, some flowered and ruffled.

The trend in fashions was distinctive. Skirts were to be full and short, just a touch above the knee. Waists were to be small, pinched. Shoulders would be wide, sleeves frequently mutton-legged. Designers had used their available material with abandon, and manufacturers as well as ladies throughout the world sighed enviously and knew it would be some time yet before they could make such lavish use of precious cloth. But the week-long showings were, to a world still celebrating the freeing of Paris, like bright and delicate spring flowers in warm sunshine after a long, cold, hard winter. Paris was free and her special genius unsullied. There were still some things right with the world.

Though newsprint was still tight and newspapers were rationed, women's editors, who had been starved for fashion news for nearly five years, had a field day with the pictures and stories emanating from the Parisian galleries and salons. It was as though Rosie the Riveter with her sometimes form-fitting coveralls had never existed.

Rosie was much in evidence though, if one cared to look. Ladies had invaded just about every phase of industrial, business, commercial and agricultural life and, as one wag put it, held every job that men once occupied except that of attendant in the men's room.

In industrial plants a new danger had been discovered in out-of-the-way storage rooms and the New England Personnel Managers Association scheduled a discussion of how to deal with promiscuity on the job. The Puritan ethic endured. Sex was not forbidden, exactly, for it was wartime, you know, but it wasn't condoned openly either, especially not on company time.

In the bigger defense cities it appeared that "on the job" was the only locale for lovemaking, the housing shortage being what it was. It was a rare bedroom on the West Coast or in the South that didn't have two, three or more beds in it that were used for eight-hour stretches, in shifts, by weary war-workers. An aircraft worker in Seattle, who shared a bedroom with three other men from his shift and surrendered it to four other workers when his time was up, complained that he slept on the most unloved-on mattress in all of America.

In Starke, Florida, six miles from Camp Blanding, which had been built almost overnight to train as many as 10,000 infantry replacements at one time, a lady who once kept chickens converted all of the coops to bedrooms and rented them for $3 a night to soldiers on pass, soldiers' wives, soldiers' girls and a few ladies of uncertain relationship but seemingly high income.

A tall person couldn't stand in the henhouse bedrooms, and they smelled fiercely of Lysol, creosote and roach spray mingled with the cloying pungency of fresh whitewash, but they were preferable by far to the bedrooms in the Blanding USO centers, where a soldier and his wife could sleep together for 50 cents apiece per night for as many as three nights, provided it could be verified that the girl was, indeed, the soldier's wife.

Having to verify the legitimacy of the union lent spice and excitement to the urgency of long separation and couples, having registered, hurried to their assigned bedrooms, there to discover that they were ceilingless and had paper-thin walls that reached up about eight feet, and that on either side were reunited husbands and wives engaged in noisy, sweaty, spring-torturing reunion on army cots that had never been constructed for such purposes.

To some of the boys and girls who had never been away from home before and whose experience with basic life was confined to the Sunday School class, it was a traumatic experience never to be forgotten and many was the "reunion" that was postponed until the soldier could get another pass and line up one of the chicken coops in Starke.

By 1944, and indeed, even before that, the off-post military business had become established and entrenched. In the town nearest every large military complex there were specialty shops catering to soldiers. Principal among them, of course, were restaurants and bars where opportunities were legion for fleecing the homesick country boys in their ill-fitting uniforms.

Inevitably there was a jewelry store running heavy to cheap trinkets, gold-colored hearts with "Sweetheart" or "Mom" written on them, service-flag pins for Mother, sweetie or wife to wear proudly, denoting a son, boyfriend or husband in the service, heart-shaped lockets for miniature snapshots that turned green in the hand of the purchaser as he paid his $3 plus tax, tasteless barrettes made in the shape or image of American flags, and awkward pins that said: "My Man is in the Army" (or Navy or Air Corps or Coast Guard or Marines or Merchant Marine).

The off-post photographer always did well. He charged something like $15 or $20 for a portrait picture in a cardboard frame, with three or four 1-1/2-by-2-1/2-inch contact prints thrown in. As soon as the recruits got the official piping on their overseas caps denoting their branch of service, and the regulation brass insignia on their lapels, Mom or wife would send the required cash and they'd hustle off to the photographer to get an "official" picture. For many, of course, it would be the last studio picture ever taken of them, and the weekend lines of waiting GI's in front of the photographer's shop were understandably impressive.

Inevitably, also, there was a hock shop. It was only one month before most GI's, fresh from civilian jobs, learned that the $30-a-month Army pay (it had been raised from $21) didn't go far, especially after there were deductions for life insurance, a wife's or mother's allowance and laundry. The net pay for a buck private trainee ran to around $24 a month. As a consequence, the off-post pawn shop had a goodly supply of wrist watches, cuff links, stick pins, class rings, watch chains, guitars, banjos, harmonicas, accordians, concertinas, civilian fedoras and dresser jewelry boxes.

Another stalwart of the boom town who did well, surprisingly, was the barber. A serviceman could get a perfectly good haircut on the post or base for prices ranging from 10 cents to 25 cents, yet, due to the delousing ceremony at his induction when all of his hair was clipped off, he had such suspicion of military barbers that he would gladly wait in line in the nearest civilian barbershop, get a quick trim with the electric clippers, and pay $1-1.50, plus the expected tip.

Although good, Grade-A ice cream was served for dessert on the posts or bases at least three times a week and the on-post PX's served the best ice cream available for a nickel, GI's would stand in line in the boom towns and pay 15 cents for a scoop of ice cream made for civilians of water, powdered milk, dehydrated and powdered eggs and artificial flavoring. It was the same with drugs. Aspirins were handed to GI's merely for the asking, yet they'd buy bottles of the most expensive brands in the drug stores in town. Rubber contraceptives were available free of charge to all who applied at the supply room on post, yet a majority of the soldiers paid $1 for three of them in the town drugstore, never noticing that they came from the same manufacturer.

A thriving in-town business was the shoe shine stand. After a weekend pass and before they returned to base, GI's would gladly pay 25 cents, if they had it left, to have their boots shined and made ready for the next inspection before the next weekend pass.

After the liberation of Rome, the invasion of France and the recapture of Paris, it became evident to the Allied powers that plans should be started to form some kind of international organization that would maintain the peace after the war ended. Accordingly, Secretary of State Cordell Hull invited diplomats from the four great powers—Britain, Russia, China and the United States—to meet at Dumbarton Oaks, in Georgetown, just outside of Washington, to prepare the groundwork for the body that would be charged with preserving the world's peace. It would be known as the United Nations Organization, at first, and then, simply, as the United Nations.

For two months the delegates met, planned, structured. Then it was announced that one day, in due course, France would become one of the Big Five and entitled to a permanent seat on the eleven-member Security Council. Among resolutions adopted: that the United Nations should have armadas of "national air force contingents immediately available" to send against any aggressor.

In December, the increasingly ill Cordell Hull sent in his resignation. It was a genuine personal tragedy, for Cordell Hull, a public servant for fifty-one of his seventy-three years, had hoped to preside at the opening session of the United Nations after the war. Appointed to succeed him was Edward R. Stettinius, Jr., forty-four.

Just before Christmas the nation was bothered by another great shortage.

There were simply no cigarettes to be purchased, anywhere. That is, for most people.

The nation's retailers who normally dealt with tobacco and cigarettes had turned into smiling liars. Under the counter they had a few cartons tucked away, not always the brands they wanted, but there were cigarettes there. They were, however, for favored customers and friends and relatives.

Before a Senate investigating committee, R. J. Reynolds Tobacco Company's chairman, S. Clay Williams, confessed that even he, on many occasions, had to walk *more* than a mile for a Camel. (His advertising slogan, brilliantly illustrated by Madison Avenue artist Roger Smith of Douglaston, Long Island, was: "I'd walk a *mile* for a Camel.")

Now not only Lucky Strike green, but just about all cigarettes, had gone to war. Home-front smokers faced a bleak Christmas and New Year's, burning their tongues on newly purchased pipes and wondering how in hell the British managed to be so fond of them.

18

From Yalta to Warm Springs
1945

It had been a tense "non-holiday" during the Christmas season as the year 1944 drew to a close. With communications perfected from both Paris and London, news of the losses in the Belgian Bulge was flashed back to Washington and Ottawa and quickly disseminated to the public. To compound the worries at home there were grave fuel shortages in the Northeast and Canada, the Middle Atlantic States and the Midwest, and the areas were gripped in one of the severest cold spells in years.

Britain was under constant assault from robot bombs, the latest generation of the "buzz bombs" that had plagued that nation for so long. The island empire, which had already been at war nearly 2,000 days and nights as the New Year rolled around, seemed to be literally pockmarked from the deadly explosives.

As the year started, the east coasts of the United States and Canada were alerted to the *probability*—not merely the *possibility*—of robot bomb attacks, and air raid wardens who had loafed through much of the past year got out their identifying armbands and tin hats and took up their posts again by night, making certain that the blackout was enforced, that curtains and blackout drapes were tightly pulled and that the only cars on the road were those with painted headlights that emitted only slits of lights. The "brownout" of inland cities, meaning that only traffic lights would be operating at night, was extended nationwide for the first time. Heretofore only cities along the coasts had been obliged to observe the precaution, and during "brownouts" some had been allowed to turn on deeply hooded and shaded streetlights.

Air raid wardens, some of them a bit officious, were the brunt of many jokes and gibes, mostly because as paunchy, bald, wizened middle-aged citizens, they didn't look like the standard movie stereotype of lean, hard military men. Many plump ladies donned tin hats and armbands and mounted sky watch atop towers, belfries and cupolas. It was comforting for those inside houses to know they were there.

Adolf Hitler broadcast the New Year's speech to his troops and his people. At times the Fuehrer's voice seemed weary, about to crack. At others it was the old shrill, exhorting cry that had such hypnotic effect on so many Germans:

> The Nationalist Socialist State, our 2,000-year-old civilization, can neither be replaced by Bolshevism nor by democratic-plutocratic ideology. This nation and its leading men are unshakable in their will and unswerving in their fanatical determination to fight this war to a successful conclusion.

Further on he added:

> I am at present speaking less frequently, not because I do not want to speak but because my work leaves little time for speeches. I have not been sleeping. I promise solemnly to the Almighty that the hour will strike when victory will come to the Greater German Reich.

As was the custom with all major speeches by Hitler, this one was beamed to the British and Irish wavelengths and to American monitors.

On New Year's Day there awaited Americans on the home front a rash of new orders reflecting the tragic turn of events on the battlefields of Belgium. The Office of Price Administration announced it was going to return rationing to meats, fats and canned vegetables, which, in the fall, had slipped almost unheralded into the point-free category. The OPA, in another first-of-the-year communiqué, announced that shoe rationing was to be revised because there would not be enough leather for even two pairs of shoes for each civilian in 1945. The War Production Board at the same time announced that the production of passenger car tires was being slashed to the bone and drivers would simply have to make do with what they had—and what they had in the way of tires was in poor shape.

As if that hadn't hit hard enough, War Mobilization Board chief James Byrnes ordered all horse and dog tracks shut up tight by January 3, with instructions to remain closed until war conditions would permit resumption of racing.

Around the nation, wherever space permitted, in post offices, railroad stations, airline terminals, bus depots and public buildings, and on telephone poles, the signs went up again:

Use it up,
  Wear it out,
Make it do,
  Or do without!

It was hardly a necessary slogan, for, in truth, there was no alternative. Almost nothing seemed replaceable.

President and Mrs. Roosevelt returned to the White House just before Christmas after spending twenty days in Warm Springs, Georgia. The President was lightly tanned and appeared rested and a bit plumper. He went right to work on his State of the Union message to Congress, in which he had several specific recommendations: universal military training to insure against World War III; a reduction in taxes after V-E Day, which he predicted would come in 1945; a big postwar building program of housing (then acutely short), bridges, roads, schools, airports, hospitals; continued efforts in building an organization for world peace.

"This new year," he wrote, "can be the greatest year of achievement in human history. Nineteen forty-five can see the final ending of the Nazi-Fascist reign of terror in Europe; 1945 can see the closing in of the forces of retribution against Japan. Most important of all, 1945 can and *must* see the substantial beginning of the organization of world peace."

In the morning of January 20, sleet fell on Washington and the skies were heavily overcast. It had snowed the night before and, attired in snowsuits, almost a dozen Roosevelt grandchildren slid and tumbled on the slope of the White House lawn. Late in the morning the crowd began to gather, bundled in overcoats and galoshes, many citizens carrying umbrellas in deference to the black and ominous low clouds.

Promptly at noon the former senator from Missouri, Harry S. Truman, stepped forward briskly and took the oath as vice president, administered by the chief justice of the Supreme Court, Harlan Fiske Stone.

When Truman had seated himself, the thirty-second man to hold the office of President of the United States rose to be inaugurated for his fourth term of office. Only those behind him on the portico of the White House could see the effort required as the President's broad shoulders and heavily muscled arms hoisted his big frame onto his polio-weakened, steel-braced legs. Capeless, hatless, he walked to the podium.

As he had in his three previous inaugurations, he placed his hand palm-flat onto a page in the old Roosevelt family Bible. As on the three previous occasions, it was opened to the thirteenth chapter of the First Epistle of St. Paul to the Corinthians, which begins, "Though I speak with the tongues of men and of angels, and have not charity, I am become as sounding brass, or a tinkling cymbal," and ends, "And now abideth faith, hope, charity, these three; but the greatest of these is charity."

As he had in his State of the Union message, the President addressed himself to the world of peace that he felt so confidently would come in 1945. A thin, misty and chilling drizzle fell on the White House steps as he delivered his inaugural address. Moisture gathered in beads on the shoulders of his coat.

"We have learned that we cannot live alone, at peace," he said. "We have learned that we must live as men, and not as ostriches, nor as dogs in the manger. We have learned the simple truth, as Emerson said, that 'the only way to have a friend is to be one.'"

At the brief ceremony's end, Roosevelt returned to his wheelchair and was assisted to the Red Room to receive 2,000 invited guests who were to have luncheon. It was the biggest reception in the twelve years the Roosevelts had been at the White House. FDR had insisted that the meal be spartan and had asked to have chicken à la king. He was overruled by the housekeeper, who wanted something a bit more sumptuous, and settled for chicken salad on crisp lettuce. There were hard rolls without butter or margarine, unfrosted pound cake (sugar was scarce) and coffee.

The President wasn't aware of it then, but that night the family, dining alone, would have the first rib roast the Roosevelts had been able to get in many months. The secret was shared by Eleanor and the housekeeper, a surprise for Franklin.

After the luncheon there was a tea for those who didn't attend the meal. Eleanor Roosevelt, sitting next to Bess Truman, who had stayed to help receive guests, advised her on how to make entertaining less taxing by learning how to relax the knees.

Unknown to most Americans, highest-echelon arrangements had been underway for several weeks for the second conference of the Big Three, Roosevelt, Churchill and Stalin (the first conference was at Teheran in 1943). This was to be held at Yalta on the Crimean Peninsula, and in a subsequent toast to peace it was named by Josef Stalin, the "Crimea Conference." Though this was the official term intended for history books, the meeting became known as the Yalta Conference, and the results thereof as the Yalta Agreements.

The President departed secretly, shortly after his inauguration. He appeared not long thereafter at Malta aboard an unnamed U.S. battlewagon, which correspondents described as "shining, polished and absolutely spotless." There he was met by Winston Churchill. It was the ninth time since Pearl Harbor that he had conferred in person with the British prime minister. Roosevelt debarked wearing a comfortable tweed cap, the kind that wouldn't blow off at sea while the battleship was under way. Winnie, as the President called his friend and ally, was wearing his own special concept of an admiral's uniform, with baggier-than-regulations-would-allow trousers, a comfortable soft jacket with brass buttons and a visored cap.

Together they took a plane to a secret Crimean airport, followed by other planes carrying staff, interpreters, advisers and some military bigwigs from both Britain and the United States.

At Yalta, Russian construction crews had been working around the clock for weeks repairing damage that German bombers had wrought. Roosevelt was put up in a white stone palace that had been built in 1911 for the last of the Romanov czars.

Premier Josef Stalin of the Union of Soviet Socialist Republics greeted his distinguished guests wearing a peaked peasant's cap and a plain but expensive-appearing peasant's shirt-jacket. He brought along with him his favorite crook-stem pipes and a supply of his pungent smoking tobacco. Next day the trio posed, smiling in the sunshine, for Signal Corps photographers, giving every appearance of men who were determined to add the word "accord" to whatever history chose to call the Yalta conferences.

It was not all work. There were some pleasant drinking sessions and some splendid (for wartime) repasts, with many laudatory and flattering toasts proposed by the leaders of the three Allied governments.

The news of the Yalta meeting was not released until all three heads of state were on their way home. Information in the first joint announcement was skimpy. In Paris, however, the provisional French leader, General Charles de Gaulle, announced that France, having been rebuked by the Yalta Conference, would handle its own affairs without outside help. It was clear that he was angry. Then it was learned that Roosevelt, realizing that de Gaulle would be upset over the fact that the Big Three did not yet trust France with a custodial role in the postwar world, even in Western Europe, had asked the provisional French president to meet him in Algiers where he had hoped to calm the general's turbulent temper, but that de Gaulle had refused to leave Paris. It was to be the first of several Gaullist blunders brought on by personal sensitivity.

On his way home, Roosevelt decided that he had better report to Congress about Yalta just as soon as possible. He authorized release of more detailed stories of the meeting just as soon as his safety was assured. He began to prepare what he was to say. Then, thirty-six hours after his return, still looking tired from the journey, he went to the House chamber to address a joint session of Congress.

There was a puzzled hush as he entered in an armless wheelchair. He had decided to leave his leg braces at the White House. He was wheeled to a red plush chair behind a table containing a dozen or more microphones and he eased himself into it and smiled at the lawmakers. There was an explosive ovation and the President began:

> I hope you will forgive me for the unusual posture of sitting down, but I know you will realize it makes it a lot easier for me in not having to carry about ten pounds of steel around the bottom of my legs and also because of the fact that I have just completed a 14,000-mile trip.

There was another crash of applause.

Then followed a fifty-four-minute speech, one of the longest and perhaps one of the most historic of his career. He spoke in almost confidential tones, conversationally. Lacking was the familiar Roosevelt oratory, the almost-nasal Rooseveltian tone.

At one point his voice nearly gave way. He soothed it with a sip of water. At another it seemed to weaken, then, as if by special effort, he brought it up to full timbre.

He had been in Yalta for eight days, he said, from February 4 to February 12, and the conference had not only achieved unanimous action but unity of thought among the Big Three:

> There will soon be presented to the United States Senate and to the American people a great decision which will determine the fate of the United States—and of the world—for generations to come. There can be no middle ground here. We shall have to take the responsibility for world collaboration, or we shall have to bear the responsibility for another world conflict.

At one point, in an ad-lib aside, he commented on the fact that "there are a great number of prima donnas in the world." This was an apparent gibe at Charles de Gaulle, as if to remind him that personal feelings shouldn't come before the peace of the world. The agreement to form the United Nations had been forged at Yalta, and Roosevelt wanted all nations to respond, and the Senate to ratify America's role in the new organization.

When he had finished, Roosevelt went back to the White House to prepare for a quick trip back home to Hyde Park for a few days of sorely needed rest. He was tired, and he looked it, but he was in good spirits and joked frequently with staff-members, as a man will do after he has completed a gargantuan task and knows that he has done it well.

Not so happy with the President's appearance was the long-time friend and neighbor of Eleanor Roosevelt, Margaret Doane Fayerweather, who was at the White House when Roosevelt arrived and said he appeared "terribly thin, worn and gray." She observed with distress that his hands shook uncontrollably.

His return to Washington was not entirely that of a unanimously supported victor. There were many, in Congress and out, who protested the Yalta "deal" that gave Estonia, Latvia and Lithuania to Stalin and the Soviet Union, and they wondered what disposition would be made of Poland and Czechoslovakia.

There were still a great many isolationists in America who did not support the idea of a world government of which the United States would be only a part. Editorial response was mixed.

Only in later years was it to be learned that Roosevelt had given deep thought to the fate of Estonia, Latvia and Lithuania, and had weighed the probability that the United States would have to go to war to wrest them from the Soviets, something he calculated America would be unwilling if not unable to do after fighting the bloodiest, most costly war in all mankind's history. Apparently "Smilin' Uncle Joe" Stalin, whose Yalta photographs made him appear like a pleased and indulgent adult host at a party for youngsters, had made it quite clear to FDR and Churchill that Russia was ready to fight her allies, if necessary, to maintain sovereignty over territories she had "won."

Moreover, both Churchill and Roosevelt knew—or felt certain that they knew—that the Russians had committed heinous atrocities in Poland with the deliberate murder of 11,000 Polish military men in the massacre of Katyn Forest. Thus, they reasoned, the Russians were not only determined about their "territories," but were capable of almost any ruthlessness in holding onto them. (It was not until 1972 that official documents were released in Britain disclosing the report that absolutely pinned blame for the Katyn massacre on the Russians. Until that time, some historians and members of the press had held the Nazis accountable for the systematic mass killings.)

Roosevelt and Churchill shared two immediate concerns that apparently, in their judgment, took precedence. These were the rehabilitation of Britain and Western Europe and the initiation of immediate steps to set up the United Nations in order to avoid World War III.

The President had other troubles on the home front as well, and after the Hyde Park respite, it was necessary to confer with congressional and administration leaders. Much of it concerned his old, staunch supporter, Jesse Jones, and his former vice president, Henry Agard Wallace.

By 1944 Henry Wallace's forward-looking social and economic ideas had begun to appear "radical" to many old-line Democrats. Republicans called him everything but a revolutionary. He had become a political liability to FDR's wartime administration. At the Democratic convention in Chicago, Roosevelt had dumped Wallace as vice president and had chosen instead a middle-of-the-roader and severe administration critic, Harry S. Truman, the senator from Missouri who had headed the wartime fact-finding committee that frequently flayed Roosevelt's policies. The move quelled dissension in the party and impressed independent voters and the many "wartime Republicans" who had decided to stick with FDR through the war if they possibly could. Now, in 1945, Roosevelt had to find a good job for Wallace. Roosevelt owed Wallace a debt, for even though he had been rejected by Roosevelt, the vice president had campaigned for him and had persuaded the CIO's Political Action Committee, to whom he was an outstanding hero, to support the President.

Thus, in January, Roosevelt had ordered one of the few firings in the history of his administration. He asked for and received the resignation of Jesse Jones, the veteran head of the Department of Commerce and its mammoth Reconstruction Finance Corporation and RFC's eight powerful and heavy-spending subsidiaries.

Then he appointed Henry Wallace secretary of commerce, and chairman of the Reconstruction Finance Corporation and all of its subsidiaries. The debt was repaid, but an old wound was reopened. Here was the house liberal back in an extremely vital position. The anti-Wallace forces rallied.

Before Wallace's appointment could be confirmed, a bill was introduced in the Senate to divorce the Reconstruction Finance Corporation—the biggest business in the world—from the Department of Commerce. Everyone knew it was Jesse Jones' idea, though it had been introduced by Senator Walter George of Georgia.

Jesse Jones did appear before the Senate committee that was deliberating the bill and he declared:

> Certainly the RFC should not be placed under the supervision of any man willing to jeopardize the country's future with untried ideas and idealistic schemes. It [RFC] is bigger than General Motors and General Electric and Montgomery Ward and everything else put together, and you don't hear much about it because it is being run by businessmen, by men who haven't any ideas about remaking the world.

Jones voiced what many of the anti-Wallace people thought: that Wallace was an amiable idealist, essentially harmless, but not to be trusted with the nation's biggest lending business.

Then Wallace appeared before the senators and said:

> There are some who have suggested that this separation of
> the lending functions from the Commerce Department is
> desirable because of my alleged "lack of experience." This
> is not a question of my lack of experience; rather it is a
> case of not liking the experience I have.

The real issue, he declared, was whether or not RFC was to be
used to help big business only, or whether its powers (and
wealth) were to be used also to help small businesses and help
carry out the President's commitment of 60 million jobs for
Americans after the war.

It was purely a political talk, but it was widely printed and
reprinted and it defined Henry A. Wallace's role in the American political and intellectual establishment for the remainder of
his career. He spoke of the President's "Economic Bill of Rights,"
which included the "right to a job" for every American; of more
jobs; of more foreign trade; of greater production; of
guaranteed annual wages for all workers; of preserving the free
enterprise system for private industry; of more homes and public housing; of better roads; of more TVA's; of more free
education; of expanded social security; of health insurance; of
public works programs for schools, hospitals, libraries, of special
attention for the poor, the ill, the handicapped. All this could
be done, he said, with lower taxes and a reduced national debt.
The implication was that it could be done with RFC money if
the agency were handled properly.

In the end, the "bill of divorcement" that divided the two jobs,
prevailed. The Reconstruction Finance Corporation was
separated from the Department of Commerce, but Henry A.
Wallace, fifty-six, an effective spokesman for the liberals, was
approved as secretary of commerce.

Many in the Democratic party were not happy about it.

It remained for Roosevelt to restore unity and calm the tem-
pers and this was his assignment as he stopped briefly at the
White House after his rest at Hyde Park and before his depar-
ture for Warm Springs for some restorative exercises and relaxation in the early spring sunshine.

Roosevelt was also worried about a United States District Court
decision in Chicago that had effectively curbed the powers he

had exercised under the War Labor Disputes Act. He was uncomfortable over the fact that the decision had meant a moral victory for his old sparring partner from the entrenched business interests, Sewell L. Avery, the crusty chairman of Montgomery Ward and Company, Inc.

Right after New Year's, Roosevelt had ordered the seizure of Montgomery Ward for the second time in seven months. This time it was because Chairman Avery had refused to obey two War Labor Board directives: first to pay retroactive raises to 17 percent of Ward's 700,000 employees; and second, to sign a union contract guaranteeing maintenance of membership.

This time the Army hadn't bodily removed Sewell Avery, though again he had refused to cooperate. Major General Joseph W. Byron had merely opened an office adjacent to Avery's, installed a Signal Corps switchboard and took over operations. Avery sat in his office with nothing to do, and finally, bored, he went off to catch some sun and less harassment at an exclusive Arizona hotel. Meanwhile his lawyers were appealing to the courts to have the Army evicted from Montgomery Ward.

In less than three weeks Judge Philip L. Sullivan of the United States District Court in Chicago handed down a decision: President Roosevelt, he said, had no power to seize the plants and facilities of Montgomery Ward and Company. The President could seize mines, plants and facilities only when they were equipped for the "manufacture, mining or production" of war-essential materials. The law did not cover businesses that were in "distribution," such as Montgomery Ward.

(The decision came as a disappointment to Miss Iona Creech of Harlan, Kentucky, who, having read in the local newspaper that the Army had taken over Montgomery Ward, mailed in her order for a "staff sergeant of 5 feet 9 inches height, dark hair, with brown eyes.")

Bothering Roosevelt more than anything else about the Montgomery Ward legal decision was the fact that just off-stage, waiting in the wings for early spring to arrive, was John L. Lewis, labor's champion Roosevelt-baiter, whose United Mine Workers union was authoritatively reported to be cooking up trouble for the White House.

Roosevelt also found time to "receive" a group of French correspondents in his office and in Harvard French he greeted them and expressed his regret at being unable to visit France on his way home from Yalta. He recalled his pre-polio youth when he had bicycled through the French countryside. He said they should forget about the reported differences between himself and de Gaulle, which were no bigger, he said, "than a thumbnail."

Then he departed for Georgia and the "Little White House," a small white cottage on Pine Mountain, near the Warm Springs Foundation for polio victims. Eleanor Roosevelt, with a full schedule of work, much of it in her husband's behalf, remained in Washington. Accompanying the President were his cousins, Laura Delano and Margaret Suckley.

For nearly two weeks the President stayed close to the cottage, resting, too exhausted to venture out into the remedial sunshine.

On the morning of April 12, ninety-six days after he had been inaugurated for his fourth term, the President seemed better than at any time since he had arrived. He was planning to go out to a barbecue in the afternoon and that evening the polio patients at the Warm Springs Foundation were scheduled to give a minstrel show in his honor. He commented happily on both prospects and said he was looking forward to them.

The plane that brought his daily mail from Washington was delayed in arriving that morning due to bad weather. When it did come, the President and his secretary, Bill Hassett, sorted it out almost gaily. Mr. Roosevelt sat beside the fireplace in the cluttered but cozy living room and his two cousins chatted happily at the other end of the room. There were the usual things to read and sign, among them the bill to extend the life of the Commodity Credit Corporation. As he put his pen to the bill he commented, as he had so many times, "Here is where I make a law." As always, it brought a quick smile to Bill Hassett.

The only appointment that day was for Mrs. Elizabeth Shoumatoff, a portrait painter who had done one portrait of Franklin Roosevelt and had received permission to do another. She had been making sketches for several days. She sat at a strategic angle and quietly sketched while the President went through the rest of his mail. Mr. Hassett took the signed letters and documents and withdrew.

All was quiet for a time. The President was reading. Suddenly Miss Suckley saw a motion near the fireplace. She glanced at the President. He had slipped sideways in his chair. She and Miss

Delano raced across the room. "I have a terrific headache," Franklin Roosevelt said, and fainted.

The ladies called his valet, Arthur Prettyman, a twenty-year Navy veteran. With a messboy summoned from duty in the kitchen, he lifted the unconscious man and carried him to his bedroom.

Doctors, quickly responding, found the President there in his austerely furnished room with its picture of a sailing ship and a ticking brass chronometer measuring off the seconds. They put pajamas on him and tried to make him comfortable. There was nothing else they could do. He had suffered a massive cerebral hemorrhage.

At 3:35 o'clock by his brass chronometer, the President's heart stopped and his breathing ended.

Within minutes the news was flashed to the outside world. It blared from radios with a stunning, stupefying clout. All regularly scheduled broadcasts were suspended. Citizens sat benumbed. Businesses closed. Theatres emptied. In the big cities, traffic slowed and halted. Offices were closed and the released employees, numbed and preoccupied with their thoughts, jammed public transportation facilities. Anyone who had anything to do with a newspaper, a news magazine or a broadcasting station rushed back to news rooms—editors, reporters, rewrite men, copy editors, photographers, printers, stereotypers, mailroom employees, librarians, secretaries, copy boys, announcers, engineers. Even the smallest dailies put out special editions.

At military posts throughout the nation, all personnel were ordered confined to the post limits. The news was especially shattering to the young; they could remember no other President.

America grieved.

Eleanor Roosevelt had checked Warm Springs early in the morning and had learned that the President partook of a good breakfast and was feeling well. In early afternoon she had gone, as guest of honor, to the Sulgrave Club tea for the benefit of Washington's children's clinics. A short time later she was summoned to the telephone. She apologized for leaving "in this way," and rushed back to the White House. In her sitting room on the second floor, Press Secretary Steve Early and Vice Admiral Ross T. McIntyre, the President's personal physician, confronted her gravely. Said Mr. Early: "The President has slept away."

Moments later Vice President Truman arrived. He also had been summoned by telephone by Steve Early. It was Mrs. Roosevelt who told him. "The President has passed away," she said.

"What can I do?" asked the Vice President.

"Tell us what *we* can do," responded Mrs. Roosevelt. "Is there anything we can do to help *you*?"

A short time later, Mrs. Roosevelt boarded a plane and flew to Georgia. Next morning, with Miss Delano and Miss Suckley riding with her in her limousine, and Fala, the President's Scottie at her feet, she followed the hearse down the wide trails, off the mountain. Whenever he had left Warm Springs, the President always rode past Georgia Hall, the foundation administration building, to shout goodbye and wave to the patients there in their wheelchairs, and Mrs. Roosevelt asked that the hearse take that route.

Before Georgia Hall the procession slowed. Mrs. Roosevelt looked out at the saddened, distraught faces of the polio victims. A Negro boy carrying an accordion stepped forward. She recognized him as Graham Jackson, who had played many times for the President. Now, tears in his eyes, he pressed out a tune. Mrs. Roosevelt knew it well. It was "Goin' Home," one of Franklin Roosevelt's favorites.

A special white-flagged train was at the tiny, sun-bleached station. Into the last car they gently placed the flag-draped casket. On Steve Early's arm, the President's widow walked sturdily into her car, immediately forward, Fala trailing on a leash. A military band played, its sad music filling the hot valley. The train's doors were closed as quietly as possible by attendants and conductors and it rolled off, toward the north and Washington.

All that day the train proceeded past silent mourners, gathered by the thousands along the right-of-way. Farmers in fields tied their horses or mules to fence posts and stood with bared heads as it moved past. In Charlotte, North Carolina, thousands stood bareheaded and silent in the station, and to one side a group of blacks sang sad spirituals in low harmony. On through Virginia the train rolled, and Eleanor Roosevelt sat straight and mute, staring out the window at the saddened people of a nation.

For three days and three nights the radios of the land were stilled except for news broadcasts and religious music. Some newspapers printed black borders around their headlines. A large number of businesses remained closed. The whole nation seemed hushed.

There was a funeral procession in Washington, the flag-draped casket on a black caisson drawn by eight white horses. Services in the East Room of the White House were attended by family and friends, the top men in the United States from all walks of life, the new President, Harry Truman, all members of the cabinet, Russia's Andrei Gromyko, Britain's Anthony Eden.

Next day, at Hyde Park, New York, in the Hudson Valley that he loved so well, Franklin Delano Roosevelt was lowered to his final resting place. Gray-clad cadets from the United States Military Academy at West Point fired three volleys. Through the greening valley echoed the lingering, sweetly sad notes of Taps. America's great soldier was at peace. He had not lived to see the final victory, nor the start of his longed-for United Nations.

19

The Way Things Were
1945

By late 1944 and early 1945 many of the things that had been "in short supply" earlier in the war were now scarce or nonexistent. Cigarettes had never been rationed, but they simply did not exist from November, 1944, through June, 1945. Whenever stores—even gas stations—received a shipment, the proprietor would post a sign, "WE'VE GOT 'EM," and the supply would be cleaned out in a few minutes at the rate of one carton to a customer. Pals of servicemen who smoked Camels, which were in shortest supply, would spend hours going from cigarette machine to cigarette machine getting one pack at a time (all that was allowed) until there were enough to mail a little packet of ten or a dozen packs to camp.

Coffee had been rationed right along, but suddenly it, too, disappeared from shelves. Butter disappeared, and so did shortening and many popular brands of soap. If you could find it, Lux was 8 cents per cake.

It was rumored that bread would soon be rationed, and tens of thousands of girls who had never boiled water or baked a potato wrote to their mothers to get recipes for homemade bread. It turned out that while it was scarcer, it never did disappear from shelves entirely, and it was not rationed, except on a "voluntary" basis by individual sellers. A great many local bakeries did close, however, as the small bakers couldn't get enough sugar, flour, yeast and baking powder to sustain their businesses.

Gasoline had been rationed all along, and so had tires and most other rubber products such as hot water bottles and the like, but as the war dragged on, it became almost impossible to find a new tire or tube in any garage or gas station. Tire manufacturers that had their own retail outlets—Firestone, General, Dunlop and others—offered the buyer some chance, but more often than not what they had to sell was a "retread," an old carcass that had new tread fused onto it. More and more often gasoline service stations trotted out the big signs that had been saved for emergencies: "NO GAS TODAY!" It made no difference how many ration coupons one had, if there was no gas to sell, there was none to be bought.

Most of these scarcities did not affect school children except for teenagers in the "predraft" group, who found their parents reluctant or even unable to allow them to use the family car for normal older-teen pursuits. (There was also the fact that many former lover's lanes had been converted to airstrips, military reservations or defense plant sites.)

There were other things about life on the home front that did affect the youngsters. In school they bought defense stamps regularly each week, from their allowances, they wore identification tags, and they had air raid drills once each week in which they were obliged to crouch under their desks. It was at school that they turned in the large balls of tinfoil they had saved from gum wrappers and smoking tobacco pouches, and by retrieving bits and pieces from sidewalks and gutters. Girl Scouts and Brownies prepared boxes of cookies, gum and candy and sent them to servicemen on duty.

At home, the kids cut the ends out of tin cans and jumped on the resulting cylinders to flatten them so they could be turned in at the nearest fire station. They also retrieved and refolded brown paper Kraft bags used for carrying groceries. *McCall's* magazine experimented and found that the average paper bag could be reused five times. Paper was extremely scarce, as Americans had learned earlier in the war. In 1945 *Newsweek* carried an ad from Kimberly-Clark which reported that it took more paper than rails to run a railroad, a verity that any file clerk could confirm. Thus, an added chore for young people on the home front was to save, bundle and tie newspapers.

Victory gardens abounded even in the vacant lots of Manhattan, Philadelphia and Chicago. A nation which had been trekking off the farm and to the cities since World War I suddenly became agrarian-minded and kids who had thought that small farm implements consisted of reel-type lawn mowers, grass clippers and hedge trimmers, were introduced to the hoe and the spading fork and learned to identify garden weeds. They sowed packets of seeds, supplied by their schools.

Women throughout America learned to "put up" vegetables

by canning. Pressure cooking, used heretofore only by the commercial canners, was introduced to the American housewife and the War Production Board issued special orders to see that there was a sufficient nationwide supply of pressure cookers, glass jars and rubber sealing rings. For many, one magazine noted wryly, wartime had enforced the eating of balanced meals, what with the outpouring of fresh vegetables.

Young people were most seriously affected in the war by the shortages that hit toy-making. Boys felt it more strongly than the girls because more of their toys had been traditionally made of metals. There was no such thing as a mechanical or electric train unless the retailer had entered the war with an enormous inventory. The same applied to ice skates, roller skates, sleds, steel-edged skis, bicycles, BB guns, toy cars, coaster wagons and tricycles.

There came into existence, as a result, a wide variety of plastic toys as Yankee ingenuity sought to fill the gap in an exceedingly demanding market. Counters in the five-and-dime stores became loaded with gaily colored items of all shapes and sizes and after some hesitation even the connoisseurs conceded that a plastic truck worked better in a sand box than did the "old fashioned" metal variety. Girls, less finicky about things, still had a good selection of dolls and doll clothes. Most little girls were just as happy with plastic ducks in their bathtubs as they had been with rubber ones. Their own accessories, such as plastic handbags and plastic barrettes for their hair, seemed to please them.

For the lady of the house, life was rather complicated even if she hadn't taken on an outside job to release a man for service. Soap, for one thing, was increasingly hard to find by 1945, and flakes or beads for dishes and laundry were in continuously short supply. Plastic plates and dishes that she bought to replace broken crockery were not as satisfactory as items made for the kids.

When the sun was bright she spent as much time as possible tanning her legs so she could avoid wear on her hosiery. With a little searching she could find a pair of nylons for sale in her size, and learning a trick from her sisters in uniform, she kept them in a glass jar to prevent deterioration. A very sexy style, used when she dressed up, was nylons with a black seam and black, pointed "clocks" at the heels. These were worn with high platform shoes with high ankle straps, and, of course, leather heels, for there was no rubber.

When she went out she wore a custom suit with high, square, padded shoulders. Quite frequently she wrapped her head in a turban, particularly if she had not had a recent "hair-do." Do-it-yourself permanent wave kits for home use had recently come onto the market and sometimes two or three housewives would get together and devote a day to giving each other permanents. If she was merely going shopping, she would often hold her hair in place with a loose net which she called a "snood." In cold weather she chose a scarflike head covering that she had borrowed from Russian peasant women and called a "babushka."

She painted her lips and nails a dark red, almost burgundy. She smoked about as much as her husband did, and usually the popular unfiltered brands of cigarettes, though some ladies preferred Virginia Ovals, which were filtered.

She wore a regular-type girdle, if needed, and avoided as uncomfortable the recently introduced panty girdles. For very special occasions she had black nylon underwear and a black bra, on the supposition that this color pleased her husband, and she called this a "dance set." She also owned a black nylon, transparent nightie for very special occasions.

She used a cream-style deodorant, washed her hair with Packer's Tar Soap, and brushed her teeth with Teel or Ipana. She was, as a result of advertising campaigns, terrified that she might have body odor (or "Beeee-Oooooh," as a foghorn voice called it on radio commercials) and halitosis, so she bathed and gargled as advised by Madison Avenue.

She liked fan magazines and women's magazines, which, among other things, informed her that if she dipped her broom in water occasionally, it would last longer, and that she should dry it in a hanging position and never stand it in a corner on its bristles.

It was she who during wartime elevated the American ritual of the "weenie roast" into the formality of the back yard barbecue with such meat-savers as slumgullion (chili without the chili powder) and spare-ribs, which, on some occasions, were purchasable without ration coupons. She learned to like liver and such things as tripe, and like her Yankee ancestors, developed delicious meals out of them.

If she was a wife living near a military post, she learned to cook good meals on a Sterno stove or a hot plate, and to conserve food without benefit of a refrigerator. Under such conditions she learned to have fun with her always-broke husband by simply sitting under a tree or taking a walk or watching a sunset or discussing a book or a recent movie. A common pastime was "planning for the future." Great dreams were built.

She liked books by Frances Parkinson Keyes and stories by Temple Bailey, Elizabeth Gouge, Brenda Conrad, Margaret E. Sangster, Nelia Gardner White, Dorothy Sanburn Phillips and Carolyn Darling.

One of her great cultural heroes was Orson Welles, whose Mercury Theatre players on October 30, 1938, had caused near panic on the East Coast by broadcasting a dramatization of H. G. Wells' fantasy, *The War of the Worlds*, over Station WABC in New York—listeners had believed Earth was being invaded by Martians. Welles, in movie theatres in 1945, was appearing in *Jane Eyre*.

Her favorite he-man on the screen depended on her age. The choice ranged from Clark Gable, the undisputed king, to Tyrone Power to Victor Mature. She shared with her husband a great admiration for the ruggedness of John Wayne who by 1945 had spent as much time in the combat uniforms of one branch of the service or another as he would have if he'd joined up with the British in 1939 and never taken a single day off. Big Duke Wayne, however, had never left Hollywood.

Younger girls wrote long letters to boys in the service whom they didn't know. Names were supplied by the USO and cooperative school boards. They, and older ladies, knitted many pairs of sometimes matched khaki socks and many more pairs of khaki mittens which were turned over to the Red Cross. Most of them tried to emulate one of their favorite movie stars in fashion, hair-style, carriage and demeanor. Sultry star Veronica Lake, who wore her long hair brushed over one eye, had to cut her tresses because so many who copied her style got their hair caught in machines. Several girls were virtually scalped.

Americans, men and women alike, thought that Norman Rockwell, whose realistic paintings graced the covers of the *Saturday Evening Post*, quite accurately defined what America was and how Americans comported themselves. His New England-flavored pictures of the family at Thanksgiving dinner, or kids around the Christmas tree, or the family seeing a soldier off on a train, or volunteers giving the old fire truck its regular Saturday bath at the fire station (with mongrel dog observing their activities closely) somehow rang true in a land that was trying to create an image for itself.

The war had given impetus to several talented and highly sophisticated writers and playwrights. These included James Agee, Clifford Odets, Sidney Kingsley, William Saroyan, Dalton Trumbo, Moss Hart and Maxwell Anderson. It presaged an era of more urbane movies with sharp dialogue and challenging themes.

For a good share of the war, however, movies were standard fare and somehow seemed to be dominated by Abbott and Costello (frequently in uniform) serving up their hoary burlesque routines in vehicles that invariably ended in a patriotic theme; and the Andrews Sisters singing close harmony to bouncy tunes in a USO or stage-door canteen or a military recreation center, invariably marching away into a fade-out to martial strains.

When Americans went to the movies they saw a newsreel, which outside the major centers had to consist of rather timeless news because it took a number of days to get the film distributed. Most such ten-minute features were saturated with propaganda, managing to leave the audience with the impression that the Japanese were subhuman and the Nazis were inhuman and that only total extermination of both breeds would permit the survival of the decent people in the free world.

A featurette that was much less slanted and relatively free of propaganda became extremely popular with movie-goers, who because of it found their horizons being widened, their perspectives broadened. It was called *The March of Time*, and was prepared by the editors of *Time* magazine. It was narrated by Westbrook Van Voorhis, whose image never appeared on screen, though he was a pleasant-faced intelligent-looking man with a military moustache (à la, say, Errol Flynn or Ronald Coleman), but his voice became known to millions, who were enthralled with his sign-off—"Time—[pause]—marches on!" He effected a resonance with the *m* in "Time" and the *n* in "on" that was virtually impossible to imitate.

Strong characterizations were taking shape in the movie scripts and in 1945 patrons were treated to such fare as *Wilson*, starring Alexander Knox; *The Story of G.I. Joe*, with Burgess Meredith portraying the beloved correspondent Ernie Pyle; *The Lost Weekend*, with Ray Milland and Jane Wyman; *Mildred Pierce*, starring Joan Crawford; *The Keys of the Kingdon*, starring Gregory Peck; *A Song to Remember*, starring Paul Muni and Merle Oberon; and *The Corn Is Green*, with Bette Davis.

Two excellent musicals were to be seen. They were *Meet Me in St. Lous* with Judy Garland and Margaret O'Brien and *Anchors Aweigh* starring Frank Sinatra, Kathryn Grayson (said to have the finest female singing voice in Hollywood) and Gene Kelly.

A Tree Grows in Brooklyn, with Joan Blondell, Dorothy McGuire and James Dunne, offered warm-hearted entertainment, pleasing to those who had not read the book and acceptable to those who had. Other good movies that year were *Laura* with Gene Tierney and Clifton Webb, *National Velvet* with Mickey Rooney and Elizabeth Taylor, *Saratoga Trunk* with Gary Cooper and Ingrid Bergman, *Spellbound* with Ingrid Bergman and Gregory Peck, *State Fair* with an all-star cast and *Valley of Decision* with Greer Garson and Gregory Peck.

For those who liked adventure there was Errol Flynn in *Objective Burma*. For those who liked the world's sexiest body and legs in combination with a pleasant singing style, there was Betty Grable singing "A Nickel's Worth of Jive" in the film *Billy Rose's Diamond Horseshoe*. For those who liked comedy there was one of the all-time bests with Danny Kaye and the graceful Vera-Ellen in *Wonder Man*. Danny Kaye's concept of a Russian baritone struggling to overcome his hay fever while singing "Otchi Tchorniya," remained in memories for years to follow. Something else again was the sturdy screen adaptation of John Hersey's book, *A Bell for Adano*, with John Hodiak as the major.

Hollywood personalities also provided interest for their fans. Starting with the youngest—Shirley Temple, age seventeen, the dimpled goldilocks who had grown up to become a silver screen bobby-soxer, married an Army Air Force physical instructor, John Agar, twenty-four, and promptly got him signed up for future roles with her studio. Judy Garland, age twenty-three, revealed she had fallen in love with the man who directed her in *Meet Me in St. Louis*, Vincente Minnelli, thirty-eight, and married him one week after she won her divorce from David Rose, the bandleader and composer ("Holiday for Strings," among many others). Mayo Methot Bogart, called "Sluggy" by her husband, Humphrey Bogart, age forty-five, won a divorce in Las

Vegas, charging extreme cruelty. It was convenient, for Bogart had already announced his engagement to his current leading lady, Lauren ("The Look") Bacall, who was to become his fourth wife.

The paperback book, born just before the war, proliferated as a device to save paper stock, and increasingly it brought pleasure not only to at-home Americans, who had to wait patiently and sometimes inactively for the war to be won, but also to Americans on duty at the outposts of civilization, for the paperback was light and inexpensive and easily mailable. Special editions of best-sellers were issued in a handy format for GI's. As a result, many reprints were read.

Readers liked and sent to best-sellerdom a number of books brought out in 1945, however. Included was one of the genuinely earthy books of the time, John Steinbeck's *Cannery Row*, a loose, amorphous, frequently candid story of some extremely strong and vibrant characters.

Kathleen Windsor's sizzling *Forever Amber*, brought out the year before, was still a best seller, and eventually reached a total sale of a million copies, alerting would-be writers everywhere to the untapped profit in stories about sex.

James Thurber, whose stories and cartoons of dogs and beleaguered males had delighted millions, brought out *The Thurber Carnival*, which among other things reintroduced a highly tickled public to *The Secret Life of Walter Mitty*. Walter Mitty, helpless in his own timidity, dreams powerful dreams of high adventure as Dr. Mitty, the famous neurosurgeon; as Commander Mitty, terror of the high seas; as Boss Mitty, the Wall Street tycoon.

More delightful nonsense was supplied readers that year with *New Yorker*-writer E. B. White's book *Stuart Little*, the story of a little mouse born to Mr. and Mrs. Frederick C. Little, a normal American couple. Adults read many meanings into the adventures of Stuart Little. Children loved him for what he was, a shy and lovable mouse who behaved very much like a normal little boy.

C. S. Forester fans—and they were legion—were delighted with the current offering in his series about Captain Horatio Hornblower. It was titled, simply, *Commodore Hornblower*, signifying a promotion for the dashing savior of the seven seas.

Sinclair Lewis contributed still another book exploring the

Midwest and boosterism—*Cass Timberlane*. It was more of a love story than Lewis' other works, and also less successful as a novel.

By far the most memorable book to hit the stalls and counters in 1945 was *Black Boy*, the autobiography of Richard Wright, thirty-six, whose forceful novel *Native Son* had been published in 1940. Already acclaimed as the most gifted living American Negro writer, Richard Wright, in 1945, was recognized as one of the greatest American writers, black or white. He brought home the passionate truth of what it was like to be a sensitive Negro youth growing up in the Deep South.

The Age of Jackson, by Arthur M. Schlesinger, Jr., which was to win the Pulitzer Prize in 1946, purportedly told the story of how Andrew ("Old Hickory") Jackson, representing the common man, kicked the Federalists out of office, and along with them financier Nicholas Biddle, but in fact drew an analogy between the forces for social change in Jackson's time and those which brought about Roosevelt and the New Deal.

Other books of the year were *The Black Rose* by Thomas B. Costain, *Captain from Castile* by Samuel Shellabarger, *Daisy Kenyon* by Elizabeth Janeway, and *The Egg and I* by Betty MacDonald.

Late in the year a university press book hit the best-seller list. It was Professor Henry DeWolf Smyth's *Atomic Energy for Military Purposes*. The Smyth report, written by the chairman of Princeton's physics department, told the story of the building of the A-Bomb.

Despite the plethora of reading fare as the war neared its end, Americans did not neglect their jukeboxes and record players. They patronized them as never before.

Musicmakers Oscar Hammerstein II and Richard Rodgers contributed several memorable tunes that year. For the film *State Fair* the pair offered "It's a Grand Night for Singing," "It Might As Well Be Spring" and "That's for Me." From *Carousel* there were the Rodgers-Hammerstein songs "If I Loved You," "June Is Bustin' Out All Over," "This Was a Real Nice Clam Bake," and "You'll Never Walk Alone."

Sammy Cahn (lyrics) and Jule Styne (music) teamed up on two very popular hits, "It's Been a Long, Long Time" and "Let It Snow! Let It Snow! Let It Snow!"

Other movies brought their share of good scores: "Aren't You Glad You're You" from *The Bells of St. Mary's*, "Dig You Later—a Hubba, Hubba, Hubba" from *Doll Face*, "Doctor, Lawyer, Indian

Chief" from *Stork Club*, "Give Me the Simple Life" from *Give Me the Simple Life*, "I Can't Begin to Tell You" from *The Dolly Sisters*, "The More I See You" from *Diamond Horseshoe*, "On the Atchison, Topeka and the Santa Fe" from *The Harvey Girls*, "Some Sunday Morning" from *San Antonio*, "You Came Along —From out of Nowhere" from *You Came Along* and "Laura" from *Laura*.

Songs that reached hit status on their own included "Autumn Serenade," "Cruising Down the River," "For Sentimental Reasons," "I'll Close My Eyes," "Love Is So Terrific," "Waitin' for the Train to Come In," "No Can Do," "Oh! What It Seemed to Be," "Rodger Young," "Symphony," "There Must Be a Way," "Till the End of Time" and "You Won't Be Satisfied."

There were two novelty songs in 1945 that gained wide popularity with the younger set. The bobby-soxers were blissfully unaware that both were, in fact, almost ancient. One of them, "One Meat Ball," was adapted from a song that was popular in Boston in the late 1850s. It in turn had been adapted from a poem in *Harper's Monthly* that had been written by an embarrassed Harvard professor who had ordered one solitary fish ball and had been told by a loud-voiced surly waiter that he couldn't have bread with it.

"Chickery Chick" ("che la, che la") was also a hit on the jukes. It, too, had an Ivy League origin. It dated back to the 1770s and was revived by students at Amherst in the 1870s for drinking parties. It was a tongue-twister and in the original version concerned a Chinese with a complicated name.

In Paris's newly reopened Opera House a new star was born, baritone Sergeant Johnny Desmond, a twenty-four-year-old Detroit boy, who simply wowed the Parisians with "I'll Be Seeing You" and "Long Ago and Far Away." They called him *"le Cremair"*—"The Creamer."

Leonard Bernstein, with his musical *On the Town* packing in crowds, took some time off to bring a triple treat to the Pittsburgh Symphony, as conductor, composer and piano soloist.

In most places where a jukebox was to be found the rest rooms were adorned with signs reflecting the fever of sloganeering that had gripped the country since Pearl Harbor. Aside from the usual recruitment posters ("Uncle Sam Needs You!") there were signs warning that waste was sabotage. Others warned: "Don't Talk!" and showed a picture of a huge ear, presumably belonging to Adolf Hitler, and admonished: "The Enemy Is Listening!" To the timid, especially little old ladies with active imaginations, these signs suggested the presence of spies everywhere, and police were kept busy with reports on suspicious-looking characters, or lights that blinked on and off unaccountably. At war's end, the FBI revealed it had collared 1,500 actual spies in the country. It didn't say how many bad leads it had followed.

Sports began to struggle back into existence in 1945, heralded with the announcement that the War Production Board, despite the energy-saving ban on the use of lights for nighttime affairs, would permit night baseball games. Shortly after that announcement, the New York Yankees came to life.

The Yankees had been on the auction block ever since the death of owner Jacob Ruppert, the beer baron, in 1939. The purchasers, it turned out, were multimillionaire Del Webb, an ex-minor-league pitcher who in 1930 moved to Phoenix and started what turned out to be an extremely successful construction business, and Dan Topping, heir to a tin-plate fortune, who was still on duty as a captain in the Marine Corps. The man who would run the Yankees as president and general manager was Colonel Leland Stanford ("Larry") MacPhail, who, it was revealed, had a lush ten-year contract. As baseball's innovative promoter, Larry MacPhail, when he was boss of the Cincinnati Reds, had painted his ballpark orange, brought in whistle-bait usherettes and introduced night baseball. More recently, as top man at the Brooklyn Dodgers, he had paid off a million dollars of debt and had won a pennant before reporting to the Army for a three-year stint.

Players who had been in uniform began to filter back onto the diamonds—Bob Feller to the Cleveland Indians, Hank Greenberg to the Detroit Tigers—often to the accompaniment of record-setting crowds to welcome them home. Greenberg's home-run hitting streak led the Tigers to the series, where they defeated the Chicago Cubs, four games to three.

In the fall, Branch Rickey, mentor of the Brooklyn Dodgers, made an announcement. He had been scouting Negro ball clubs for three seasons past, he said, and he had decided to sign on a man he thought was a great player, Jackie Roosevelt Robinson, former all-America halfback at UCLA, who had been playing sensational shortstop for the Kansas City Monarchs of the Negro American League.

The first Negro player in the major leagues knew that a special burden rested on him. Modestly he said, "There is no possible chance I will funk it for any other reason than that I am not good enough." He turned out to be better than merely "good enough."

As in 1944, the football season was one of the most avidly watched on record, and as in 1944, the team most watched was Army, whose two sensational backs, Felix ("Doc") Blanchard and Glenn ("Junior") Davis, held forth with lightninglike terpsichorean specialties, seemingly untouchable to opposing players.

Army, ranked No. 1, trekked to South Bend to face Notre Dame, ranked No. 2, and came away with a 48-0 victory. A couple of weeks later, Army went to Penn State, and chalked up a 61-0 victory. In the traditional Thanksgiving Day Army-Navy game before 102,000 fans in Philadelphia's Municipal Stadium, Blanchard scored three touchdowns and Davis ran across for two, giving the Army another unbeaten season with the final score Army 32, Navy 13.

The U.S. Golf Association did not schedule the U.S. Open for 1945. One reason: there were no golf balls. Prewar golf balls were selling as high as $60 a dozen, and very few were to be found. Reprocessed golf balls, some of which had gone through the rejuvenating mill three times, were getting scarce. A WPB directive permitting the manufacture of 500,000 dozen new golf balls with synthetic rubber centers could in no way meet the customary annual demand of 3 million dozen new balls. Besides, experts found that those with neoprene centers fell fifteen yards short on a 225-yard drive.

On Broadway there were some excellent and well-patronized shows. These included Tennessee Williams' *Glass Menagerie, Carousel, On the Town* and Maurice Evans in *Hamlet*.

20

Mild Man from Missouri
1945

He was a slightly built man, lean, bespectacled. He wore carefully cut gray hair, and appeared to be a neat, cautious dresser. He was nervous, as anyone would be under the circumstances, and he looked worried. His hazel eyes reflected an expression of sadness and extreme gravity.

It took only one minute for Chief Justice Harlan Fiske Stone to administer the oath of office. It was 7 o'clock at night at the White House. Eleanor Roosevelt and Steve Early had left to fly to Warm Springs. Members of the cabinet had streamed in, along with the heads of the war agencies. The White House secretariat was dissolved in grief.

Harry S. Truman, the thirty-third President of the United States, made no bold statements, pledged no great promises. He shook hands gravely and turned to the great mahogany desk in the oval study that had been Franklin Roosevelt's until that day. It was cleared of the knickknacks that FDR had collected and treasured. On it now were Harry Truman's things, a worn Bible, a thesaurus, showing evidence of much use, and a thumbed, leather-bound pictorial history of the United States. Nothing else. It was a place to work.

The sixty-year-old man sat down gingerly. Someone showed him what the three buttons were for, and how they summoned secretaries. (He never did care to use the buttons, but preferred to go to the door and request a secretary to step into his office.)

The new President was well-known on Capitol Hill, having been in the Senate since 1934. But only in recent years had the public been learning of the man. He had made a nationwide name for himself as head of the Senate investigating committee that bore his name. The Truman committee was credited with keeping the war effort as honest as possible, and this was conceded to be a Herculean task.

Son of a Missouri farmer, Harry S. (the S was an initial only;

Harry was given no middle name) Truman went through high school only, and then set about making a living. The farm did not attract him and he went to Kansas City. He was a timekeeper for the Santa Fe Railroad. He wrapped newspapers for the *Kansas City Star*. He clerked for a while in two banks. He didn't like any of those jobs and decided that the farm wasn't so bad after all. He returned home, donned denims, and went to work. It had taken him five years to learn that he didn't like the city. He stayed on the farm from 1906 until he was mobilized in the National Guard in World War I.

A longtime guardsman, he was sent to France as a captain in the artillery. He won a commendation for coolness under fire (a quality he was to display as well in the White House) and returned home as a captain. At the time of his ascendancy to the presidency and commander in chief, he held a colonel's commission in the Army Reserve.

After the war, Harry returned home to Independence, Missouri, and in June of 1919 married Miss Bess Wallace. With added responsibilities, he decided to join with a friend and open a haberdashery in Kansas City. It failed.

At about this time he became interested in politics and soon got to be a county judge—an administrative post, not a judicial one. For a number of years he remained a minor politician until Boss Pendergast decided to run him for the Senate. With Pendergast's nearly absolute control of the state's political machinery, it was as simple and as easy as that. In 1940, Harry S. Truman was elected to his second six-year term.

As he began his second term, the nation was gearing up for defense and the frenzy with which government money was being thrown around evoked strong memories in Harry Truman of the great waste during World War I. With the patriotic zeal of a veteran and the zest of a politician who sees his big chance, Truman organized the Senate investigating committee that bore his name.

For four years he scouted out shortages, prodded up production, made manufacturers and the Army and Navy strictly accountable for the money spent on the war, and in that short time, Harry Truman's name became known from coast to coast. By the time the 1944 Democratic convention rolled around, Roosevelt had considered him a logical choice for second place on the ballot.

281

Now, on April 12, 1945, he was President. The people of the world were anxious to discover just what kind of man he really was. They didn't have to wait long.

First of all, the White House secretariat learned that he was an early riser and unvarying in his punctuality. If he scheduled a caller for 9:30 A.M., he was waiting for him. If another was scheduled for 9:45, the President was through with the first caller and was awaiting the next. He was as neat about his offices as he was about his person. There was no clutter in Harry Truman's life.

Those who had to deal with him found him plain-spoken, direct, decisive, unshakably midwestern in his manner and view, solid, though not stolid. He was Apple Pie American. He had no time for sophistry or cant.

They found him calm, even-tempered, hard to rile. They liked his wry humor and blunt similes. They liked it when he revealed that before dinner he favored a bourbon with branch water. That was, after all, a native American drink.

Harry Truman had inherited more than the presidency. He was heir to a war. He went about his business with calm efficiency.

He set the tone of his administration on his first day of work when he greeted the press corps by shaking hands all around and asking: "Did you ever have a bull or a load of hay fall on you? If you have, you know how I felt last night. I felt as though two planets and the whole constellation had fallen on me. I don't know if you boys pray, but if you do, please pray God to help me carry this load."

That was Harry Truman, the new man at 1600 Pennsylvania Avenue, blunt, to the point, no sham or pretense.

The war that Harry Truman inherited was unmistakably headed for victory. As he took the oath of office, American, British, Canadian and French troops had crossed the Rhine at numerous points and were spreading out into Germany. General George S. Patton, Jr.'s Third Army was lancing toward Berlin. On the Eastern Front, the Russians were storming and recapturing Vienna, the Austrian capital of 2 million that the Nazis had decided to doom. A new commander in chief but an old artilleryman, he knew that it wouldn't be long before the final white flag was delivered by the Nazis.

In the Pacific, the Allies had begun to close in on Japan. In bold, island-hopping moves, they had taken the Solomons, New Guinea, the Gilberts, the Marshalls, the Marianas, and finally the Philippines. MacArthur had returned to Corregidor. Now, as the new commander in chief took over, the U.S. Navy had assembled the largest fleet in the history of man to capture Okinawa, from which it would be possible easily to carry out aerial bombing of Japan.

In the spring of 1945 there were some amusing tidbits from the battle areas to cheer and titillate the folks on the home front.

One such was the story of Marine Sergeant Willson Price, a Navajo who succeeded in completely baffling the Japanese by developing a code based on the Navajo language. In the entire Pacific area, throughout the war, the Americans had been troubled because it seemed apparent that the Japanese had cracked the U.S. code. More, the Japs had highly skilled and seasoned teams of men who could not only listen to American radio and telephone messages, but could intercept them and relay them inaccurately. They had Japanese who spoke in Brooklynese, Deep South, midwestern, New England, Plains western, Texas, and even Lake States accents. They could drop their *r*'s like a Bostonian, slur them like an Alabaman, flatten their *a*'s like a Michigander saying "waater" or speak of "erl tankers" like native New Yorkers.

The Yanks had taken to using words with a lot of *l*'s in them as most Japanese had difficulty pronouncing the *l*. But Sergeant Price went one step further and developed a Navajo code, and the Marines immediately assigned 200 additional Navajos to monitor the circuits. The Japs never figured it out, even after they discovered it was Navajo, and the story had been printed.

(Master Sergeant Willson Price retired from the Marines in the summer of 1972 after thirty years of service. He accepted his honorable discharge in San Diego with plans to open a television repair shop in Santa Ana, California.)

Then came the story from Europe of how the Germans had raged against the defense lines at Bastogne in the Belgian Bulge with a force that outnumbered the Americans four to one, but sustained losses that outnumbered American casualties four to one.

In the foxholes around Bastogne's perimeter were officers and men of the 101st Airborne Division (the Screaming Eagles) of Patton's Third Army and they knew their business. On the first night of the attack the Germans succeeded in rendering a blow that could literally cripple any fighting force—they captured the entire U.S. surgical unit. The wounded Americans would have to shift for themselves.

For nearly a week the Germans circled the completely surrounded town, firing round after round of artillery into its center. In the dark cellars, the wounded crouched alongside the civilians—some 3,000 of them. Yet, whenever the Nazi forces probed, they encountered fierce Americans who exacted great costs in lives. It was like probing into a huge nest of rattlers.

Finally, tired of the "insane Americans," the German commander experimented. He sent a team through the lines carrying a white sheet and a surrender proposal. The offer: surrender within two hours. The choice: "annihilation by artillery." It was delivered to Brigadier General Anthony Clement McAuliffe, acting commander. He gave the order a quick scan, sat down at his small, littered desk and wrote out a reply:

> To The German Commander:
> NUTS!
> The American Commander

He handed it to the envoy.

"Vas is das?" he asked.

For the blindfolded German, the American interpreter provided enlightenment. "It means the same as 'GO TO HELL,'" he said.

Next day a line of Sherman tanks rolled into Bastogne. The lead tank's turret opened and out popped a bandaged head sporting a huge black eye, but the man gave the proper password. The man with the shiner was Lieutenant Colonel Creighton ("Abe") Abrams, commander of the 4th Armored Divison's rescue force.

About this time, too, there was circulated the story of how General Patton—the true Hollywood hero of the war in Europe—got the rain to stop during the offensive that was launched in the winter by Nazi General von Rundstedt.

Rundstedt had scheduled his offensive wisely, apparently timing it when a long rainy spell was predicted. No Allied planes flew. Tanks that were desperately needed to check the Nazi assault were bogged down in mud.

On the third day of this frustration, Patton called in one of his chaplains.

"I want a prayer to stop this rain," the general ordered. "If we got a couple of clear days we could get in there and kill a couple hundred thousand of those krauts."

"Well, sir," said the chaplain, "it's not exactly in the realm of theology to pray for something that would help to kill fellow men."

"What the hell are you—a theologian or an officer of the U.S. Third Army?" Patton roared. "I want that prayer!"

The prayer was forthcoming. It was printed on small cards and distributed to the troops. Next day the sun shone. Von Rundstedt's offensive was smashed.

Tales like these, apocryphal or true, cheered and entertained home-fronters, who by the spring of 1945 were almost as weary of the war as the men on the fighting fronts. As Rosie struggled out of bed at 5 A.M. to get to her riveting job at 6, she had to remind herself how tough it was for the man with the gun whom she was replacing on the production line, and how weary the British must be, who had been at war since 1939. The war seemed more than ever like an especially stubborn toothache, unrelievable, unending.

It showed in the faces of citizens, more and more of whom returned at night to homes that displayed a black-bordered serviceman's flag in the window. Americans, without realizing it, had acquired a pinched and tired look as though harassed by great and mystical powers beyond the control of man. The figures were piling up: Official Army and Navy reports listed 1,002,887 casualties. More than 600,000 American men and women had been wounded; more than 60,000 were missing; more than 75,000 were listed as prisoners; more than 250,000 had died in battle. People remembered that World War I dead had totaled 126,000.

The headlines showed that the war was being won. The Russians were closing in on Berlin. The American and British Allies had the Nazis bottled up before the city. Okinawa was under siege. Then, in the last week of April, came news of the inglorious end of Benito Mussolini, the first of the Fascist dictators. To the angry, still-battling Allies, it was a satisfying death.

In early 1945 the German Army still controlled northern Italy, but it was retreating fast. With the Nazis, living under an uncertain kind of house arrest, was Benito Mussolini, who had been forced out of power by his crumbling government back in 1943. With Mussolini was his mistress, Clara Petacci, the twenty-five-year-old daughter of a Rumanian family.

On Sunday, April 22, Milan's railway workers went out on strike, obviously the beginning of a revolt against the German garrison in the city. By Wednesday, April 25, demonstrations against Germans and Fascists were in full force. A group of Italian partisans went to Mussolini's rooms and demanded that he surrender to them.

"The Germans have betrayed me," he shouted. Then he asked for one hour's time in which to complain to the German High Command. The extension was granted, and Mussolini and Clara Petacci seized the gift of time to flee into the hills. At 9 P.M. he was spotted near Lake Como on the Swiss border, apparently intent on getting into the "safety" of Germany.

At 6 o'clock the next morning, April 26, Mussolini and his ladyfriend, disguised in German officers' overcoats, joined a German truck convoy and headed northward. He got as far as the village of Dongo when he was spotted by partisans and held for arrest.

A partisan commander known only as "Eduardo" sent ten men and an officer to handle the affair. They found Mussolini and Miss Petacci in a cottage on a hillside overlooking the village. The Duce, spotting the men, thought they had come to free him.

Coldly, the partisan chief informed the dictator that he was under arrest.

"Let me save my life," he pleaded, "and I'll give you an empire." The men laughed. Busily they rounded up the other members of the Duce's party, sixteen in all, and bundled them off to the village.

Mussolini had already been tried in absentia and found guilty and sentenced to death. The other sixteen *Fascisti* were "tried" on the spot, and also sentenced to death.

The dictator, his mistress and the sixteen were lined up before a firing squad. Mussolini's last words were: "No! No!"

The bodies of the eighteen were loaded into a moving van and trucked off to Milan, where, at 3 A.M. Friday, they were ignominiously dumped into the Piazza Loreto square. All Friday morning the Milanese came and looked at the bodies. Then they erected a scaffold and hanged Mussolini and Miss Petacci by their feet. All day long, and all Saturday, people came and spat upon the swinging upended corpses. No one bothered to protect the blonde Miss Petacci's modesty. Many men raged past to kick at the dictator's shaven head. A woman appeared with a pistol and emptied it into the cadaver of the dictator. "Five shots," she cried. "One for each of my murdered sons!"

Next day the corpses were dragged through the streets like sacks of potatoes, and delivered to a mortuary.

It had been twenty-two years earlier in Milan, not far from Piazza Loreto, that Mussolini had launched his Black Shirt march on Rome to become the first Fascist dictator.

Two days after Mussolini was taken captive, Russian forces advancing from the east closed in on the Reich Chancellery building housing the government in Berlin, and that same day Adolf Hitler closeted himself with his mistress, Eva Braun, in a bunker deep in the heart of the ruined building, and committed suicide.

Within two days, two of Europe's dictators had perished. The war was speeding to an end like a Hollywood melodrama.

Totally defeated, Germany struggled on for a few days more, then, on May 6, capitulated; two days later, May 8, its representatives signed the articles of unconditional surrender in bomb-devastated Berlin. V-E Day had come. Europe's war was over.

It was Harry Truman's sixty-first birthday, and the natal gift was peace, or at least the approach of peace. He had known that V-E Day was coming and for a week had been prepared with his speech. In the Oval Room, flanked by his family, his cabinet and his aides, Harry Truman first read his speech to an assemblage of about 200 newspapermen. Then, at 9 A.M. eastern war time (2 P.M. Berlin time), he went on the radio and informed the nation that V-E Day had come. His voice was clear, unemotional, matter-of-fact. He began: "The Allied armies, through sacrifice and devotion and with God's help . . ."

Though it was early morning, America began a frenzied celebration. The streets filled. School classes were dismissed. Horns and noisemakers were scouted from attics. Members of marching bands got together and began impromptu parades. Offices were emptied and their usual occupants tumbled out into ever-thickening crowds. War plants cut back on their frantic schedules and released workers to join in the fun.

Servicemen in uniform were seized and hugged and kissed by

women passersby and embraced in bear hugs by men who were openly crying in jubilation. Bars and taverns rapidly filled up and mayors of some cities considered ordering emergency closing, then thought better of it.

In the bigger cities radios were hooked up to amplifiers and the news was blared out into the streets. New York's Times Square became so jammed by noontime that those few who did want to return to work couldn't get through. Caught in the crush of cheering, shouting, yelling people, they gave up and joined in the celebrating. The joyful news flashed in lights around and around Times Tower.

The radios carried accounts of the celebrations in London, in Paris, in Montreal, in Toronto, in Vancouver, in Amsterdam, in Stockholm. There was even a broadcast from Moscow. The Allied world went wild with joy.

In stateside military posts, enlisted personnel were confined, lest they be tempted to overcelebrate. The PX's did remain open later than usual, however.

Harry S. Truman had been in office twenty-six days when V-E Day was celebrated. There were big things ahead, among them the signing of the charter of the United Nations and the Potsdam Conference with Churchill and Stalin. Senators Tom Connally and Arthur Vandenberg were already in San Francisco, helping draft the UN charter.

In the last week of June, while Washington broiled and steamed under a locked-in heat wave, Harry Truman slipped off for a week's relaxation. He went to another Washington, one with a more amenable summertime climate. As the guest of State of Washington Governor Mon Wallgren, an old Senate buddy, the President put aside the cares of office, taking long walks in the fir-scented air, trying a hand (unsuccessfully) at fishing in Puget Sound in a stretch of water famed for its salmon, and paid a visit to Governor Wallgren at the State Capitol, where he sat down at the organ under the great dome and played Beethoven's Minuet in G and the "Blackhawk Waltz." When this was well received, the President, the governor and Press Secretary Charlie Ross sang (to Mr. Truman's accompaniment) "Peggy O'Neill" and "Melancholy Baby."

From Tacoma, the President went to San Francisco to witness the scene that, more than any other, Franklin Roosevelt had wanted to see, the signing of the World Charter of the United

Nations. It would have to be ratified by the various nations, but that seemed assured. Truman knew that his own Senate was strongly in favor of it. A world organization to keep the peace was now in existence.

The Japanese were resisting bitterly in the Pacific. They were exacting a tremendous toll from Allied soldiers in their island-hopping course to the invasion of the Japanese mainland. Only now were the reports on the excessively high casualty figures coming back to the home front. Printed in just about every periodical in the free world was the combat photograph of four marines raising the Stars and Stripes atop Mt. Suribachi on Iwo Jima. It had been taken by Associated Press photographer Joe Rosenthal of San Francisco, a slight, bespectacled man of thirty-three, who was to win the Pulitzer for his picture—a candid shot.

It was a graphic reminder of the fierceness of the fighting in the Pacific and the toll in American lives.

As Truman returned from San Francisco to Washington he received word that at last Okinawa had fallen to the Americans. The Japanese, said Fleet Admiral Chester Nimitz, had ended all "organized resistance." That meant that pockets of resistance continued and that a mopping-up operation was underway. The cost of the island, needed as the last jumping-off place to Kyushu, Japan's southernmost main island, 370 miles away, was: Japan—98,564 men killed and 4,500 captured; U.S.—6,990 dead or missing, and 29,598 wounded.

The President also knew that much of Tokyo had been bombed to the ground. Over 46 percent of the built-up area of the city had been reduced to ashes and more than 4.5 million people who had lived in the area were homeless. But still the Japanese fought on, fiercer than ever before, in their determination to stave off the ultimate defeat.

On President Truman's desk was the most highly confidential report of all time. It detailed the findings of a group of American scientists of a long and costly research project to solve the secret of atomic fission, a project that Truman, when he was a cost-cutting senator, was completely ignorant of.

The report told of plans to explode an atomic bomb in the desert at Alamogordo, New Mexico.

As he prepared for a leisurely eight-day cruise to the Potsdam Conference, President Truman issued orders for the continued build-up of the biggest invasion fleet ever assembled in any waters, 1,400 ships and 100,000 men, but he also told the scientists to go ahead with their experimental detonation of the A-bomb.

On the day he arrived at Potsdam, July 16, he was notified by code that the Alamogordo test had been made that day and that it was highly successful.

President Truman was face to face with the gravest decision ever to confront a leader of men or nations.

21

The New Age Dawns

It may have started as early as 1939 in Germany. That's about the time that American and British scientists began to give some thought to splitting the atom. In 1941 the British had recognized the potential power of nuclear fission and had set top scientists to work on it in great secrecy. In the most confidential exchange of verbal information in the war, Winston Churchill had told Franklin Roosevelt of the British project.

The following year, 1942, a British-Norwegian volunteer force conducted a raid on a port in Norway and discovered a heavy-water plant where the Germans were busily engaged in creating an essential constituent of a nuclear weapon. Churchill conferred with his scientists, and then with Roosevelt. The only conclusion that could be drawn was that the Nazis were a bit ahead of both the British and Americans in exploring the atom. Worse, Britain, threatened with invasion at any time, subjected to nightly bombing raids, was hardly the place to experiment with the chain effects of nuclear reaction.

Roosevelt had already suggested that the British, Canadians and Americans pool their scientific brains and set up a project in the United States to see it through to its finish. There was a precedent for this. The British had invented radar in the war's earliest days and finding no place to manufacture it, had sent it first to Canada, then to the United States, sharing its secret with both.

Quickly the plans were drafted to consolidate the work in the United States and the War Department was handed the most supersecret assignment of all time. It was known as the Manhattan Project. It had first call for any military specialists. If a civilian specialist was needed he was simply appropriated. Mathematicians, chemists, physicists and other scientists began to disappear from laboratory, industrial plant and classroom, all to report to the "Manhattan Engineer District," most of them in total ignorance of what it was. The physicists knew that back in 1939 Roosevelt had appointed an Advisory Committee on

Uranium, but since nothing had been heard of it since, it was assumed that it had petered out, and surely that it had nothing to do with a Manhattan "Engineering" (as it was called) District. Of the 65,000 persons who ultimately worked on the Manhattan Project, very few knew, until the end, the purpose of their labors.

The top physicists, who did know, were horrified at the thought of what they were doing, but they knew that if the Allies didn't get there first, the results would be even more horrible to contemplate.

Where was the Manhattan Project? It was taking form in Oak Ridge, Tennessee; at Pasco, Washington; at the University of Chicago; at Los Alamos, New Mexico; at dozens of isolated laboratories in industrial plants and universities; and in quiet, isolated rooms in the facilities of Eastman Kodak, E. I. du Pont de Nemours and Company, Union Carbide and others.

Reports on the progress, coming in piecemeal, were channeled only to Franklin Roosevelt and thence to Winston Churchill and Canada's prime minister, MacKenzie King. Important discoveries were reported from the University of Chicago, where the project was called the "Metallurgical laboratory." Heading it was Dr. Arthur H. Compton. He was assisted by nuclear physicist Enrico Fermi.

In Oak Ridge, Tennessee, huge plants were constructed, housing strange machinery. A new city sprang up around this mysterious industrial complex. It was called Dogpatch, after the hometown of Al Capp's comicstrip character, Li'l Abner. It was in the Oak Ridge facility, in an atmosphere resembling a staging area, that scientists produced the supply of U-235 that would be used to detonate the first bomb.

Meanwhile, on a squash court underneath the stands of the University of Chicago's football field, scientists working only scant feet away from strolling students, manufactured the supply of plutonium that would be the ultimate explosive. Taking form was the world's first atomic pile. It was a strange apparatus, graphite bricks with uranium embedded in their corners. The scientists were exploring deep into unknown and perilous territory, guided on a theory only. The idea was that as the bricks were set in place there would come a certain point when the chain reaction would start spontaneously. Hopefully it could be stopped short of "critical mass" or holocaust by the insertion of cadmium strips or rods to break the chain.

The reaction started. Instruments gave an alarm. It was going too quickly. The cadmium strips were inserted. The reaction was stopped, a split second before disaster. The Atomic Age was born. It was a spine-chilling experiment; the first necessary step. Years of theory had at last resulted in tangible proof.

As the Fermi experiments were being conducted, work was being rushed on a gigantic plutonium plant near Yakima, Washington. Plutonium might replace uranium as an explosive. It was highly secret, of course, so secret that those working on construction of the plant had no idea of what they were building and even the architects and superintendents couldn't inform them, but nevertheless, the scientists there were obliged to call in more physicists. The reason: exploration of the unknown.

According to nuclear theory, the atomic piles should generate radiation at once, thus creating radioactive elements whose nature was unknown, perhaps dangerous and poisonous to any form of life. It was believed that a working atomic pile could never again be approached.

What was needed, therefore, was a method for operating "piles" by remote control, where the operators would be working behind absolutely impervious protective shields. Accordingly, the possessors of some of the most imaginative brains of the world were collected, screened, and put to work. The assignment: a safe manufacturing process for plutonium, to make the atom bomb.

Brand-new elements managed to escape and plague the experimenters. These isotopes were dangerous, all the more terrifying because it was not known exactly what their "half-life" might be. The cooling water was found to be radioactive and it had to be purified before being released back into the river. A gadget was invented to measure radioactive dust in the air. Geiger counters ticked off the level of radiation in corridors. Workers had to be checked constantly to guard against contamination. All workmen wore special badges containing film. This film, when developed, would reveal radiation contamination.

While the huge plants for production were being built, another group of distinguished physicists, headed by Professor J. Robert Oppenheimer of the University of California, assembled at the New Mexican town of Los Alamos. They were to put together, and try out the science fiction weapon—the A-Bomb. Up to now the work on splitting the atom had been ticklish business. To the Los Alamos men it was deadly. Not only was there the danger of blowing up their own unit, but the transcending fear that, with one mistake, they might blow up the United States, the Earth, or even the Solar System.

On the morning of July 16, when Harry Truman was at Potsdam, the Los Alamos physicists gathered in a ranch house near Alamogordo on the New Mexican desert. Tensely they watched while physicist Robert Bacher, formerly of Cornell University, made the final connections.

The bomb was clamped down to a steel tower laden with measuring devices. More than five miles away the scientists lay flat on the ground behind an earthen embankment, their eyes shielded by black goggles, and waited.

Dawn had barely come to the desert. A hovering thunderstorm gnashed its teeth and moved away toward the hills in the distance. At an instrument panel dug into the cold sand a radio voice counted out destiny: "Minus six minutes, minus five minutes, minus four minutes." At "minus forty-five *seconds*," machines took over the controls. The watchers dug deeper into the sand; the next fifteen seconds were the tensest moments of their lives.

Then suddenly, there was an unbelievable roar—sustained, earth-rocking. The entire world seemed filled with the brightest light man had ever seen. In Albuquerque, nearly 125 miles distant, the sky was bright as high noon on a cloudless day.

The scientists, peering anxiously over their barricade, saw an enormous pillar of colored cloud and fire belching eight miles into the sky.

Where the bomb had been detonated there was a gaping, smouldering crater. There was nothing remaining of the tower and concrete blocks. The heat, at five miles, was unbearable, and the scientists hugged the cool sand, their special protective clothing protecting them from burns.

At Potsdam, with the results of the Alamogordo test in his mind—and knowing that Clement Attlee, Britain's new prime minister, also had been informed of the accomplishments in the desert—Truman sat down to help shape postwar policy. The

Japanese war would be pressed to its conclusion, with the Allies accepting nothing but unconditional surrender. Four armies, British, French, Russian and American, would occupy defeated Germany under the command of Supreme Allied Headquarters, whose chief was to be General Dwight D. Eisenhower.

The Truman policy took form at Potsdam. In broadest terms, it was to offer friendly help and guidance in ending the differences that plagued America's European friends, and at the same time to offer substance and practical assistance in putting Europe back on its feet. There would be no "Morgenthau Plan" (a study commissioned by Roosevelt) depriving Germany of all industry and turning it into an agricultural economy. Instead there would be tangible help from still-rich America to clean up the devastation and rebuild modern nations in France, Germany, Italy and—of course—in Britain.

Flying in the plane that had carried Franklin Roosevelt to earlier Big Three meetings, President Truman had left Antwerp and swept at low altitude over ravaged northeastern France and northwestern Germany, and he knew that the task of reconstruction would be gigantic.

In Potsdam Castle, where the Russians had planted a profusion of red flowers in the shape of a giant star, Harry Truman sat down at a circular mahogany table with Premier Josef Stalin and Prime Minister Winston Churchill (to be replaced later by the new British Premier, Clement Attlee) to enunciate his policy, the policy that was to become the spirit and the scope of the Potsdam Conference. It was the first time since Woodrow Wilson went to Versailles twenty-seven years earlier, that a U.S. President had journeyed abroad in the quest for peace.

Before he came home, President Truman was confronted with a terrible problem. The Japanese were defeated but they would not quit. Repeated bombing strikes at Tokyo and other major industrial centers had leveled the buildings but not the spirit of the Japanese people. Then came an intelligence report: The Japanese had amassed an army of 2 million men in the vicinity of Tokyo to fight off the impending invasion.

Quickly, Truman asked for estimates of casualties from such an invasion in light of the latest intelligence. The figures were astronomical for Americans, even greater for Japanese.

With the weapon that would surely end the war, was he not

morally obligated to use it and put an end to this slaughter? Harry Truman made a decision.

The dreadful new bomb was flown to a spot in the Pacific and transferred to the U.S.S. *Indianapolis*, which landed them at Saipan on July 26. Then, quickly, the plans were made.

The Potsdam Conference ended on August 2 and President Truman flew home the next day. Quickly he checked with Saipan and learned that the bomb was ready. Again he checked with his military advisers. The Japanese were resisting more doggedly than ever and were battling fiercely in China and Indochina.

Truman gave the order that only he could issue.

On the morning of August 6, one lone Superfortress flew toward Hiroshima. Aboard were ten people, including one newspaperman, the brilliant William L. Laurence, science writer for the *New York Times*. All wore welder's goggles to protect them from what they knew would be blinding light.

The bomb-run over the city was short. At exactly 9:15 A.M., Major Thomas Ferebee, bombardier, pressed a toggle switch. "Bomb away," he reported, as the single missile dropped toward Earth. Colonel Paul Warfield Tibbets, the pilot, took back the controls. He banked the plane to turn her broadside to the city below. All eyes strained through the black goggles and the plexiglass windows.

It took less than sixty seconds, then the men aboard the big B-29, which was named *Enola Gay*, were literally struck by the great white flash of light, stronger by far than the light of the morning sun. It was so strong that the men reported feeling a "visual shock."

A few seconds later the shock wave from the blast reached the *Enola Gay*, now several miles away, and tossed it like a toy plane made of balsa wood. What did the crew say at this momentous point in history, the dawn of an entirely new era? It is recorded that they looked back in silence. One said, "My God!" It seemed the only fitting remark.

Bill Laurence wrote up what the men of the *Enola Gay* saw, though his story was not to be released by the Army until a month had passed:

A giant ball of fire rose as from the bowels of the earth. Then a pillar of purple fire, 10,000 feet high, shooting skyward. At one stage it assumed the form of a giant square totem pole, with its base about three miles long. Its bottom was brown, its center amber, its top white. Then, just when it appeared as though the thing had settled down, there came shooting out of the top a giant mushroom that increased the height of the pillar to a total of 45,000 feet. The mushroom top was even more alive than the pillar, sizzling upward, a thousand Old Faithful geysers rolled into one.

Hiroshima had been the home of more than 325,000 people, and there were thousands more in a nearby quartermaster depot. In the instant of the bomb's explosion, 80,000 people died, according to estimates made by the United States at the time, though the Japanese government later revised the figure upward to 200,000 persons, including those who died of aftereffects from the holocaust of nuclear fire. Many simply vanished from the earth, only their shadows, captured photographically by the strange other worldly light of nuclear radiation, remained, eerie pavement runners of the last days of the city. Many others were cooked where they stood, their clothes burned off, each body bloated into one huge blister.

Many buildings merely disappeared into vapor or dust. Thousands were leveled. All greenery of any kind vanished for miles. A total of 4.1 square miles—60 percent of the city's built-up area—was completely destroyed.

Next day President Truman asked for air time to make an important announcement:

> Sixteen hours ago, an American airplane dropped one bomb on Hiroshima, an important Japanese army base. That bomb had more power than 20,000 tons of TNT. It is an atomic bomb. It is a harnessing of the basic power of the universe. What has been done is the greatest achievement of organized science in history.

It took no mathematician to realize that with the new, dreadful weapon, one plane could wreak the destruction that it would have taken 2,000 B-29s to do only twenty-four hours earlier.

Of the Japanese, President Truman observed:

"If they do not now accept our terms, they may expect a rain of ruin from the air, the like of which has never been seen on this earth."

There could be no question that the President of the United States meant what he said. Still the Japanese remained mute.

Three days after the bomb was dropped on Hiroshima, another Superfortress, the *Great Artiste*, set out on a similar mission, the destination, Kokura, another industrial complex. Bad weather had broken out over the coast of Japan and when he got to Kokura, Major Charles W. Sweeney found that it was socked in solid. He had just enough gas to try for one run over his second-choice target, Nagasaki. The bomb-run was begun on instruments, but then, right over the target, there was a hole in the clouds so that the bombardier, Captain Kermit K. Beahan, was able to aim by sight.

This was a more powerful and more "efficient" bomb than the one dropped on Hiroshima. Plutonium had been used instead of uranium, and there was an improved detonating system. Three days after its use, the first atom bomb was already shelved as obsolete.

The new bomb exploded near ground-level and blasted a gaping crater. The crater contained some of its destructiveness. It leveled only one square mile of the Kyushu seaport, but it killed 35,000 people and injured 60,000.

Truman waited for what he knew must come, a Japanese appeal for peace.

Four days after the bomb-drop at Hiroshima, early in the morning, just as the President was about to leave his rooms in the White House, a War Department messenger arrived with a radio dispatch that had been broadcast by Radio Tokyo and picked up on the West Coast and teletyped to the Pentagon. It was not official, but it was the most joyous news Harry Truman could imagine ever receiving. He read the message:

> In obedience to the gracious command of His Majesty the Emperor, the Japanese Government are ready to accept the terms enumerated at Potsdam on July 26, 1945 with the understanding that the said declaration does not comprise any demand which prejudices the prerogative of His Majesty as a sovereign ruler. The Japanese Government hope sincerely that this . . .

There it stopped, broken off in mid-sentence.

President Truman knew that the real message from the Japanese government, the offer to surrender, was en route through diplomatic channels. He went on about his day's work.

One of his first appointments of the day was with Representative Mike Mansfield of Montana, a congressional expert on Asian affairs. Mansfield did not believe that the United States should guarantee to leave intact the "prerogatives of His Majesty as a sovereign ruler." Truman said that's the way he felt, too.

With various callers during the day, the President checked over those "prerogatives" that the Japanese wanted preserved for the emperor. In the main, there were four:

1. The emperor was to remain the central authority of civilian government.

2. The emperor was to remain as supreme commander of the Army and Navy.

3. The emperor continued to have supreme authority in foreign affairs, which included declarations of war and the making of treaties, including treaties of surrender.

4. The emperor was to remain head of the state religion (Shintoism).

It was the first three prerogatives that bothered the President. Yet it was the imperial issue that meant he would have to continue the war or accept a compromise peace. Truman saw that there was no way to conclude the war without unconditional surrender. At last the official version of the Japanese offer arrived through channels. The President turned it over to the Department of State.

It was about twenty-seven hours after Radio Tokyo's offer had first been read by Mr. Truman that transmitters in Saipan, Honolulu and San Francisco beamed directly to Tokyo were broadcasting the Secretary of State's reply. The official version, meanwhile, was going back through the diplomatic pipelines. The State Department message said:

> From the moment of surrender the authority of the Emperor and the Japanese Government to rule the state shall be subject to the supreme commander of the Allied powers, who will take such steps as he deems proper to effectuate the surrender terms.

The Emperor will be required to authorize and insure the signature of the surrender terms and shall issue his commands to all the Japanese military, naval and air authorities to cease active operations and to surrender their arms.

The ultimate form of government of Japan shall, in accordance with the Potsdam declaration, be established by the freely-expressed will of the Japanese people.

The armed forces of the Allied powers will remain in Japan until the purposes set forth in the Potsdam declaration are achieved.

It was to require seventeen hours for the official version to get to Tokyo through the sluggish diplomatic channels, but it wasn't long after it arrived that President Truman got his answer. He called in the press and said, simply:

"I have received this afternoon a message from the Japanese Government, a full acceptance of unconditional surrender."

Official records show that the Japanese sued for surrender on August 10. It wasn't until four days later, however, that the President of the United States could announce officially that the Japanese had accepted unconditional surrender.

It was three years, eight months and seven days after the sneak attack on Pearl Harbor. More than 75,000 American lives had been expended in the Pacific. Japanese casualties were calculated to be 1,219,000.

It was at 7 P.M. Washington time that President Truman made the momentous announcement, a time agreed upon with London and Moscow, but millions of Americans knew the news was coming. There had been intimations of it all day on the radio. Moreover, they could *sense* it.

Thousands had gathered outside the White House, pressed up in a solid mass against the fence, and chanting "We Want Truman! We Want Truman! We Want Truman!" Again, Times Square was packed with people, waiting for the news to be flashed in the traveling letters atop the old Times building. America prepared, waited, for its own "private" war to end.

A few moments after 7 P.M. eastern war time (an hour ahead of standard time) the news was official. Throughout the continent, great cheering erupted. From Key West to Bellingham, from Eastport to San Diego, from Glace Bay to Vancouver, a whole people went mad with joy. There was dancing in the streets. Bars served free drinks to whatever servicemen could be dragged in off the streets, some of them adolescent teetotalers. The horns on harbor vessels filled the air with satisfied grumbles. Church bells pealed, beckoning people to come give thanks, many of whom responded. Motorcades sprang up on quieter city streets, and with horns blaring, drivers paid a loud final salute to gas rationing and tire shortages. Servicemen in downtown areas, their faces smudged with lipstick, exposed wide, happy grins for press photographers.

At many domestic military posts the gates were again locked, as they were on V-E Day, to prevent too much celebrating by the happy GI's, but again the PX's stayed open later than usual, dispensing gassy, weak 3.2 beer. Old noncoms knew where the real stuff was hidden, anyway, and those who were friendly with officers got liberal handouts from the officers' club bar. In the towns and cities, MP's and SP's turned their backs on whatever they saw servicemen doing, short of mayhem.

Until midnight the world seemed frenzied and maddened with joy. Then, with the advent of a new day, the first day of peace, the nation sobered and entered the postwar world.

At military emplacements throughout the world, war-weary men and women looked homeward expectantly, forgetting about the dreary chore of occupation, unmindful of the military verity that no land is conquered until the boots of the conquerors tread the soil and keep it secure. Prepared and waiting at the Pentagon, however, was a "point system," based on months of service and time in combat, which would allow for the orderly withdrawal and discharge from service of the weary, and the replacement of them with fresh troops still being drafted.

Preparations for the homecomings filled the hours of relatives and wives and sweethearts back on the home front. Some 12 million Americans had donned the uniform and their return would be a joyous reinvasion of the homeland, even though a large number of them would be different in many ways, some painfully so.

Vastly different was the home front to which they would be returning, though a majority of home-fronters seemed unaware of the enormous changes that had taken place in five years. The America of 1945 seemed centuries away from the America of 1940. For one thing, the United States, already the world's leading industrial nation, multiplied its lead many times, with plants, factories and shops crowding landscapes, along almost every port and on the banks of almost every river. At the same time, the U.S. had become the world's leading agricultural producer, and growing things filled the rich heartland of the nation.

Men would return to women who had changed. The retiring, naive, unsophisticated smalltown girl had vanished. Many had traveled to distant points to be with their servicemen husbands or boyfriends, and had learned to fend for themselves in using the crowded wartime transportation facilities and the jammed housing accommodations. They had learned to work in factories and retail shops. They had learned to live with anxiety and gnawing fear. Almost all had learned to cope with homefront wolves who preyed on loneliness. Most had been steadfast and faithful. Those who had slipped a little, were able to hide it well. A goodly number had written "Dear John" letters to boyfriends or husbands overseas, but the vast majority had not, despite long separations.

Those who were to return later in 1945 would find their womenfolk wearing dresses that reached almost to their ankles, a shock to some who remembered leaving them in dresses that came exactly to the knees.

Even gray-haired mom had changed. She was more modish, somehow, certainly more sophisticated. She, too, had worked in the factories, the shops, even the gas stations, to release a man for war or war work. She had traveled a lot, too, and seen much more than she had ever seen before her son left.

Old dad, too, was a man with a broader perspective, a harder drive, possessed of a built-up momentum from the war that seemed to keep going. He had learned how to relax, too, forced by the arduous work of the war years, and he played at golf, at fishing, at boating, at card games, something he did less often before the war. He had more money. He knew more about politics and international problems, and he discussed his viewpoints readily. He was convinced America was the greatest land in the whole world. Hadn't everyone just proved it—the young who fought and the rest of the Americans, who provided the food, the clothing, the ammunition and the materiel of war for, let's see three nations—no, four, if you count France.

Broadway was alight again and lines queued up before the box offices. Movie theatres were aglow with new marquees and brilliant displays. The jukes still blared the latest music, blues, sweet, country, jazz and swing. The magazines were fatter than they had been for years, as were the newspapers, more dignified now without the black war headlines.

The home front had changed. All America had changed. It would never be the same again.

22

The Peace Crisis
1945

In a great many ways, Harry Truman's *real* presidency began
with the war's end. The great tasks he had inherited were done.
Before him lay the challenging future of peace. If the world had
changed beyond recognition and the home front had undergone
great upheavals, so, too, had the American presidency. It would
never be the same again.

America was now the leading military and economic power in
the world. The leaders in every capital, even in remote and aloof
Moscow, looked to Washington and to the man residing at 1600
Pennsylvania Avenue for guidance, for support and for material
help.

It was apparent to Truman that marshaling the forces for
peace would require as much careful planning, as much organizing and possibly almost as much money as waging the war.
There was one thing Truman was dead set against, however, and
it came from his prudent background and from his years on the
Senate's wartime watchdog committee: waste. He would not
tolerate wastefulness in the American economy, and he would
scout it out in foreign spending.

Almost before the last gun had been silenced, the question of
extending lend-lease was before the President. An immediate
decision was required because pressure was already mounting
on the White House with requests from foreign embassies for
more dollars.

Britain presented an urgent problem. She needed almost
everything, from foodstuffs to heavy machinery, and she could
not buy in the American market until her own economy was back
on its feet. Therefore she needed dollars, and fast. The same
applied to France, whose whole industrial economy had either
been ransacked by the Nazis or devastated by the bombs and
shells of the Allies. Russia had petitioned Truman for $6 billion

in postwar credits. China had made a formal presentation, requesting extension of its lend-lease help.

Truman listened long to his advisers—Secretary of State Jimmy Byrnes, Treasury Secretary Fred M. Vinson, War Mobilization Director John Snyder, Fleet Admiral William Leahy, Brigadier General Harry Vaughan. He listened hard. He thought hard. He made no comments.

Then, after the case for extension of lend-lease had been presented, Harry Truman set his jaw and made a declaration. The United States must not contribute further to its reputation of being a Santa Claus, he said. He wanted lend-lease held to a minimum now, and as soon as possible and practical, he wanted it ended.

Nine months before Pearl Harbor, lend-lease had been devised by Franklin Roosevelt as a means for furnishing food, munitions, armaments, tools and technology to the nations that were to become our wartime Allies. Now, only days after the war's end, his successor in office had ordered the program junked.

In all, the United States had spent $40 billion for lend-lease. Harry Truman thought it was enough.

Immediately the political analysts made a reappraisal of Harry Truman. They decided he was probably a fiscal conservative. They were to learn, quite soon, that it didn't pay to categorize or label Harry Truman, that he had his own mind, one that didn't necessarily follow the textbook philosophies, and that he had his own methods, which fit into a long-range, overall plan to which he had devoted considerable thought.

In England, Prime Minister Clement Attlee informed the House of Commons of Truman's decision and admitted that the British government was totally unprepared for such an announcement. The Labour government seemed challenged by this new President in Washington. Opposition leader Winston Churchill, who *had* lived to see his war won but who had lost the premiership to Attlee, arose to rescue Attlee from the awkward situation. "I cannot believe," he said, "that this is the last word of the United States. I cannot believe that so great a country would proceed in such a rough and harsh manner." Churchill had voiced the thoughts of leaders in Paris, Moscow, Berlin, Rome, Seoul, Manila, Saigon, Tokyo and Peking, and in many smaller capitals.

Of course Harry Truman had not cut off U.S. aid. He had merely substituted one form of aid for another (three forms: direct aid, International Monetary Fund and Export-Import Bank) and had shown the world (and Congress) that he respected the U.S. dollar.

Congress, a few weeks before, had already approved the Bretton Woods Agreement, the first and, economically, the most significant postwar instrument for restoring world stability. The complicated monetary plan was to remain in almost unaltered usage until the fall of 1971, when President Richard M. Nixon was to devalue the dollar and suspend redemptions of gold. At the time of its approval, Congress also appropriated $8.8 billion to the International Monetary Fund and $9.1 billion to the World Bank.

Yet to come was President Harry S. Truman's first peacetime message to Congress, which would give insight into his long-range plan and cause the analysts to start up their labeling machines and place him just a little left of center, perhaps a nudge farther to the left than Roosevelt had been. It was a time of great ideological name calling. The labeling of people was gaining popularity. The press used a form of shorthand, in which people were flatly called "leftist," "rightist," "isolationist," "internationalist," "populist," "obstructionist," "centrist," "procapitalist," "militarist" and so on, *ad infinitum et nauseam*. By leaping back and forth from right to left, the industrious man from Missouri caused infinite problems among the labelers.

First on the agenda, however, was V-J Day, the actual surrender of Japan. Long before, the Allies had chosen the man who would enter and occupy the modern world's most complicated and complex country, General of the Army Douglas MacArthur. President Truman, with a show of sentiment, requested the general to have the final, formal surrender on the decks of the Third Fleet battleship named for the President's home-state—the U.S.S. *Missouri*.

In Manila, MacArthur's staff received the first envoys of Japan's surrendered government with icy dignity, put the members of the party up in the hastily repaired Rosario Apartments, and got down to business. MacArthur had established his headquarters in Manila's City Hall.

Armed with a half-dozen cartons of American cigarettes, which he had purchased with cash from a large bankroll of U.S.

currency, Lieutenant General Torashiro Kawabe led his delegation to the City Hall foyer, where he bowed low before Lieutenant General Richard K. Sutherland, MacArthur's chief of staff. Sutherland led the six ranking members of the Japanese delegation to a conference room with four other staff generals and Rear Admiral Forrest P. Sherman.

MacArthur was obviously not in the mood for conciliatory gestures. First he had insisted that when the Japanese delegation flew to Manila their planes use the identifying radio code call of "Bataan." This rubbed salt into the Japanese wounds. Then, when Kawabe insisted that everything in the surrender terms be spelled out at least twice for clarification, MacArthur snapped: "The directive from this headquarters is clear and explicit and is to be complied with without further delay." That was that.

The Japs had a brief nap and then were awakened to be handed a sheaf of two dozen pages of explicit surrender orders, were packed back onto their planes and sent back to Tokyo, after which MacArthur issued an announcement for the waiting world:

> In my capacity as Supreme Commander for the Allied Powers I shall soon proceed to Japan with accompanying forces composed of ground, naval and air elements. Subject to weather that will permit landings, it is expected that the instrument of surrender will be signed within ten days. It is my earnest hope that pending the formal surrender, armistice conditions may prevail on every front and that a bloodless surrender may be effectuated.

To the ground, naval and air elements, he issued the specific orders for an "invasion" of Japan to be conducted with no firing, but with fingers on the triggers, ready for any development. He was not unmindful that Japan still had 2.5 million men under arms on its mainland, many taught since childhood to hate Americans.

The 4th Marines waded ashore at Yokosuka, laden with battle gear and bandoliers of ammunition. It was the final beachhead of the war and they took it standing up, advancing warily against an enemy that never materialized. The 11th Airborne Division, also fully armed and on the alert, dropped down on the Atsugi airfield. Soon transport planes began to land with precise timing and long lines of military personnel poured out. A military band stood ready off the apron of the airstrip, and then the transport plane *Bataan* dropped down and taxied to the ramp. MacArthur alighted and took the salute of his troops, then his stern, chiseled face broke into a broad smile. He shook hands with the members of the military band, calling the men by their names. That night he dined with his junior officers for the first time since December 7, 1941.

Transport planes landed at four-minute intervals, disgorging countless troops. In steady columns that stretched over the horizon, battleships, cruisers, destroyers and surfaced submarines advanced into Tokyo Bay. Both U.S. and British flags flew on the craft.

In short order, marching American soldiers and marines, eight abreast, swung down the streets of Tokyo. Children laughed and waved. Adults huddled indoors or hid in the corrugated iron boxes that served as homes for those who had been bombed out. Men on the streets, many wearing the tattered remnants of uniforms, glared at the Yanks with open hostility. There was no look of guilt, no look of fear, only resignation. Japan had quit.

Leading the armada in Tokyo Bay was the U.S.S. *Missouri*. It had been scrubbed, holystoned, polished and repainted until it seemed mint-new. The verandah deck was as sparkling as a surgery. On the morning of September 2, Tokyo time (September 1 in the United States), military dignitaries began to arrive, all high-ranking. Britons, Russians, Chinese and Americans, wearing their dress uniforms and all of their decorations. They represented all the armed services, land, sea and air. Each was accorded full military courtesy as he was piped aboard, saluted the bridge and saluted the officer of the deck, and to martial music was escorted to the verandah deck to a witnesses' position determined by his rank.

At nine o'clock the Japanese were piped aboard, a small delegation headed by the silk-hatted foreign minister, Mamoru Shigemitsu, who limped on his wooden leg and leaned heavily and tiredly on his cane, and the chief of the Imperial General Staff, Yoshijiro Umezu, solemn-faced. Umezu was known to many of the general officers who stood on the deck and received his salute. He was still a soldier, though a defeated one. He knew, as the Japanese people did not, that Japan had lost the war long before the atom bomb had been dropped.

Four minutes after the Japs arrived, MacArthur stepped briskly from a cabin, stood stiffly erect and read the surrender document in his deep, clear, carrying voice. His hands trembled slightly with emotion. He half-turned and faced the Japs, fixed them with a hard glance and said: "I announce it my firm purpose to insure that the terms of surrender are fully, promptly and faithfully complied with."

MacArthur handed the document to an aide. It was placed on the long table, which was draped with a rich, heavy cloth and served by two straight-backed chairs. The aide nodded at Shigemitsu.

The foreign minister doffed his silk hat, placed it on the table's edge and peeled off a glove. Painfully he limped to the chair, leaned his cane against the table, and signed. Umezu took off his gloves, declined the chair, and bending his slight, stocky frame forward, affixed his signature. It had taken four minutes. Next MacArthur signed, and the document was valid.

Slowly he said, "Let us pray that peace now be restored to the world and that God will preserve it always."

He turned to the Japanese and said: "These proceedings are closed." Thus, on September 2, 1945, the world was at last at peace. The Allies had carried out the mission proclaimed by Franklin D. Roosevelt, to beat the enemy in their homelands and to exact unconditional surrender. World War II was over.

While the drama was unfolding in Tokyo Bay, Harry Truman, back in Washington, was working on his first message to Congress. It was to be 16,000 words in length, the longest since Theodore Roosevelt's 20,000-word message in 1901. When Congress got the Truman message, "all Hell broke loose," as Bert Andrews of the *New York Herald Tribune* was to report. It was Truman's plan for peace and prosperity. It needn't have surprised congressmen, for much of what was in the document had been said by Truman before. He had merely correlated his thinking, put it all down in writing and named it the "Fair Deal." The labelers were stunned: here he was again, bouncing from right of center to left of center without any warning. Complained Minority Leader Joe Martin: "Not even President Roosevelt ever asked as much at one sitting. The scenery is new and there is a little better decoration, and he does dish it out a little easier. But it's just a plain case of out-New Dealing the New Deal."

But the Republican-oriented stock market jumped three points at the news of the President's message and reached its highest level since 1937.

Truman had asked for a multibillion-dollar public works program to rebuild the nation. He wanted a "full employment" act with a council of economic advisers to advise on public spending if a slump seemed to loom on the horizon. He asked for a Fair Employment Practices Committee to make sure that workers got proper representation. He said that the 40 cent minimum wage rate was "obsolete and should be junked." Most of all, he said that the nation should make sure there was a job for every man who wanted one. He foresaw that with proper spending and management, America would experience "the greatest peacetime industrial activity we have ever seen." Instead of lend-lease, there would be direct foreign aid in the form of low-interest loans.

Generally, the public liked what it heard, and members of Congress, sniffing the winds of the country, decided to try to give Harry Truman what he wanted. They also settled down to a lengthy debate on a tax bill to give the President a "new and lower" tax structure, as he had requested.

This turned out to be the biggest tax cut in the nation's history, but it was hardly the bill some people had hopefully expected. Taxes would not return to their 1940 prewar level. Business got $3.3 billion relief with the elimination of excess profits taxes and a slight reduction of 2-4 percent in corporate rates, but still, any business would pay the government 38 cents of every dollar earned over a $50,000 profit.

Some 12 million low-income Americans, who had been paying small taxes, would pay none under the new bill. Others, in the middle-income brackets, would pay slightly less. Computed on net income after deductions, the new bill called for these payments:

Reading the bad news about the new tax tables, Americans learned the harsh truth that Harry Truman had been trying to pound home—that peace was going to be just as expensive as war. The total cost of war, it seemed, did not end with the cessation of hostilities; it went on and on, and the bill would have to be met by everyone who worked or had an income.

Net income	Single person	Married man, two children
$ 2,000	$ 285	$ none
3,000	484	190
4,000	693	380
5,000	921	589
6,000	1,169	799
8,000	1,719	1,292
10,000	2,346	1,862
15,000	4,270	3,638
20,000	6,645	5,890
50,000	25,137	24,111

Particularly angered were those in the higher brackets. They were obliged to pay just about half of their income to Uncle Sam. When it was called a "victory tax" it had seemed less onerous. But victory, after all, had been won. It hadn't been paid for, though.

However, most home-fronters were delighted with the speed at which the United States returned to peacetime living. Wartime controls were lifted faster than most people had expected. Overnight the meat crisis ended and butchers' display cases were filled, even though ration books were tossed away. Towering stacks of tires appeared beside gas stations and garages. There was plenty of gas. Stores advertised shoes. One could get any brand of cigarette he wanted. Scarce canned goods reappeared. Home oil-delivery companies began to advertise new oil burners: "Don't reconvert from coal back to your prewar oil burner."

Truman had put the word out in Washington in a firm order: "Decontrol as fast as you can." Businessmen who went to the nation's capital expecting to stay weeks winding down their contracts, returned home in a few days, their business completed. Truman also put all federal employees back on a forty-hour week to reduce costs. He warned department heads that they had better get ready to plan cuts in personnel.

To symbolize what he was doing, the President removed the model of the M-1 Garand rifle that had sat on his desk during the war, and replaced it with a small model plough.

Summer resorts stayed open late into the season to accommodate those who decided to take their "first real vacation since Pearl Harbor." They did a booming business. The Atlantic Coast Line and the Seaboard Air Line railroads reported that their Florida-bound trains were booked solid right up to the New Year.

And still, in 1945, all Negroes traveling south on the rail lines, had to detrain in their nation's capital, and climb into Jim Crow cars for their trip farther southward on the Richmond, Fredericksburg and Potomac Railroad before joining up with either the Coast Line or Seaboard carriers.

Lake resorts in the northern and midwestern states stayed open until first frost, serving luscious roast beef and steak dinners and genuine scotch whiskey and genuine British gin martinis to celebrating guests. It was the same in western vacation spots and, as a by-product of USO troop shows, cabaret shows were introduced to places in Reno, Las Vegas, Arrowhead Lake and Lake Tahoe and in various lounging locations nearer the Coast, and stars were imported from screen and radio and pressed into emergency service.

America began to relax. Americans began to spend their money. For the first time in history, leisure-time industries came into existence in a big way and were taken seriously. The war had been over only scant weeks before it was apparent that Americans were intending to take to recreation just as seriously as they had taken to waging the war. Fun is the goal and damn the cost, was a nationwide thought, if not a slogan.

There were infants, babies and small children everywhere. Whether in uniform or out, we had reproduced in abundance during the war years, and in the fall of 1945 the tots and youngsters accompanied their parents on their "end of the war" vacations, requiring new services, different accommodations.

Restaurants along highways quickly stocked bottle warmers, cans of baby food and high chairs. Hotels and the new motels (a wartime development) bought inventories of cribs and trundle beds and rearranged room plans for connecting rooms. Pablum and other baby foods were offered on menus. "Reliable baby sitters available" appeared on promotional material.

A surge of mobility got underway in September and continued for the rest of the year. Returning veterans who had already traveled thousands of miles felt impelled to keep right on moving, right across the face of America. Wives and girlfriends who had dreamed of vine-covered cottages spent the first months of peace breathing the exhaust fumes of aging cars that were pressed into a last fling before retirement to the junkpile. After all, by October the auto manufacturers were advertising that new models would be coming off the war-perfected assembly lines shortly after the first of the year. There was no need to baby the old buggy any longer, and it was sensible to squeeze out the last mile.

Those with breakdowns—and they were legion—had to spend long hours and sometimes many days in strange places, waiting for parts to be repaired or replaced. Reluctant to put new tires on an old hack that would be traded in next spring, auto-owners pored over acres of used tires, trying to find some that might last the few required months. Even second-hand batteries enjoyed a brisk demand. Seat covers were bought in huge lots to cover up worn and abused upholstery. Many driving gadgets appeared—magnetic ash trays, rubber-suctioned compasses, felt covers for steering wheels, oddball-shaped items (dice cubes, for instance) for stick-shift levers, kewpie dolls for dashboards.

Returning servicemen felt rich with dollars they hadn't been able to spend in the service, and many were laden with savings they had accumulated by selling. PX watches to enemies and Allies alike, by selling cigarette rations that they didn't use, by fashioning gadgets, such as watch bands, out of scrap material, and by winning in the inevitable and continuous crap games. And when they got home, many of them received cash bonuses from their grateful states and communities.

Those who had waited for them had usually put aside some of their war-plant earnings, too, so that pooled, their resources allowed them to have the big fling that had been postponed for many for five long years. It was not necessary to be overprudent. Uncle Sam had promised to underwrite the mortgage on the new home that would be required by the vet and his family. He had also promised to pay for his college education if he didn't have one. It was Yankee Doodle Dandy all over again, nearly two hundred years later, living it up with a big, golden insignia stitched over the left-hand breast pocket of his uniform, which he called a "Ruptured Duck" and which meant that he had been honorably discharged, having fulfilled his obligation to his nation.

Perhaps it all turned too good too soon. Perhaps the bounty

313

from the great American horn of plenty poured forth too many goodies. When wage and price controls were ended abruptly, some conservative economists had worried about an immediate surge of inflationary prices and a quick rise in wages, but it had not happened—at least not right away.

Prices did begin to nudge up in the fall, though not alarmingly. The real threat of inflation was just a bit off in the future, presaged by the fact that almost every organized labor union had served notice on its management that it wanted to negotiate a new contract just as quickly as possible. Real estate prices did begin to show a quick upsurge.

Almost immediately labor unrest began to rock the nation. It seemed to spring up everywhere at once—textile workers and rubber workers in the Northeast, steelworkers in Pennsylvania and Ohio and Indiana, auto-workers in Michigan, truck-drivers in Wisconsin, farm equipment workers in Minnesota and Wisconsin, worried aircraft and shipyard workers on the West Coast and in Gulf ports. Strikes and threats of strikes began to fill the headlines: silk mills shut down in New Jersey, rubber plants closed in New York, cotton mills shut in New England, woolen plants closed by strike in Pennsylvania, a slowdown in rubber plants in Ohio, strike after strike in parts companies in Detroit and Chicago and across the border in Hamilton. A wheel plant closed. A transmission factory shut tight. An ignition manufacturer struck.

In strike-blasted Detroit, unemployment mounted and so did anger. Cops had to wade in to try to stop a union picketline set up around a meeting hall in which rabble-rouser Gerald L. K. Smith's followers were berating the turn of events, and violence broke out. As good union men fell under a rain of nightsticks, anger flared out over the pickets and cops alike, turning both into a mob. Quickly the riot spread through Detroit and just as quickly it turned into a racial affair with both blacks and whites seizing the opportunity to settle war-shelved animosities.

There had been race riots earlier in the war. Americans had been sickened by them. They didn't expect them again. Now a new generation of kids had come along, who had learned about living together and learning together in the loose harmony that prevailed during the war years, when muscle and sweat were needed and it mattered not the color of the body that yielded them.

Within hours high school kids were rioting, white and black side by side, in New York, Chicago, Gary, Detroit, Pontiac. Wholesale hooliganism prevailed. Stores were ransacked. Buildings were burned. Cars were overturned and some were set afire. Heads were cracked. Bones were broken. Windows were smashed.

In the White House, Harry Truman faced a whole new crisis and he was not at all sure the Congress would be with him. He envisioned a whole new, higher plateau of wage levels in America, something that would cause a whole new, higher level of prices. He saw it as necessary for the postwar world with its high postwar taxes. But would Congress go along? He guessed he'd have troubles. He guessed right.

About this time, the President encountered racial problems of his own. Beauteous, bosomy, brown Hazel Scott, who played one of the finest boogie-woogie keyboards in the nation, was booked to play in Constitution Hall in Washington. The executive committee of the ancestor-adoring Daughters of the American Revolution, owners of the hall, decreed again, as it had earlier, that the hall could be used for "white artists only."

The next morning a special messenger brought a note from the White House to the desk of New York Congressman Adam Clayton Powell, Jr., Miss Scott's new husband. It was a response to Powell's demand for "action" against the DAR. In the note, Truman said that while he could not interfere with a "private enterprise"—which indeed the DAR was, and is—he recognized that "one of the first steps taken by the Nazis when they came to power was to forbid the public appearance of artists and musicians whose religion or origin was unsatisfactory to the *master race*." Moments later Powell received a telegram from Bess Truman, the nation's First Lady. In it she said, "I deplore any action which denies artistic talent an opportunity to express itself because of prejudice against race or origin."

But that afternoon Bess Truman attended a DAR tea in her honor. Asked by a reporter if she might be a guest at similar teas at another time, Bess asked, "Why not?"

Stung, Adam Clayton Powell shouted, "From now on, Mrs. Truman is the *Last* Lady!"

Those close to Mrs. Truman said she was hurt deeply by the remark. She had not intended to slight Powell or Miss Scott. The DAR tea was a traditional affair, and she had gone as a matter of courtesy and duty, one of the nebulous yet necessary chores of the wife of a political figure, in this case, the nation's First Gentleman. The President had not even been aware of her appointment schedule for the day. Yet the incident garnered headlines across the land and added greatly to the unrest.

Among other things it brought out the bigots, among them Mississippi Senator Theodore (The Man) Bilbo, who praised Mrs. Truman for her stand against the Negroes—praise she did not want, since she had not meant it to be a "stand." Lines were drawn. Back to the antebellum level went some of the nation's philosophical and ideological discussions. The firm, businesslike, plain man in the White House, who had no prejudices of his own, could see his control of the nation slipping through his fingers. He was worried. He was angry. Most Americans had never seen Harry Truman when he was angry; he was supposed to be unruffleable. They were to learn.

Right after that Harry Truman instituted a new regimen in the White House. It was a tough working day, a serious working day. All work and no play. He let the mood trickle into other areas of government, too, and made comments like, "Let's cut out the foolishness and get back to work." Everywhere in Washington and in regional government offices, people stiffened up, toughened up, sobered up. The celebrating was ended. The serious business was at hand. A stern President was at the helm. He was also an angry President.

How did the people respond to Harry Truman? He was a bit of an enigma, a bit unfathomable, but they liked him. Poll after poll gave him the highest ratings in popularity ever accorded a President since such surveys started, and no one seemed to be able to figure out why this was so. Only in later years did the analysts realize that it was because Harry Truman was *real*. He didn't pretend to be anything other than what he was, a darn good politician from Missouri.

He was to come up with such expressions as "The buck stops here," indicating *his* desk, and "If you can't stand the heat, stay out of the kitchen," meaning the White House itself. These things endeared him to a plain, unpretentious people who were instinctively suspicious of foreigners, easterners, Ivy League graduates and, in some cases, contract bridge players. Harry Truman was a man's man, a politician's politician, a plain man's plain man, yet he embodied something of greatness in his very bearing and in his words, something vaguely Lincolnesque, something remotely Jacksonian. He was from river country and from plains country, and he made no effort to hide it; he was proud of it. He did not pretend. That made him more than acceptable to most. If ever anyone were to take the title of "Great Commoner" from William Jennings Bryan, it would be Harry S. Truman. He had a pleasant wife and a cute America-fresh daughter. He ran his office with American efficiency and knowhow. He played poker. He drank bourbon. He wasn't even a good fisherman. In 1945 he fit "like a duck's foot in the mud."

He bothered some, however, back in the Bible-Belt land of his birth. The first honorary degree to be offered to Harry Truman, who had no earned degree, was an LL.D. from Baptist Baylor University in Waco, Texas. But the Texas Baptist General Convention in Fort Worth voted against it with 4,500 nays. "No Baptist school should confer a degree on a man who likes his poker and drinks his bourbon," declared the chairman of the convention's Civic Righteousness Committee. "I know that we all agree that no man, even the President of the United States, could be a good Baptist and drink his liquor." Baylor thought about this for a while, but decided that, no matter, it would give Harry Truman the degree anyway. The President, a Baptist himself, though now decreed to be backslid because of a liking for cards and a touch of native spirits, made no mention of religion in his acceptance speech.

A *Fortune* poll showed that 75.6 percent of the people thought he was doing a good-to-excellent job on foreign policy; 58.9 percent liked his domestic programs; 64.7 percent thought he was doing a fine job in handling Congress.

The dust of war was still unsettled when the new secretary of state, Jimmy Byrnes, reshuffled the State Department, naming as under secretary and key man, Dean Gooderham Acheson, fifty-two, who had resigned as assistant secretary three days earlier because he couldn't afford to live on the $9,000-a-year salary. He was persuaded to come back to tougher responsibilities for a $1,000-a-year raise.

A tall, immaculately dressed, self-contained man, wearing a carefully groomed mustache, Dean Acheson looked stage-cast for the role of diplomat, elegant and cool. He could back it up. The son of an Episcopal bishop of Connecticut, he had gone to Groton and Yale, served as a naval ensign in World War I and took his law degree at Harvard, where he was an honor graduate. Supreme Court Justice Louis D. Brandeis immediately hired him as clerk, and after his apprenticeship he went on to a large and powerful Washington law firm.

Acheson was to mind the store while Secretary Byrnes went off to London to confer with the foreign ministers of the world's five great powers to settle the peace terms for World War II and adopt the initial covenants that would go to the United Nations. It was to be, perhaps, the most sensitive meeting of the war years, and there were still those in America who worried that they were represented by a comparative amateur who would be dealing first-hand with those experienced foreign diplomats.

To London's bomb-damaged Lancaster House Byrnes brought Benjamin V. Cohen, the New Deal's wonder-boy; Manhattan lawyer John Foster Dulles, the leading Republican foreign-affairs expert, who would himself one day become secretary of state; and a shipload of specialists. Jimmy Byrnes, himself, brought two valuable assets. First, he had been at Yalta, the key conference of the war, and had taken shorthand notes of the meetings to compile, eventually, the best record of the conference. Second, he knew the functionings of the United States government better than most. He had been a congressman for fourteen years, a senator for ten, a Supreme Court justice for sixteen months, the economic stabilizer for eight months and the war mobilizer for twenty-two months, before becoming secretary of state. He was an untypical diplomat, a simple man with simple tastes. He described his personal goal as "two tailor-made suits a year, three meals a day and a reasonable amount of good liquor."

The Democrat President and the predominately Democratic Congress were embarrassed just after V-J Day with the disclosure of the story of how Franklin Delano Roosevelt helped his son Elliott get a $200,000 loan and then arranged for it to be settled for two cents on the dollar. The deal came to light through the House Ways and Means Committee, which was asked to make a decision about a tax question. Should the lender, John A. Hartford, president of the Great Atlantic and Pacific Tea Company, be permitted to take a $196,000 income tax deduction for his loss on the loan? By a straight party-line vote the Democratic majority voted to allow the deduction.

Republicans and old Roosevelt-haters howled "Unfair!" The record was to show that they were justified.

John Hartford testified that back in 1939, Elliott Roosevelt, seeking to finance his Texas State Network, Inc., a radio chain, had come to him and asked to borrow $200,000. He said he had come at the suggestion of the President. To prove it, Elliott got the President on the telephone.

Hartford said, "I said 'Hello, Mr. President,' and I heard a familiar voice, a voice I had heard over radio many times, say 'Hello, John,' and I told him that Elliott was in my apartment and asked him what did he think about this $200,000 loan Elliott wanted to make in connection with the radio business, and the President said that he was entirely familiar with it, and that it looked good, and gave assurance to me that it was a sound business proposition and a fine thing. He said he would appreciate anything I could do for him."

Hartford added candidly: "After the President was so enthusiastic about it, I felt that I was on the spot and I had to make a decision right then and there, and I did not want to do anything to incur the enmity of the President."

The record showed that at the time the loan was made Congress was *considering* a chain-store tax that would have cost A & P $6,625,000 annually. It did not pass the law.

Three years later, with Elliott off at war as a brigadier general in the Army, President Roosevelt got into the deal a second time and sent Jesse Jones to settle the loan. No payments had been made, either in interest or on the principal. Jones gave Hartford $4,000 and got back the Texas State Network stock that Hartford had been holding as security.

It turned out that at the time that Jesse Jones retrieved the stock, Texas State Network was beginning to prosper and showing signs that in short time the stock would be worth the full $200,000. By the time the matter got before the House Ways and Means Committee Texas State Network was a flourishing and profitable company with Elliott's ex-wife, Mrs. Ruth Googins Roosevelt Eidson, as its president. She and their children got all of the stock.

It was not the first time Elliott Roosevelt had embarrassed the Democrats. Earlier in the year three servicemen—a sailor en route home to visit his just-widowed mother, and an Army sergeant and a Seabee, both on emergency furlough to visit critically ill wives—were "bumped" off a plane at Memphis airport because their No. 3 Priorities had been topped by a No. 1 Priority. They were told that some "critical material" was coming aboard and their spaces on the plane were needed.

They stood and watched as a huge crate occupying three seats' worth of space was trundled to the transport. In it was a big, 115-pound tawny dog. On the crate, sure enough, was the No. 1 Priority sticker. The label revealed that the crate and the dog were the property of Colonel Elliott Roosevelt, the son of the President, and that it was consigned to Faye Emerson Roosevelt, his actress wife, in Hollywood, California. Questioned about it in London, later, Colonel Roosevelt explained that it was a pedigreed English bull mastiff named Blaze Hero, and he had bought it as a gift for his wife.

As the leaves began to turn to gold on the deciduous trees, the giddy new world of civilian industrial production began to open up. The War Production Board, after forty-three months of restrictive regulations, suddenly and startlingly told manufacturers they could make all the automobiles they wished. The restrictions were also removed from a host of other items that had been tightly controlled.

The restrictions were off electric dishwashers, ironers, washing machines, electric shavers, pots and pans, radios, photographic film, storage batteries, tires, pottery, toys, paper napkins, paper handkerchieves, suits, dresses, shoes, phonographs, records, cameras, projectors, lawn mowers, garden tools, shop tools.

With a whoop, Americans took to the highways, enjoying noisy blowouts and banging their vehicles together until the National Safety Council had to issue stern warnings to reduce the roadside carnage.

Most of the items freed from control would not be available to the public until Christmastime, and the new cars would not really arrive until after the first of the year, but the horizon looked bright to consumers, even though labor disputes were flaring everywhere.

To ease some of the pressure on the scarce supply of civilian goods, the Army, the Navy and other wartime purchasing agencies decided to sell their war-hoarded government goods to the nation's retailers. There were at least $90 billion worth of leftovers, many of them unusable by civilians. There were 40,000 surplus homing pigeons with little pigeons pecking through eggs every minute, and thousands of dogs, mules and horses. A surplus chimpanzee had been sold, but the Surplus Property Board still had $50 million worth of sixty-inch searchlights that it wanted to get rid of and 10 million pounds of contraceptive jelly. There was a warehouse full of Elizabeth Arden black face-cream used by soldiers for night attacks and now useful only to burglars.

At least $600 million worth of usable civilian goods was released from the government warehouses right after V-J Day. Gimbel's immediately announced a sale on Army DDT sprayers good for killing any insect from spiders to mosquitos to ants to tsetse flies, and was cleaned out almost immediately.

In New York City the advent of butter pats on restaurant tables and the appearance of genuine scotch whiskey was celebrated with restraint.

The big remaining problem was housing. Every major American city was jammed. In Atlanta 2,000 people answered an ad for a single apartment. Throughout the country people were living in their cars. The nation was short at least 4,660,000 homes and contractors estimated it would take ten years to fit supply to demand.

President Truman asked Congress for price ceilings on both old and new houses and he called for priorities that would channel 50 percent of all building materials into the construction of houses costing $10,000 or less, after it was found that most such materials were going right to industry. The Senate voted unanimously to turn 75,000 units of war housing over to veterans and their families, to remodel government dormitories to house 11,000 more families and to redo Army barracks to provide room for 14,000 more. But it was a tiny, albeit helpful, remedy for a gigantic problem.

In late summer an Army B-25, flying from Bedford, Massachusetts, to Newark, New Jersey, crashed into the tower of the 102-story, 1,250-foot high Empire State Building, and burst into flames. It was flown by a pilot who was unfamiliar with the New York skyline. Three persons aboard the plane and ten persons inside the building were killed as the huge torch burned in the world's highest blaze—915 feet above street level.

Even a child could see, however, that worldwide civilian aviation was here. Round-the-world airplane service was inaugurated on September 28 when a Globester of the Air Transport Command left National Airport, Washington, and returned on October 4 after completing a global trip of 23,279 miles in 149 hours and 44 minutes. A month later an A-26, flying westward, circumnavigated the globe in a flight covering 24,859 miles in 96 hours, 50 minutes.

The military was chalking up some impressive records. A C-69 Army transport plane flew from New York to Paris, 3,600 miles, in 14 hours, 12 minutes. A B-29 flew from Honolulu to Washington, D.C., 4,640 miles, in 17 hours, 21 minutes. An O-54 Air Transport Command plane was flown from Tokyo, Japan, to Washington, D.C. on November 1, in 31 hours, 25 minutes. That same day Brigadier General Frank A. Armstrong brought a flight of four B-29s nonstop from Tokyo to Washington, a distance of 6,544 miles, in 27 hours, 29 minutes.

As fall deepened, labor unrest mounted. No industry was exempt from strikes and threatened strikes. Violence broke out in spots, like electrical storms in a wide and spreading low-pressure area.

At one time 420,000 workers were idle. A wildcat strike at the Kelsey-Hayes Wheel Company in Detroit kept 50,000 from their jobs and halted the conversion efforts of the automobile industry. Then John L. Lewis' United Mine Workers, striving to get recognition of its foremen's union, called a strike at 127 soft-coal pits, throwing 53,500 more out of work, and threatened a general strike of 450,000 miners. Pit by pit, more coal fields were closed until 210,000 soft-coal miners were idle.

Then Lewis heard a rumor: Truman was prepared to denounce him publicly for the strike. Truman, it was known, was getting angrier by the minute. Lewis decided not to court a public spanking and called off the strike after four weeks and the loss of 13 million tons of coal production urgently needed by factories and homes.

All this time, the cleverest union leader of them all was at work drafting revolutionary demands. He was Walter Reuther, Vice President of the CIO's United Automobile Workers and director of UAW's General Motors Division. He was planning a strike, not for the customary reasons but for a 30 percent pay increase for production workers, and he had prepared figures and projections to show the beneficial effect a 30 percent pay increase in the giant motor industry would have on the entire economy by stepping up wages across the whole spectrum and moving the nation to a higher level of abundance.

Reuther wanted to strike General Motors, though his boss, UAW President R. J. Thomas thought it should be postponed. Right after Thanksgiving, however, 200 delegates of the UAW voted unanimously to support Reuther and to close down General Motors. It was the first big strike of the postwar period. It was to idle 175,000 men and women on GM's production lines.

After the General Motors strike had gone on for two weeks Harry Truman finally lost his temper. He had been holding it in check all fall and now, as Detroiters and workers at other GM plants around the country faced the bleakest Christmas since the depression, he let the nation learn that the mild Missourian could also get a mad-on.

With no advance notice he sent a plan to Congress for settling future strikes and said he would apply it immediately, without benefit of law or of permission from Congress, to end the General Motors strike. Without waiting for congressional reaction, he called upon General Motors strikers to go back to work, and promised to appoint some fact-finders to arbitrate the issue. He didn't *ask* them to return to their jobs; he *ordered* them, as their President.

His plan was based on the Railway Labor Disputes Act, which for nearly twenty years had worked to stave off strikes on the nation's railroads. It called for establishment, on the President's orders, of a fact-finding commission to investigate any major strike, with power to subpoena all books and records. It would report directly to the President. It ordered a thirty-day cooling-off period during which no strike could be called.

CIO President Philip Murray nearly blew the fuses on the nation's radio sets: "It is legislation that can have but a single purpose, the weakening of labor unions, the curtailment of the right of free men to refrain from working when they choose to do so. The CIO shall mobilize its entire membership to defeat this specific measure and all similar attempts directed against labor." Said John L. Lewis of the Truman proposal: "It is an evil, vile-smelling mess."

In the Congress, Senator Robert A. Taft and Representative Fred Hartley thought it was time the Wagner Labor Relations

Act was augmented with some safeguards to protect the public interest. They thought Truman was moving in the right direction but that he needed a new law with teeth in it.

Not in 1945 would the General Motors strike be settled. It dragged on into January, but did not, as many feared, spread to the other manufacturers. By January showrooms were featuring new models from all the other manufacturers—Fords, Lincolns, Mercurys, Chryslers, Dodges, Plymouths, DeSotos, Packards, Studebakers, Jeeps, Nashs, but no Cadillacs, Buicks, Oldsmobiles or Chevrolets.

Just before Christmas, however, the United Steelworkers voted to call a general strike of the steel industry on January 14. This would mean that the entire auto industry would also close down. There were 800,000 steelworkers in 1,100 plants, but there were 3 million additional workers in other industries who depended on steel for their production jobs. (The strike was called and settled the following month.)

President Truman, still testy about the way Americans were abusing or misusing the first months of peace, served up a special "Christmas present" for General Motors, again setting an entirely new labor policy.

Walter Reuther was insisting in his negotiations with GM that he get a 30 percent raise for his workers unless "shown the arithmetic" to prove that such a raise would force higher car prices.

President Truman's special present arrived at the negotiating table in the form of a mimeographed statement:

> In appointing a fact-finding board in an industrial dispute where one of the questions at issue is wages, it is essential to a fulfillment of its duty that the board have the authority, whenever it deems it necessary, to examine the books of the employer in order to determine the ability of the employer to pay. In view of the public interest involved, it would be highly unfortunate if any party to a dispute should refuse to cooperate with a fact-finding board.

Immediately, General Motors decided to reopen negotiations with the union. Left for the future was the uproar in legal and labor circles that the Truman memorandum would have. The President did not say wages should be based entirely on ability to pay. It was a "relevant fact." It might be used by unions to justify demands that would cut down profits for the most efficient companies. Also, it might be used by incompetent managements to justify substandard wages.

As a result of all of the strikes, the first postwar Christmas contained a great many "promises." You'll get your new camera (or bicycle or skis or refrigerator or sled or model train) just as soon as it arrives at the store, Love, Santa." Even so, it was the gayest Christmas in four years, and grateful for their peace, Americans made the most of it.

They prepared for the biggest, brassiest, noisiest, gayest New Year's celebration of the century, however, and made elaborate plans. Manhattan bars planned to stay open until dawn. Across the country roadhouses had their bright lights and neon signs adjusted. Bars were stocked with the real stuff, and for those with more exotic tastes, genuine French champagne was back. The stiff white shirt, last worn on New Year's Eve, 1940, was to appear in abundance. Horns, confetti, paper streamers, crazy hats—all the paraphernalia of gaiety and zany madness—were trotted out to welcome in 1946, the first real year of peace.

And during the last week of the year, U.S. Army Signal Corps experts prepared for a bold experiment to take place the following month—sending a radar beam to the moon.

Bibliography

Books

Aaron, Daniel, and Bendiner, Robert. *The Strenuous Decade*. Garden City: Doubleday & Co., Anchor Books, 1969.

Adams, Henry H. *1942, The Year That Doomed the Axis*. New York: David McKay Co., 1967.

Adams, James Truslow. *The March of Democracy*. Vol. 6. New York: Charles Scribner's Sons, 1945.

Asbell, Bernard. *When F.D.R. Died*. New York: Holt, Rinehart & Winston, 1961.

Bergman, Peter M. *The Chronological History of the Negro in America*. New York: Harper & Row, 1968.

Brown, William B., and others. *America in a World at War*. New York: Dell Publishing Co., 1964.

Buchanan, A. Russell. *The United States and World War II*. Vols. 1 and 2. New York: Harper & Row, 1964.

Catton, Bruce. *The War Lords of Washington*. New York: Harcourt, Brace & Co., 1948.

Childs, Marquis. *I Write from Washington*. New York: Harper & Brothers, 1942.

Cleaver, Eldridge. *Soul on Ice*. New York: McGraw-Hill Book Co., 1968.

Davies, Joseph E. *Mission to Moscow*. New York: Simon & Schuster, 1941.

De Seversky, Alexander P. *Victory Through Air Power*. New York: Simon & Schuster, 1942.

Dos Passos, John. *State of the Nation*. Boston: Houghton Mifflin Co., 1943.

Flower, John. *Moonlight Serenade—A Bio-discography of the Glenn Miller Civilian Band*. New Rochelle: Arlington House, 1972.

Geddes, Donald Porter, ed. *Franklin Delano Roosevelt, a Memorial*. New York: Pocket Books, 1945.

Goodman, Jack, ed. *While You Were Gone*. New York: Simon & Schuster, 1946.

Green, Abel, and Laurie, Joe, Jr. *Show Biz from Vaude to Video*. New York: Henry Holt & Co., 1951.

Hope, Bob, with pictures by Glanzman, Lou. *So This Is Peace*. New York: Simon & Schuster, 1946.

Hosokawa, Bill. *Nisei*. New York: William Morrow & Co., 1969.

Howe, Quincy, ed. *The Pocket Book of the War*. New York: Pocket Books, 1941.

Ickes, Harold L., *The Autobiography of a Curmudgeon*. New York: Quadrangle Books, 1943.

Jones, Ken D., and McClure, Arthur F. *Hollywood at War*. Cranbury, N.J.: A. S. Barnes. 1971.

Kernan, W. F. *Defense Will Not Win the War*. Boston: Little, Brown & Co., 1942.

Krooss, Herman E. *Executive Opinion—What Business Leaders Said and Thought on Economic Issues, 1920's—1960's*. Garden City: Doubleday & Co., 1970.

Lash, Joseph P. *Eleanor and Franklin*. New York: W. W. Norton & Co., 1971.

Lawson, Ted. *Thirty Seconds over Tokyo*. New York: Random House, 1943.

Lerner, Max. *Public Journal*. New York: Viking Press, 1945.

Lincoln, C. Eric. *The Negro Pilgrimage in America*. New York: Bantam Books, 1967.

Lingeman, Richard R. *Don't You Know There's a War On?* New York: G. P. Putnam's Sons, 1971.

Lippmann, Walter. *U.S. Foreign Policy*. Boston: Atlantic-Little, Brown & Co., 1943.

Lynd, Robert S., and Lynd, Helen. *Middletown in Transition*. New York: Harcourt, Brace & Co., 1937.

Mattfeld, Julius. *"Variety" Music Cavalcade, 1620-1961*. (Revised). Englewood Cliffs, N.J., Prentice-Hall, 1962.

Mauldin, Bill. *Back Home*. New York: William Sloane Associates, 1947.

———. *The Brass Ring*. New York: W. W. Norton & Co., 1971.

Miller, Douglas. *You Can't Do Business with Hitler*. Boston: Atlantic-Little, Brown & Co., 1941.

Millis, Walter. *Arms and Men*. New York: Capricorn Press, 1956.

Nelson, Donald M. *Arsenal of Democracy*. New York: Harcourt, Brace & Co., 1946.

Perkins, Frances. *The Roosevelt I Knew*. New York: Harper & Row, 1946.

Polenberg, Richard. *War and Society*. Philadelphia: J. B. Lippincott, 1971.

Pyle, Ernie. *Here Is Your War*. New York, Henry Holt & Co., 1943.

Reston, James B. *Prelude to Victory*. New York: Alfred A. Knopf, 1942.

Sandburg, Carl. *Home Front Memo*. New York: Harcourt, Brace & Co., 1941, 1942, 1943.

Settle, Irving. *A Pictorial History of Radio*. New York: Grosset & Dunlap, 1960, 1967.

———, and Laas, William. *A Pictorial History of Television*. New York: Grosset & Dunlap, 1969.

Sherwood, Robert E. *Roosevelt and Hopkins*. New York: Grosset & Dunlap, 1948.

Spaeth, Sigmund. *A History of Popular Music in America*. New York: Random House, 1948.

Stettinius, Edward R., Jr. *Lend-Lease, Weapon for Victory*. New York: MacMillan Co., 1944.

Summers, Harrison B., ed. *History of Broadcasting, Radio to Television*. New York: Arno Press and the New York Times, 1971.

Willkie, Wendell L. *One World*. New York: Simon & Schuster, Pocket Books, 1943.

Wish, Harvey. *Contemporary America*. New York: Harper & Brothers, 1945.

Young, Roland. *This Is Congress*. New York: Alfred A. Knopf, 1943.

Magazines

(Anonymous). "V. . .- Mail—Letters to Our Boys Via Film." *Collier's*, October 17, 1942.

———. "Wings for a War." *Life*, January 30, 1939.

———. "Short-Wave Radio War Uses a New Kind of Geography." *Life*, May 15, 1939.

———. "Rumania Has Oil Trouble." *Life*, February 19, 1940.

———. "U.S. Army Tries Out Its Newest 'How' and 'AA' Gun." *Life*, April 15, 1940.

———. "Elmer Davis Attempts to Explain the War." *Life*, July 27, 1942.

———. "Soldiers' Wives Give up Home and Job for Camp Life With Husbands." *Life*, October 12, 1942.

———. "Washington Newsletter." *McCall's*, July, 1942.

———. "Washington Newsletter." *McCall's*, July, 1944.

———. "God and the Gestapo." *Redbook*, March, 1940.

———. "Dream Power." *Saturday Evening Post*, February 8, 1941.

———. "Baiting a Trap in Bataan?" *Saturday Evening Post*, April 4, 1942.

———. "The Admiral Who Called the Turn." *Saturday Evening Post*, April 4, 1942.

Bainbridge, John. "Schoolmaster of the Sky." *Woman's Home Companion*, March, 1943.

Bosworth, Allan R. "Civil Air Patrol." *Liberty*, July 11, 1942.

Burdett, James H. "Vegetables for Victory." *Woman's Home Companion*, April, 1942.

Cades, Hazel Rawson. "Take Care." *Woman's Home Companion*, March, 1943.

Churchill, Winston S. "The U-Boat Menace." *Liberty*, May 10, 1941.

Courtney, W. B. "Here's Your Horsepower." *Collier's*, May 1, 1943.

Creel, George, and McCandless, Comdr. Bruce. "Mr. McCandless Takes Over." *Collier's*, January 30, 1943.

Dangerfield, George. "Winston Churchill." *Life*, January 9, 1939.

Davis, Forest, and Lindley, Ernest K. "How War Came." *Ladies' Home Journal*, July, 1942.

Demers, Sgt. Larry. "I Was Eighteen, Too." *Woman's Home Companion*, March, 1943.

Devore, Robert. "Paratrops Behind Nazi Lines." *Collier's*, September 18, 1943.

Dorsey, Biddle, and Kiesling, Barrett C. "The Massawa Miracle." *Collier's*, November 13, 1943.

Dos Passos, John. "The Listening Post." *Woman's Home Companion*, April, 1942.

Eliot, Major George Fielding. "The Finnish Line Breaks." *Life*, March 18, 1940.

Ford, Corey. "Remember Dutch Harbor." *Collier's*, May 1, 1943.

Gaskill, Gordon, "Eavesdropping on the World." *American Magazine*, July, 1941.

Gervasi, Frank. "Hitting Hitler's Oil Barrel." *Collier's*, September 18, 1943.

Goslin, Phyllis, and Goslin, Omar. "Cannon and/or Butter." *Woman's Home Companion*, May, 1941.

Greenbie, Marjorie Barstow. "Steps to Victory." *Woman's Home Companion*, May, 1942.

Hamilton, Frederick L. "How You Look to the Japs." *American Magazine*, May, 1942.

Hartley, Howard. "Fortress in the Sky." *Collier's*, April 19, 1941.

Hauser, Ernest O. "Son of Heaven." *Life*, June 10, 1940.

Henderson, Harry, and Shaw, Sam. "Invasion Gun." *Collier's*, September 18, 1943.

Henderson, Leon. "The War and Your Pocketbook." *American Magazine*, October, 1941.

Hoover, Herbert. "Feed Hungry Europe!" *Collier's*, November 23, 1940.

———. "We'll Have to Feed the World Again." *Collier's*, December 5, 1942.

Hoover, J. Edgar. "Big Scare." *American Magazine*, August 1941.

Johnston, Alva. "Billion-Dollar Plane Builder." *Saturday Evening Post*, November 27, 1943.

Josephson, Matthew. "Production Man." *New Yorker*, March 8, 1941.

Kahn, Pvt. E. J., Jr. "The Army Life." *New Yorker*, November 15, 1941.

Karig, Walter. "How We Can Lick the U-Boat Menace." *Liberty*, July 11, 1942.

Kinsolving, Lucy Lee. "Speak American, Lady." *Woman's Home Companion*, May, 1943.

Knaust, Elizabeth. "The ABC of Nazi Propaganda." *Redbook*, November, 1939.

Kraus, Rene. "Dictators Despise Each Other." *Redbook*, February, 1940.

Landy, Rear Admiral Emory S. "Ships, Ships, Ships." *American Magazine*, May, 1942.

Lardner, David. "Wherever the Money Is." *New Yorker*, December 13, 1941.

Listowel, Judith. "Every Englishwoman at Work." *Woman's Home Companion*, July, 1941.

Lockridge, Patricia. "The Unconquerable." *Woman's Home Companion*, May, 1942.

Loewy, Raymond, and Reese, B. Smith. "Looking Backward to the Future." *Collier's*, November 13, 1943.

Lubell, Samuel. "Higher Taxes or Else." *Saturday Evening Post*, November 27, 1943.

Markey, Morris. "Coast Guard." *Liberty*, July 11, 1942.

———. "Let Freedom Ring." *McCall's*, October, 1940.

Marshall, Gen. George C. "A Message to the Women of America." *Ladies' Home Journal*, August, 1941.

Martin, Jackie. "Will He Get My Letter?" *Woman's Home Companion*, May, 1943.

Maugham, W. Somerset. "Inside Story of French Collapse." *Redbook*, October, 1940.

———. "The Refugee Ship." *Redbook*, October, 1940.

Maxwell, Anne. "We Won't Let Them Starve." *Woman's Home Companion*, May, 1943.

Moriss, Tech. Sgt. Jack. "From This Day Forward." *McCall's*, October, 1944.

Morris, Frank D. "Beach Boys." *Collier's*, May 1, 1943.

Murphy, Mark. "The Chance." *New Yorker*, November 15, 1941.

Oursler, Fulton. "The Duke of Windsor Talks of War and Peace." *Liberty*, March 22, 1941.

Panter-Downes, Mollie. "Letter from London." *New Yorker*, February 5, 1941.

Porter, Sylvia F. "Your Part in Price Control." *Woman's Home Companion*, November, 1942.

Pratt, Theodore. "Evacues à la Americaine." *New Yorker*, May 20, 1942.

Pringle, Henry F. "What Do Women of America Think about War?" *Ladies' Home Journal*, July, 1938.

Ralston, Louise Bird. "He's in the Army Now." *Woman's Home Companion*, May, 1941.

Reynolds, Quentin. "Letter to a Man with a Boy in Ireland." *Collier's*, October 17, 1942.

Reynolds, Robert R. "The Weak Link in Our Defense." *American Magazine*, September, 1941.

Sherwood, Robert E. "The Front Line Is in Our Hearts." *Ladies' Home Journal*, August, 1941.

Smith, Helena Huntington. "It Pays to Listen." *Collier's*, January 30, 1943.

Smith, Katharine. "Miracles from Milk." *Woman's Home Companion*, April, 1942.

Sternberg, Fritz. "Can a Blockade Beat Hitler?" *Redbook*, June, 1940.

Stowe, Leland. "How a Few Thousand Nazis Seized Norway." *Life*, May 6, 1940.

Taub, Walter. "We Saw Hamburg Die." *Collier's*, September 18, 1943.

Taylor, Frank J. "The Klystron Boys." *Saturday Evening Post*, February 8, 1941.

Taylor, Tom. "The 4-4 Plan." *McCall's*, September, 1943.

Thompson, Dorothy. "How to Destroy Civilization." *Ladies' Home Journal*, January, 1939.

Tivey, Patrick. "How to Get Along Under Fire." *American Magazine*, May, 1942.

Treanor, Tom. "We Never Lose a Nazi." *Collier's*, November 13, 1943.

Van Der Grif, Cornelis. "Under Jap Rule in Java." *Collier's*, May 1, 1943.

Van Loon, Hendrik Willem. "Woe to the Conquerer." *Redbook*, January, 1939.

Van Passen, Pierre. "How Long Will the War Last?" *Redbook*, October, 1941.

———. "If Japan Fights." *Redbook*, March, 1941.

———. "Prelude to a Tyrant, Part I." *Redbook*, April, 1940.

———. "Prelude to a Tyrant, Part II." *Redbook*, May, 1940.

———. "The First Soldier of France." *Redbook*, February, 1940.

———. "Whom Hitler Reassures He Destroys." *Redbook*, September, 1940.

Walker, Charles. "More Deadly Than Bombs." *McCall's*, April, 1940.

Wallace, Henry A. "The Price of Your Freedom." *American Magazine*, July, 1941.

Watts, Stephen. "All Fighting Men Together." *New Yorker*, April 25, 1942.

Wells, H. G. "Berlin Should Be Bombed." *Liberty*, February 3, 1940.

West, Rebecca. "Around Us the Wail of Sirens." *Saturday Evening Post*, February 8, 1941.

Wiese, Otis L., Editor. "Youth Speaks on the Air." *McCall's*, February, 1940.

Willkie, Wendell L. "What Kind of Life Do We Americans Want?" *Life*, November 4, 1940.

Williams, Wythe. "Germany's Secret Plans for Invading England." *Liberty*, March 29, 1941.

Winter, Ella. "Are Children Worse in Wartime?" *Collier's*, March 13, 1943.

Wolfert, Ira. "The Japs Tried to Drive Us Crazy." *Collier's*, November 13, 1943.

Newspapers, News Magazines

Time, all issues, 1940-45.
Time Capsule, editions of 1940, 1941, 1942, 1943, 1944, and 1945.
New York Times files, 1940-45.
New York Times Index.
Newsweek, all issues, 1940-45.
Providence Journal-Bulletin files, 1940-45.
Chicago Tribune files 1940-45.
Danbury News-Times files, 1940-45.

Index

333

335